# COURTS

## A COMPARATIVE AND
## POLITICAL ANALYSIS

# MARTIN SHAPIRO

THE UNIVERSITY OF CHICAGO PRESS
CHICAGO AND LONDON

To J. A. C. Grant, Foster Sherwood, and Currin Shields
in whose undergraduate courses this book began.

MARTIN SHAPIRO is professor of law at the University of California,
Berkeley, where he teaches in the Jurisprudence and Social Policy Program. Formerly professor of government at Harvard University, he is
president of the Western Political Science Association.

THE UNIVERSITY OF CHICAGO PRESS, CHICAGO 60637
THE UNIVERSITY OF CHICAGO PRESS, LTD., LONDON
©1981 by The University of Chicago
All rights reserved. Published 1981
Printed in the United States of America
85 84 83 82 81      1 2 3 4 5

Three chapters in this book have been published previously in slightly
different form: chapter 1 appeared in Fred I. Greenstein and Nelson W.
Polsby, eds., *Handbook of Political Science*, vol. 5 (1975), pp. 312–71,
published by Addison-Wesley Publishing Company, Reading, Massachusetts; chapter 2 in *North Carolina Law Review* 55 (1977): 577–
652; and chapter 5 in *California Law Review* 68 (1980): 350–81.

Library of Congress Cataloging in Publication Data

Shapiro, Martin M
  Courts, a comparative and political analysis.

  Includes bibliographical references and index.
  1. Courts. 2. Judicial process. I. Title.
K2100.S5      347'.01      80–18263
ISBN 0–226–75042–6

# C O U R T S

# CONTENTS

# PREFACE

This book has two purposes and so ought to have two prefaces. The first is very short and is addressed to those who teach courses in judicial process, comparative legal systems, and the like. This book has been written with an eye to such courses. It does not presuppose any previous knowledge of law or of the legal systems it examines. It is written in as direct a style as I can manage. Chapter 1 presents an overview of the conflict resolution, social control, and lawmaking activities of courts and of the relations between trial and appellate courts both as fact and law finders. The remaining chapters describe the common law, civil law, imperial Chinese, and Islamic legal traditions. The general propositions of chapter 1 are as applicable to American courts as to those of other nations and the chapter concludes with a brief survey of communist courts. So this book may be supplemented conveniently with additional materials on American or communist courts or both.

The second preface is more complex. I think it is fair to say that comparative law has been a somewhat disappointing field. For the most part it has consisted of showing that a certain procedural or substantive law of one country is similar to or different from that of another. Having made the showing, no one knows quite what to do next. Or, alternatively, comparison consists of presenting descriptions of a number of legal systems side by side, again with no particular end in view. The law reformer can sometimes use the knowledge built up in these ways to suggest the transplantation of a foreign legal device that seems to work better than a native one. His opponents will then use their comparative sophistication to show that most devices are too intimately connected with their own legal systems to travel well.

This book takes the hardly novel position that the comparative method is a substitute for the experimental method, not a terribly satisfactory substitute but one pressed upon us by the impossibility of putting laws and nations in test tubes and bubble chambers. The rationale of the book is simple. A number of propositions about courts are offered. My own position toward each of the propositions is then tested against the "worst case," that is against that body of known legal phenomena most likely to falsify my position. The accumulated scholarship of comparative law is used as a catalogue for searching out these worst cases. The purpose is to move toward a more general theory of the nature of judicial institutions.

Accordingly, chapter 1 first sets out the four propositions that define the conventional prototype of courts: independence, adversariness, decision according to preexisting rules and "winner-take-all" decisions. The conventional prototype can be most easily challenged by emphasizing the social control and lawmaking facets of the judicial function. The challenge is easiest in those realms partly because the prototype was really developed by focusing on a different function of courts, that of conflict resolution, and partly because assertions that courts are primarily engaged in social control and lawmaking are, and are intended to be, flat contradictions of elements of the conventional prototype. Precisely because I believe that the four prototypic propositions are incorrect, or at least incomplete and misleading, chapter 1 is devoted largely to the realm of conflict resolution, in which the best case can be made for them. It seeks to demonstrate that even in this realm courts are much less independent and adversarial than the prototype suggests and much less prone to follow preexisting legal rules or arrive at winner-take-all decisions. The main theme of this portion of the chapter is that courts seek to elicit the consent of the parties to their judgments by introducing important elements of mediation and compromise rather than simply imposing legally authoritative decisions in which the party whom they declare to be legally in the right wins and the loser is compelled to obey the court's command. More generally I argue that mediation and litigation are invariably intimately interconnected and interactive rather than distinct alternatives for conflict resolution.

Chapter 1 then does briefly survey social control and lawmaking by courts. In the process emphasis is placed upon the role of courts within political regimes. More particularly, the proposition is put forward that appeal, which is usually viewed as a process for the vindication of individual legal rights, is more properly seen as a device by which central political regimes consolidate their control over the countryside.

In each of the succeeding chapters a particular legal system is chosen for analysis because it is most likely to contradict a particular position I have adopted in chapter 1. Chapter 2 places my challenge to the judicial independence theme of the conventional prototype of courts in the context of English judicial experience. It does so because the conventional wisdom proclaims that it is in England that judicial independence has most clearly developed and flourished. Chapter 3 places the conventional prototype's insistence that judges decided by the application of preexisting legal rules in the context that appears to be most favorable to it and least favorable to my questioning of it. That context is the civil law system in which judges are supposed to be strictly bound by codes.

Because I have asserted in chapter 1 that mediation and litigation invariably intermingle rather than maintain themselves as distinct alternatives, chapter 4 deals with the traditional Chinese legal system, which is often presented as having chosen the mediation and rejected the litigation alternative. And given that I have argued in chapter 1 that appeal is all but universal because it serves the purposes of hierarchical regimes, chapter 5 is a study of the one major legal system that is reputed not to have appeal at all, that of traditional Islam.

Both prefaces may now join hands in the thanksgiving ritual. Portions of the materials in this book have appeared previously in the *North Carolina Law Review* and the *Handbook of Political Science* published by the Addison Wesley Publishing Co. and appear here by their kind permission. Indeed Fred Greenstein, who together with Nelson Polsby edited the *Handbook,* is responsible for having goaded me into producing what is now chapter 1.

Most of my writing has flowed pretty directly out of my experiences as a student and a teacher so that I confess to being a bit puzzled by the research versus teaching bout featured in the academic ring. I owe a great deal to my undergraduate political science department at U.C.L.A., to three of whose members this book is dedicated. One of my former colleagues in the School of Social Sciences at U.C. Irvine says in a preface that there must be something special about a school and a dean, Jim March, who will buy a grand piano for a sociology lab. My own improvisations at Irvine were of a different sort but equally tolerated. And my continuing thoughts on the subject of this book are encouraged by my colleagues in the Law School at Berkeley and the Political Science Department at U.C. San Diego, whose joint tolerance allows me to temper the rigors of Berkeley law with occasional immersions in the warmth of San Diego political science.

Barbara Shapiro has made some contributions to this book, not all properly credited in the footnotes. Our daughter Eve, however, is not a fan of history and social studies.

# 1　THE PROTOTYPE OF COURTS

Students of courts have generally employed an ideal type, or really a prototype, of courts involving (1) an independent judge applying (2) pre-existing legal norms after (3) adversary proceedings in order to achieve (4) a dichotomous decision in which one of the parties was assigned the legal right and the other found wrong. The growth of political jurisprudence[1] has been characterized largely by the discovery and emphasis of deviations from the prototype found in the behavior of particular courts, showing how uncourtlike courts are or how much they are like other political actors. While some political scientists and many lawyers have continued to protest against this approach, they have done so largely by reasserting the prototype.[2] Such a tactic is unconvincing because, if we examine what we generally call courts across the full range of contemporary and historical societies, the prototype fits almost none of them. Defense of the prototype thus seems fruitless. A study of courts that is essentially the measurement of deviance from a type that is rarely approximated in the real world would appear to be equally fruitless.

## The Logic of the Triad in Conflict Resolution

Perhaps it would be wise to begin over, employing a root concept of "courtness" but more freely accepting the vast variety of actual social institutions and behaviors loosely related to that concept without worrying about where "true courtness" ends and something else begins. For in reality there are few if any societies in which courts are so clearly delineated as to create absolute boundaries between them and other aspects of the political system.

The root concept employed here is a simple one of conflict structured in triads.[3] Cutting quite across cultural lines, it appears that whenever two persons come into a conflict that they cannot themselves solve, one solution appealing to common sense is to call upon a third for assistance in achieving a resolution. So universal across both time and space is this simple social invention of triads that we can discover almost no society that fails to employ it. And from its overwhelming appeal to common sense stems the basic political legitimacy of courts everywhere. In short, the triad for purposes of conflict resolution is the basic social logic of courts, a logic so compelling that courts have become a universal political phenomenon.

1

The triad, however, involves a basic instability, paradox, or dialectic that accounts for a large proportion of the scholarly quarrels over the nature of courts and the political difficulties that courts encounter in the real world. At the moment the two disputants find their third, the social logic of the court device is preeminent. A moment later, when the third decides in favor of one of the two disputants, a shift occurs from the triad to a structure that is perceived by the loser as two against one. To the loser there is no social logic in two against one. There is only the brute fact of being outnumbered. A substantial portion of the total behavior of courts in all societies can be analyzed in terms of attempts to prevent the triad from breaking down into two against one.[4]

CONSENT

The most fundamental device for maintaining the triad is consent. Early Roman law procedures provide a convenient example.[5] The two parties at issue first met to decide under what norm their dispute would be settled. Unless they could agree on a norm, the dispute could not go forward in juridical channels. Having agreed on the norm, they next had to agree on a judge, a third person who would find the facts and apply the previously agreed upon norm to settle their dispute. The eventual loser was placed in the position of having chosen both the law and the judge and thus of having consented to the judgment rather than having had it imposed on him.

The almost universal reluctance of courts to proceed in the absence of one of the two parties is less a testimony to the appeal of adversary processes than it is a remnant of this emphasis on consent, of both parties themselves choosing the triad as the appropriate device for conflict resolution. In early stages of English law, courts were frequently thwarted by the absence of one of the parties, and medieval procedure is full of elaborate devices for enticing or compelling the unwilling party into court rather than proceeding without him.[6] Modern British and American practice still prefers extended delay to the absence of one of the parties, and in many tribal societies the anthropologist encounters the same reluctance to proceed without all three members of the triad and comparable devices to cajole or coerce attendance.[7]

All of this can, of course, be put in the form of the classic political question: Why should I obey? The loser is told that he should obey the third man because he has consented in advance to obey. He has chosen the norm of decision. He has chosen the decider. He has thus chosen to obey the decision.

THE MEDIATING CONTINUUM

Nearly every triadic conflict resolver adds another device to consent in order to avoid the breakdown into two against one. This device is the avoidance of the dichotomous, imposed solution. In examining triadic conflict resolution as a universal phenomenon, we discover that the judge of European or Anglo-American courts, determining that the legal right lies with one and against the other of the parties, is not an appropriate central type against which deviance can be conveniently measured. Instead he lies at one end of a continuum. The continuum runs: go-between, mediator, arbitrator, judge. And placement on the continuum is determined by the intersection of the devices of consent and nondichotomous, or mediate, solution.

The go-between is encountered in many forms. In tribal or village societies he may be any person, fortuitously present and not connected with either of the households, villages, or clans in a dispute, who shuttles back and forth between them as a vehicle of negotiation.[8] He provides communication without the dangerous physical contact between the disputants that would otherwise be required. In more modern guise we find him as the sovereign offering "good offices" in an international dispute or the real estate broker shuttling between seller and prospective buyer and carefully keeping them apart at the negotiation stage. The go-between seems to operate in a pure consent, pure mediate-solution situation. He cannot function at all unless both parties consent to his offices and the solution reached is the product of free negotiation between the parties and is mutually satisfactory. And in theory, all resolutions offered and accepted are purely those of the parties themselves.

In reality, however, the go-between is not a mindless communicator. He exerts influence by "rephrasing" the messages he delivers. He may manage to slip in a fair number of proposals of his own. And by his characterization of the flexibility or inflexibility of each side to the other, he may strengthen or weaken the bargaining position of one or the other.

The mediator is somewhat more open in his participation in the triad. He can operate only with the consent of both parties. He may not impose solutions. But he is employed both as a buffer between the parties and as an inventor of mediate solutions. By dealing with successive proposals and counterproposals, he may actively and openly assist in constructing a solution meeting the interests of both parties.[9]

The distinction between mediation and arbitration in any particular society is a matter of legal nuance and often the subject of bitter controversy, particularly in such areas as labor arbitration. Often too the distinction is made between voluntary and binding arbitration. For our purposes we may treat arbitration generically and speak of it as involving less consent by the parties and less mediate solutions than mediation. Persons are not normally compelled to consent to arbitration. In this sense the arbitrator, like the mediator and the go-between, cannot function without the consent of both parties. In modern societies, however, arbitration clauses frequently appear in contracts so that the consent is somewhat attenuated. It is not consent of the moment to the arbitration of the moment but advance consent to future arbitration in general. Yet even such contracts almost invariably specify that the two parties must in each instance agree on who the arbitrator shall be.

The key distinction between the mediator and arbitrator, however, is that the arbitrator is expected to fashion his own resolution to the conflict rather than simply assisting the parties in shaping one of their own. And his solutions are not purely mediated in a number of senses. First, arbitrators, unlike mediators and go-betweens, usually work with a relatively fixed set of legal norms, analogous to that of the early Roman judge. The parties have consented to, or themselves constructed in advance, the norms to which they will now be subject. If in a given dispute one party has violated these norms more than the other, it is not expected that the arbitrator arrive at a compromise solution purely on the basis of the interests of the parties and quite apart from their obedience to the preexisting norms. Moreover, arbitration is frequently "binding" either by statute or under the terms of the contract. The arbitrator has the legal authority to impose his solution on both parties even if one or both do not voluntarily consent to the solution."[10]

Nevertheless, societies tend to turn to arbitration in situations in which, although overarching legal norms may exist, the most salient concerns are the interests of the two parties, neither of which is assigned greater legitimacy than the other. Mediate solutions acceptable to both parties are the goal, and, as a practical matter, few arbitrators would find much employment if they did not develop a record of providing such solutions.[11] Of course this is all the more true in "nonbinding" arbitration, in which the parties need not accept the arbitrator's resolution. In American labor law, for instance, a distinction is often made between "rights" arbitration and "interest" arbitration. In most labor-management contracts there are some provisions that set out with a relatively high degree of specificity the rights and duties of the two parties in relation to one another. When a dispute under one of these provisions is submitted to arbitration, both parties expect the arbitrator to decide who was legally right rather than provide a mediate solution. The same union and company may submit other kinds of disputes not covered by such precise contract terms to the same arbitrator and expect mediate solutions.

When arbitration is in no sense binding, it merges with mediation. When arbitration is binding, both in the sense that the two parties must go to arbitration on the demand of either and must then abide by the arbitrator's holdings, it tends to merge into judicial judgment. This is particularly true in instances such as "rights arbitration," when the arbitrator is expected to reach a legally correct rather than a mediate solution even though the "law" is that created by a mutually agreed contract between the parties. When arbitration is binding and dichotomous solutions are expected, then the "arbitrator" in fact becomes a kind of private judge, that is one who judges rather than mediates but does not hold the governmental office of judge. The very fact that he does not hold such an office but is chosen by the parties, rather than imposed on them, preserves a greater element of consent that continues to distinguish him from the official judge.

Recently one of the favored tactics for relieving delay in the civil courts has been the adoption of systems of compulsory arbitration in which suits involving relatively small amounts of money are assigned to "arbitrators" rather than tried before a judge. Such a system is not really one of arbitration but one of cheap judging. The arbitrator is expected to arrive at the same decision under the same law as would a judge. The parties usually do not choose the arbitrator. He uses simpler procedures and carries a lower overhead of courtroom costs than a judge and thus handles more cases at smaller cost. Such systems thus allow the appointment of a great many temporary judges by avoiding constitutional, statutory, and budgetary limitations on formal judicial appointments.[12]

### THE SUBSTITUTION OF LAW AND OFFICE FOR CONSENT

In turning now to judges, we return to the problem of consent and to our Roman example. As societies become more complex, they tend to substitute law for the particular consent of the parties to a particular norm for their particular dispute. They also substitute office for their free choice of a particular third man to aid in the resolution of their dispute. The earliest Romans might seek the aid of anyone in formulating a norm. They came more and more to turn to city officials for this assistance. The Praetorian Edict, which was the closest thing to a civil code that Rome as a city attained, long took the form of a series of norms that such an official announced he would supply to contending parties at their request. It was initially not a body of preexisting law but a catalogue of "ready-made" goods that replaced the still earlier practice of "tailoring" norms for each pair of disputants. As the practice grew under which each of the new praetors reenacted the edict of his predecessors, we can literally see what begins as a system of free legal advice to mutually consenting parties becoming a set of preexisting compulsory legal rules. A parallel development can be seen in the writings of the jurisconsults, which begin as professional legal advice to the praetors and litigants and end as operative parts of the Code of Justinian.[13]

The key factor in the shift from consent to law is specificity. Ethnographic and sociological materials make clear that in only a very limited number of special situations do litigants literally make their own rule of decision free of all preexisting norms.[14] At the very minimum there is a social sense of appropriateness or natural justice, of how we always do things or what we never do, of the sort suggested by the Tiv informant who says of what we would call a lawbreaker that he "spoils the tjar."[15] We may express this consensus in terms of custom or fundamental principles of ordered liberty or, as the Tiv does, as a psychic harmony of men and nature. It creates the constraints under which prospective litigants shape a norm for themselves. Indeed, much of judicial ritual, particularly in the holding of public trials, consists of reminding the litigants that as good men they must consent to the overarching norms of their society. Yet the more nebulous these norms, the greater the element of immediate and real consent in achieving a precise working rule for a particular case. At one extreme we find two disputing villagers working with an elder to settle the ownership of a pig according to the ways of the ancestors. If any rule of decision is actually formulated, it is likely to arise out of the adeptness of the elder in eliciting the face-to-face consent of the parties. At the other extreme we find litigants in a modern industrial state who discover at trial that their earlier behavior was governed by a detailed preexisting rule, even the existence of which was unknown to them at the time and which they consent to only in the generalized, abstract sense that all citizens agree to live under the laws of the state. The judge, then, unlike the mediator, imposes "his" rule on the parties rather than eliciting a consensual one.

Moreover, the parties may not specifically consent even to who shall impose his rule or decide under it. The most purely consensual situation is one in which the disputants choose who shall assist them in formulating a rule and who shall decide the case under it, as the Romans initially did. In most societies, however, there seem to be instances in which it pays to choose a big man to do these tasks, whether a government official like the urban praetor or, as among the Papuans, the owner of many pigs.[16] The disputants may turn to the big man because he knows more of the law and custom, because he has the economic, political, or social power to enforce his judgment, or because his success or high position is taken as a symptom of his skill and intelligence at resolving disputes. Beyond and perhaps out of this tendency to consent to judging by big men, many societies develop the office of judge so that the parties do not choose their judge. If they choose to go to court at all, they must accept the official judge. The ultimate step, of course, is in those instances in which a legal system not only imposes the law and the officer of the law but also compels one or both parties to resort to legal processes, as in a criminal trial or civil suit. The judge, then, unlike the mediator, imposes himself on the parties rather than being chosen by them.

He also may impose his resolution of their conflict. It is possible to envision a system in which the parties were compelled to accept the rule of decision and the person of the judge but were not compelled to accept his decision. Compulsory nonbinding arbitration sometimes comes down to this. That is, the parties may be compelled by statute or a contract provision to go to arbitration if a contract provision is in dispute, but the same statute and/or contract may not compel them to accept the arbitrator's award. Under the divorce procedures of many jurisdictions, ranging from some of the American states to many Communist countries, those seeking a divorce must first submit to "marriage counseling" by persons either licensed or employed by the government. They need not accept the "advice" of the counselor they are compelled to see. But they may only proceed with the divorce after they have heard the advice and rejected it. In some societies the losing party to one litigation might refuse the decision and resort to another forum or accept banishment. Appeal and pardon processes sometimes exhibit this feature, as for instance in "de novo" appeals, in which the dissatisfied party may get an entirely new trial from a higher court.

Nevertheless, in general, judges may impose a final resolution independent of the consent of the parties. Even when the third man must gain the consent of the parties to his resolution, as for instance the mediator must, it is possible for him to propose a dichotomous solution—one in which party A wins all and B loses all. But for obvious reasons he is unlikely to do so. When the specific consent of the parties is not required, such resolutions are more feasible. The go-between has little or no enforcement power. The mediator may do somewhat better by bringing to bear general social sentiment in favor of resolution. We often distinguish the arbitrator from the mediator on the basis that the arbitrator's decisions are subsequently enforceable by court action. Judges are furthest along the spectrum toward complete enforcement, typically having means to tap the organized forces of coercion in the society to enforce their solution. Moreover, where the judge is administering a detailed body of law whose building blocks are concepts of legal right and obligation, such resolutions are at least partially dictated by the rules of decision he has imposed on the parties.

Curiously enough it is precisely the need to elicit the consent of the loser to a decisional process that has been largely imposed on him that may lead to a decision stripping him of everything. To the extent that he believes that a third person whom he has not chosen is exercising discretion in behalf of his opponent, he may deny the legitimacy of the whole judicial system. Mediate solutions that split the difference between the two parties in various ways are likely to expose judicial discretion most clearly. Thus judges may find it preferable to issue dichotomous solutions, denying their discretion by arguing that under the preexisting law one party was clearly right and the other clearly wrong. The losing party may be unhappy with the resolution, but so long as he accepts the legitimacy of the "law," he may not perceive the judge as acting with his opponent.

The substitution of law and office for consent entails very major destablizing pressures on the triadic structure. For it was essentially his consent at every preliminary stage that enabled the losing disputant to continue seeing the triad as a triad rather than as two against one. If the loser does not specifically consent in advance to the norm, he must be convinced that the legal rule imposed on him did not favor his opponent. Thus the yearning for neutral principles of law found among contemporary lawyers.[17] And if he did not consent to the judge, he must be convinced that judicial office itself ensures that the judge is not an ally of his opponent. Thus the yearning for a professional and independent judiciary.[18]

Yet it is frequently difficult or impossible to convince the loser of these very things. First of all, many disputants are in a position to know or suspect that the law to be applied in their cases does favor their opponents. Most laws in most societies favor some classes of persons and disfavor others. Second, where the judge is a governmental or religious officer, then a third set of interests quite independent of those of the two disputants is interjected. One or both prospective litigants may perceive that the interests of the government or the church is contrary to his own. It is for these reasons that the judges and their professional defenders in most advanced societies spend such a large proportion of their dialectic and ritual talents promulgating and defending the prototype noted at the beginning of this study. Contemporary courts are involved in a permanent crisis because they have moved very far along the routes of law and office from the basic consensual triad that provides their essential social logic.

COURTS IN THE MEDIATORY CONTINUUM

Having said all these things, if we could now focus exclusively on judging in any further discussion of courts, the path would be fairly clear. However, if we turn to the work of those persons and institutions to which we normally award the titles judges and courts, we shall see that in reality they are simply at one end of a spectrum rather than constituting an absolutely distinct entity. Courts are clearly the least consensual and the most coercive of triadic conflict resolving institutions. The conventional prototype of courts has concentrated so heavily on the coercive aspects of courts, however, that it has tended to isolate judging unduly from other styles of conflict resolution. It is because elements of mediation and remnants of consent are integral to most court systems that the conventional prototype of courts is often misleading. Courts share with their fellow triadic conflict resolvers along the continuum the need to elicit consent. Among other things this means that mediating is not to be seen as an antithesis to judging but rather as a component in judging. Most judicial systems retain strong elements of mediation.

In chapter 4 we shall examine one of the longest-lasting judicial systems in history, that of imperial China. It so intimately intermingled mediation with imposed, dichotomous conflict resolution that it has often been mistakenly characterized as an entirely mediatory judicial system. In the English legal system discussed in chapter 2, we shall discover that, even before the Normans conquered England, the ideal of Anglo-Saxon jurisprudence was a resolution mutually agreed by the parties under supervision of, and recorded by, a court. Dawson has pointed out that arbitration played a very large role in the development of English equity in the sixteenth and seventeenth centuries and in the judicial business of the Privy Council. In the Roman formulary procedure described earlier, it appears to have been fairly common for the praetor to serve as or suggest an arbitrator rather than a judge to the contending parties. In these instances we use the term arbitration rather than mediation because the third party is supposed to take account of the legal rights or claims of the contending parties in framing a solution for their approval.

Indeed, it would not be difficult to move about the world's legal systems endlessly multiplying the examples of the intermingling of mediation and judging. Communist legal systems might seem to have a special penchant for "comradely mediation" between fellow members of the working class, since communists define law as an instrument of class oppression. Indeed, both in the West and in China, we encounter comradely courts that seek to resolve family, neighborhood, and work place disputes without formal judicial proceedings. But we also discover that these bodies tend to mix mediation with imposed solutions backed by the coercive authority of the party and the state. Moreover, comradely courts are almost invariably embedded in a conventional court structure staffed by professional judges applying law, or sometimes party policy that is treated as an integral part of law. Most communist states now operate their economies on a system of supply contracts entered into between industrial enterprises. Contracting parties engaged in a dispute are confronted by a range of arbitration and judicial proceedings quite similar to those in noncommunist states. Indeed, more generally, mediation and arbitration in the context of the opportunity to go into court if the parties cannot come to agreement is a typical pattern encountered in both communist and capitalist states.

Mediate solutions are most feasible when the disputed matter is divisible or can be converted into something divisible. At first glance it would seem to be injury or trespass that would be least amenable to mediation and most subject to the rule of "an eye for an eye." The common law system has often been taken as the model of dichotomous resolution, since it is a "strict" law system seeking to assign legal right to one of the parties and legal wrong to the other.[19] Yet the insistence of the common law that the central and usually sole remedy is money damages and that no resolution is possible unless one party can show he has been damaged in a compensable way reveals another dimension. The common law consistently converts indivisible disputes, that is, disputes over injury to person and property and disputes over the fulfillment or nonfulfillment of obligations into disputes over sums of money. Mediate solutions are always possible in disputes about money. Even a judge who must declare that one party is legally right and the other legally wrong need not resort to winner-take-all solutions. Typically he will award money damages that amount to more than the looser wants to pay but less than the winner claims he deserves. Moreover, where the Anglo-American law has developed equity as a means of resolving conflicts through remedies other than money damages, that is, through equitable decrees ordering someone to do something, it invokes the doctrine of "balancing of equities." That doctrine requires an equity court to shape remedies so as not to impose costs on one of the parties that far outweigh benefits to the other. In short, below the facade of dichotomous solution presented by Anglo-American courts lies the potential for mediation.

That potential is frequently realized in the courtroom itself, for instance when judge or jury reduces the amount of a damage award because the plaintiff, while legally right, was himself partly at fault. More fundamentally, money damages are mediatory because they allow the loser to substitute a money payment for the performance of some action to which he is strongly averse or for the acceptance of some distasteful retribution like suffering the loss of an arm because he has taken off someone else's.

However, in modern Anglo-American law systems, and for that matter in Continental ones, the area of mediation often moves outside the courtrooms. The bulk of conflict resolution through legal channels occurs by negotiation between the parties and their attorneys under the compulsion of eventual court proceedings should negotiations fail. To dismiss the vast bulk of conflict resolution by law in modern societies as somehow extrajudicial would both direct the student of courts away from the central phenomenon and lead to fundamental distortions of reality. For previously announced judicial rules and anticipation by the disputants of the costs and benefits of eventually going to trial are key parameters in such negotiations. They are not free bargaining based solely on the wills and immediate resources of the parties, but legalized bargaining under the shadow supervision of an available court.[20] Such negotiation is not purely mediatory, because the bargain struck will depend in part on the "legal" strength of the parties, that is, predictions of how each would fare in court. Yet such negotiations aim at, and in most instances achieve, a solution sufficiently satisfactory to both parties to avoid litigation. Failed negotiations may end up in court, where their judicial resolution sets the parameters for further negotiations. Thus the principal arena of modern legalized dispute settlement intimately intermixes elements of mediation and dichotomous solution, consent and judicial imposition.[21]

Conventional American legal scholarship has continued to draw a sharp line between mediation or negotiation on the one hand and judging defined by the prototype on the other. Two American scholars have recently delivered major attacks on that line.[22] Eisenberg has noted that, in both legal and anthropological literature, negotiation typically has been characterized as a matter of free bargaining determined entirely by the interests and power of the parties. In contradistinction to negotiation, litigation is usually seen as highly constrained by legal rules and principles. So far in this chapter, we have been concentrating on the elements of mediate settlement retained by judges engaged in litigation. Eisenberg is interested in the other side of the coin. He argues that, particularly when negotiation is carried on with the prospect that litigation may follow, negotiators invoke a great many rules and principles derived from the legal system and the more general set of social norms. Eisenberg finds major "continuities between the processes of dispute-negotiation and adjudication." While he deals largely with the diadic structure of negotiation between two parties, much of what he says would also apply to the triadic structure of mediation. Most importantly, his work shows that in actual, working legal systems, mediate solutions and legal rules are so intimately combined that the study of courts cannot proceed realistically without attention to both.

When Eisenberg comes to note the differences between negotiation and litigation, he places particular emphasis on the "binary" aspects of litigation. In part he is referring to the aspect of dichotomous, winner-take-all decision about legal right and wrong we have already noted. He also points to another aspect of dichotomous decision that we have not examined so far. Later in this chapter we shall note the important role of courts as fact finders. Even where facts cannot be established with certainty, Anglo-American courts typically make definitive findings of fact and treat them as certain even though they are established only by the preponderance of evidence.[23] This artificial dichotomy between the legally true version of the facts and the legally false one is, of course, closely related to the other dichotomy between legal right and wrong. For in order to assert that one party is certainly legally right and the other wrong, the judge must pretend that he knows with certainty what the factual situation was.

Later in this book we shall see that the desire for factual certainty marks most legal systems. In chapter 5 it will be noted that the standards of proof were so high in Islamic courts that a second court system had to be established to handle the bulk of cases in which those standards could not be met. In chapter 3, however, we shall see that French judges are far more willing than English and American judges to admit formally that they cannot be sure what the true facts of the case are. Instead of adopting the "binary" tactic of Anglo-American judges, they often openly admit that the facts remain unproved. Then they resort to an elaborate set of rules of presumption that determine which party is to win the case when the facts are uncertain. For instance we shall see that when a vehicle is involved in a damage situation, and it cannot be established with certainty what happened, French law presumes that the operator of the vehicle is responsible for the damage done.

Coons has attacked the binary fetish of American courts. He proposes that in certain instances the judge admit that the facts are indeterminate and then make decisions that give a 50–50 split to the parties instead of finding entirely for one of the other. Because both parties are supposed to be equal before the law, they should be treated equally by the judge in situations in which the crucial facts that would establish who was legally right and who wrong cannot be established with a reasonable degree of certainty. Coons offers the example of A, B, and C, who are hunting together. B and C fire at the same time. A loses an eye to a stray piece of bird shot. It cannot be determined with any degree of certainty whether the shot came from the gun of B or C. Should A get no compensation because he cannot prove whether it was B or C who injured him. Would it not be more just if he were awarded a sum of damages and B and C each ordered to pay half of them.[24] Coons relates his proposal to the mediation style of the Far East which we shall examine in chapter 4.

The work of Eisenberg and Coons shows that the prototype of courts and, particularly, the sharp disjunction between litigation and other modes of dispute settlement are being brought into question. They both describe and prescribe mixtures of imposed office and law with more mediational, consensual elements. In doing so they mirror a great deal of the reality of actual court systems that has been somewhat obscured by viewing courts through the conventional prototype.

Judicial striving for consent can be found everywhere in court procedures and proceedings. In criminal law, plea bargaining is the mediation of the interests of prosecution and defendant. Ethnographic materials, including those on American trial courts, give us numerous examples of judges proposing one solution after another and, by threat, persuasion, and the application of the social pressure brought by the audience, moving both parties to at least profess satisfaction with one of them.[25] Indeed, most of the conventional attachment to adversary proceedings is based not on the desire to heighten the level of conflict in judicial proceedings, but quite the opposite, on the need to have both parties present before the judge if he is to have any chance of creating a resolution to which both parties will consent. Every effort is made to preserve the appearance that the parties voluntarily come before the court. A striking feature of European and Anglo-American court systems in general is the extent to which the complaining party in civil suits must shoulder the burden of getting the other side into court with relatively little assistance from the court itself.

Perhaps more fundamental than these remnants of mutual consent to trial is the almost universal phenomenon that at least one of the disputants must choose to go to court. Only in isolated instances, such as the authority of the Soviet procurator to intervene in civil disputes,[26] are judicial services imposed on disputants neither one of whom wants them. In this sense while the parties no longer choose their particular law and their particular judge, at least one of them must choose the law and the courts.

In a substantial proportion of civil proceedings courts are used to settle contractual disputes in which the parties have in fact created the detailed rules of decision for themselves when they initially wrote the contract. Here again the partial phenomenon suggests the more general one. It is not only in contract disputes after all that the parties in consultation with the judge make the law. More often than not what we would label adversary proceedings are rituals in which three law speakers, the judge and the two parties or their attorneys, speak on until arriving at some verbal formulation of the law synthesized from their various versions. This can be seen at the simple level of a debate among tribal litigants about what the customs of the people truly are[27] and at the elaborate level of appellate opinions constructed out of bits and pieces of the opposing briefs.[28] Most courts make some law as they go along, and when they do so it is usually with the assistance of the parties.

Along the dimension of enforcement too we find the judge less far from the mediator than one might expect. In most societies courts have had only the most rudimentary enforcement mechanisms, often only a melange of voluntary compliance and self-help. Courts typically do not monitor compliance, and they reintervene to exact compliance only at the request of one of the parties. The reintervention often takes the form of a simple repetition of the previous order. The successful suitor even in a modern industrial society frequently finds that the decree is only the first in a long series of painful, expensive, and often inconclusive steps aimed at getting his remedy. Courts, we are repeatedly and rightly told, have neither the purse nor the sword. Perhaps more important, they rarely have the administrative resources to follow up on their resolutions. Most court systems seem to operate on the assumptions that both parties consent sufficiently to comply voluntarily at least as long as some vague threat of further judicial action is maintained.

It is hardly surprising that most judges spend a good deal of time as mediators. It might once have been argued that the emphasis on mediation in oriental courts was wholly or largely a result of Confucianism or the like, so that the oriental judge as mediator was a peculiar and culturally determined phenomenon. Structural rather than cultural factors, however, seem to be at the root of the matter. Even where law and courts are accorded a high level of legitimacy, true adversary proceedings culminating in a dichotomous verdict are an optimal mode of conflict resolution only for parties who in the future need have no relations or only arm's length relations with one another. For those who must maintain close economic or social relations, proceedings according to the prototype of courts are unlikely to be satisfactory. Given the substitution of law and office for consent, the loser will rarely feel sufficiently satisfied with the most extreme form of the judicial process to fully reenter those relations with the winner. And the less legitimacy is accorded the regime of which the court is a part, the less capable it will be at restoring a working relationship.

There are some societies where even those in close and continuing relationships are willing to accept dichotomous solutions with good grace. We generally find, however, highly mediatory styles of judging in agrarian villages, with a strong tendency on the part of the villagers to avoid the more courtlike courts of the central regime. Frequently there is an adoption of mediatory styles even by the courts of the regime. The classic Chinese situation may represent an extreme upward percolation of mediatory styles.[29] The medieval English arrangement may be more typical. There the large landowners, who were not only at arm's length but often at sword's point, resorted to the king's common law courts for strict law judgments of disputes with one another. However, when conflicts arose between lord and tenant or between tenants in the context of communal or partially communal agricultural production, they were generally resolved either in the lord's own or the communal (hundreds) courts. There a bailiff or group of elders worked in more mediatory style.[30] On the other hand, in seventeenth-century England and colonial and nineteenth-century America, where there were large numbers of individually owned and operated agricultural units producing for a cash market, there seemed to be specially high levels of litigation.[31]

The tendency toward mediation even by formally structured courts is not limited to communal agricultural settings. In modern Japan, for instance, which imported a highly adversary and dichotomous judicial style along with the German Civil Code, mediation continued as the basic judicial mode in the villages. Adversary litigation became more prevalent with urbanization and most prevalent in auto accident cases in which the parties had no continuity of relationships. Yet the major Japanese industrial cartels engage in relatively little litigation with one another or their sub-contractors.[32]

In Western societies as well, firms that must maintain continuous business relationships are not prone to litigation. Continuous business relation is usually expressed legally by contracts. It is precisely in contract relations that formal instruments of mediation and arbitration have exhibited tremendous growth in modern industrial states. Perhaps more important, as we noted earlier, negotiation under the umbrella of and within the restraints imposed by potential adversary proceedings with dichotomous solutions has become the principal mode of legalized conflict resolution in industrialized societies. And out-of-court settlement has become a major mode of resolution of even those conflicts that reach the stage of law suits. In criminal law, too, where the prosecutor has come to perceive his relation with criminals as a continuous one, plea bargaining has become the dominant mode of resolution in at least one highly urbanized, industrialized society, the United States.[33] Indeed, many observers trained to the prototype of courts are shocked by the informal, familial, conciliatory, and mediatory style of most American criminal proceedings.

Another clear example of the relation of mutual interdependency to the choice of mediatory rather than strict judicial proceedings is, of course, the endless proliferation of mediation and arbitration arrangements throughout the Western world for the resolution of labor-management conflicts.

In short, if one were to review all societies, or even to confine oneself to modern industrial and commercial states where one would most expect to find the prototypic court, one discovers that legal processes are not necessarily or entirely court processes, if we confine our definition of court to the prototype. For we frequently find intermediate rather than dichotomous resolutions. We find them aimed at the mutual satisfaction of the parties and conducted by their chosen representatives and often by a chosen third. We find them completed through procedures emphasizing mutual conciliation rather than adversary confrontation.

To put the matter another way, judges tend to share the same means of conflict resolution with other triadic figures, and most of those we would label judges engage in a great deal of mediation. Moreover, the substitution of law and office for consent has not been total even for those judges who act most independently of the wills of the parties in acquiring and resolving conflicts. As a result, even from the perspective of conflict resolution, where the prototype of court would seem to be most clear, we encounter grave difficulties. If we accept the prototype, we must admit that most of those we call judges do a lot of nonjudging. And we must confine the area of judicial studies to a very thin slice of the real world and one so arbitrarily sliced that it would appear senseless to most of the participants.

In this discussion we have focused on the commonalities between mediators and judges, particularly in the mixing of consent and coercion. In chapter 4 another point about the close relation between mediation and judging will be illustrated at length. It is no coincidence that in most developed legal systems, we encounter mediation and litigation side by side. Neither can function well without the other. Litigation facilities are very expensive. The opportunity to settle a large share of disputes by mediation reduces the costs of courts to proportions the political regime is willing to bear. Conversely, without the threat of litigation if mediation fails, parties to mediation would be far less willing to accept mediate solutions. Most mediation is far less consensual than in looks. Behind it lies the threat of litigation.

Thus even if we remain strictly within the area of conflict resolution, the conventional prototype of courts must be substantially modified by an appreciation of the important role of mediation within systems that proclaim themselves judicial. A substantial share of the legal conflicts in most societies is resolved not by dichotomous but mediate decision, either rendered by a court itself or under the shadow of potential court proceedings. Much of what courts do is not adversarial in the sense of encouraging or requiring disputations between the two conflicting parties. It is enough that both parties present their views to one another and a third or with the option of going to a third. The style of the interchange may be cooperative, benevolent, or even familial rather than one of ritualized trial by battle. Moreover, where courts preserve a more or less mediatory style, they may subtly mix preexisting legal rules with rules that emerge from the interaction of the parties. To the extent that there are preexisting rules, they may be ones created by the parties themselves in a contract. After the final settlement, less may depend on those rules than on a newly emerging agreement or understanding or set of subrules that is suggested or elicited in the very process of settling the dispute.

Only the prototypic element of judicial independence remains relatively pure in the context of conflict resolution. For neither of the conflicting parties is likely to accept anything other than pure mediation from a third who is tied to his opponent. That is, so long as the third exercises any independent influence over the outcome, he must demonstrate his independence of the party who achieves the more favorable outcome if he is to achieve the consent of the less favored. It is when we turn from conflict resolution to social control that the independence element of the prototype comes into serious question.

The basic tension to be found in courts as conflict resolvers lies in their need to persuade the parties that judges and laws they have not chosen nonetheless constitute a genuine, neutral third. Most of the ties courts maintain to the mediator, and many of the hiatuses of coercive power that we observe in the procedures of courts for acquiring the parties and imposing and enforcing verdicts, stem from this tension.

### Social Control

The conflict resolution role of courts has not been given pride of place here because it is the sole, "natural," or "correct" role of courts. We began with the conflict resolution aspect of the work of courts for three reasons. First, everyone seems to agree that conflict resolution is a basic task of courts. When we move, as we are about to, from conflict resolution to social control and lawmaking, we leave that consensus. Many students of courts would look at social control as a much more neutral function than that presented here and some would deny that courts do or should engage in lawmaking. Second, it is in the sphere of conflict resolution that the most favorable case can be made for the conventional, four-element prototype of courts presented at the beginning of this chapter. We have now seen that, even in that context, the prototype is misleading particularly in its third and fourth elements. Next we shall see that the first two elements of the prototype must be seriously questioned in the context of social control and lawmaking. Third, excessive emphasis on the social control and lawmaking aspects of the work of courts is likely to result in overstressing the role of coercion and underplaying the role of consent in the judicial sphere.

More important, such emphasis may lead to an artificial compartmentalization of judicial role that in turn may lead to a misunderstanding of crucial problems of judicial legitimacy. If the people or the regime approve the substance of the social control and/or lawmaking that courts do, the perceived legitimacy the courts may increase. Indeed it may increase quite independently of any legitimacy the courts acquire in the realm of conflict resolution. Yet the basic social logic of courts as conflict resolvers is so strong, particularly where links to consent can be maintained even as law and office are substituted for direct consent, that courts would be foolish not to enlist this conflict resolution social logic in behalf of their social control and lawmaking activities. Conversely, their social control and lawmaking activities may either emphasize or deemphasize the potential conflict between direct consent and its partial replacement by law and office. So social control and lawmaking activities may weaken or strengthen the social logic of courts in the conflict resolution area. The conflict resolution, social control, and lawmaking functions of courts must be seen as mutually interdependent. If we wish to view conflict resolution as first among equals, it is because the social logic or the triad may be a more constant source of legitimacy than popular support of the substantive policies embodied in the courts' social control and lawmaking activities.

While an analytical distinction can be drawn between the conflict resolution and social control activities of courts, in practice they are almost inevitably intertwined. Particularly in dealing with go-betweens and mediators or with judges chosen by the parties and employing a rule formulated by the parties, one may encounter a resolution which appears to be based solely on the interests of the parties, unconstrained by overreaching social norms, customs, or laws. But even when mutual consent of the parties is the dominating concern, the two parties will usually find themselves mutually consenting to the proposition that their conflict should be governed by some general norm of the society to which they belong. While our two early Romans may have occasionally invented a wholly new legal rule for themselves, most of their energies were no doubt directed at achieving an agreed verbal formulation of a Roman tribal usage or custom. It was to gain assistance in this task that they later turned to a praetor.

Thus even absent the imposition of law and office, the resolution of disputes through reference to a third is likely to entail the enforcement of broader norms on the parties either directly or as bounding constraints. Only the go-between shuttling between parties embedded in two quite different societies is likely to be acting without exerting any social control over the parties.

It is of course in the substitution of office and law for consent that the social control aspects of courts become most evident and most clearly create tensions with conflict resolution. When the two parties must go to a third who is an officer, it is as evident to them as to the observer that they are no longer going to a disinterested third. Instead they are introducing a third interest: that of the government, the church, the landowner, or whoever else appoints the official. To be sure, even the Papuans who mutually choose a "big man" to settle their disputes do not expect him to be neutral in the sense of having no interests of his own. Indeed the bigger he is, the broader is likely to be the web of his interlocking social and economic interests among the various genetic, economic, and social units to which the disputants belong. But the requirement of mutual consent allows the Papuans, like modern corporations in search of an arbitrator, to settle on a third who will not see his interests, whatever they may be, as parallel to those of one but not the other of the parties.

When litigants do not freely choose their judges, a number of alternatives arise. First, when both parties perceive the interests of the regime to be hostile to their own, the parties will not go to the official court. Indeed, considering the whole of human experience, this avoidance of courts because they represent the interests of others or outsiders is more the norm than the exception. Second, when both parties perceive the interests of the regime to be complementary or irrelevant to their own, they may go to court. Thus the bailiff of an exploitive, foreign, and hated feudal lord may be the perfect judge for two serfs in conflict over the rightful possession of a cow precisely because the lord doesn't care which of them milks it so long as he gets half the milk.

Third, when one of the parties perceives the interests represented by the judge as hostile to his own and favorable to his opponent, litigation may occur if the other party or the court has sufficient coercive resources to bring the reluctant party in, but the basic social logic of the court will disappear. Should the self-perceived underdog actually lose, he will see the situation as two against one and the role of the court not as conflict resolver but as coercer.

This phenomenon is, of course, clearest in criminal law, where coercion against one of the parties is at a maximum.[34] It is equally operative, however, in many noncriminal matters where the law clearly favors one class of parties over another. In most legal systems once a legal debt has been voluntarily incurred, the law greatly favors the creditor over the debtor who cannot or will not repay. The debtor correctly sees judges hearing debt litigation as essentially engaged in enforcement of the law through the harnessing of public authority to the efforts of the creditor to collect. Thus in most debt actions the debtor simply does not appear in court for the litigation and loses by default.[35] He correctly sees the judge as precommitted to his opponent's side. When a class of legally disfavored litigants has the political strength, it may attempt to prevent the courts from acting at all. In America indebted farmers have from time to time gotten "mortgage moratorium" laws through state legislature. Such statutes prevent judges from making mortgage foreclosure orders for a certain period of time. American labor unions belonged to the winning New Deal political coalition in 1932. They quickly used their new political power, first to strip federal judges of the power to enjoin strikes and later to set up a new body of law favorable to labor and a new court, the NLRB, to enforce it. They perceived the old law and its judicial enforcers as favorable to management.

It is to counteract these perceptions of judges as part of a two against one rather than a genuinely triadic structure that the prototype stresses the "independence" of the judge. More of the resources of legal scholarship and argumentation are spent on building up the ideology of judicial independence than on any other part of the prototype precisely because the court's basic social logic as triadic conflict resolvers rests on this element.

In the most basic and usually the least important sense, independence would mean that the judge had not been bribed or was not in some other way a dependent of one of the parties. But when we ensure this kind of independence by creating the office of judge within some governmental structure, in a far more important sense he is not independent, for he is a dependent of those for whom he holds office. Thus explicators of the prototype have come to define independence not so much as independence from the contending parties as independence from those to whom the judge owes his office. They stress the institutional separation of courts from the remainder of the political system.[36] To make independence in this sense the touchstone of "courtness" is to measure from the most deviant case. Looking at all known societies, we find a number of typical locations within the political structure for judging. One is the whole body of the tribe, the folkmoot, in which, far from having separate judges, the entire polity does the judging.[37] In tribal societies organized under strong chiefs, the chiefs judge with or without the assistance of the elders and the body of tribesmen.[38] In village societies the elders do much of their own judging.[39] In feudal societies the feudal magnates do much of the judging. In empires almost invariably the administrator of the geographic unit is the judge in those matters not delegated to or retained by the conquered peoples. In short, the universal pattern is that judging runs as an integral part of the mainstream of political authority rather than as a separate entity. In those societies in which sovereignty can be located, the sovereign judges. In those in which political authority is not clearly concentrated, those who hold the dispersed authority judge.

### JUDGING AND ADMINISTRATION

The congruence of administering and judging must be specially noted. Indeed, the observer who did not so firmly believe in the independence of judging might take judging for a special facet of administering. Both the judge and administrator apply general rules to particular situations on a case-by-case basis. Both tend to rely heavily on precedent, fixed decisional procedures, written records, and legalized defense of their decisions. Both are supplementary lawmakers engaged in filling in the details of more general rules. Both are front-line social controllers for more distant governing authorities. And in a startling number of instances both are the same person, and a person who draws little or no distinction between administering and judging.

The most striking example is the imperial administrator. The all-purpose geographic officer is the mainstay of empire, whether he be British district officer or the Chinese mandarin described in chapter 4. Such officers are there to keep the peace and collect the taxes—not unrelated functions. And for better or worse, in practice the imperial prefects are also the imperial judges. While in very wealthy empires, and at the higher levels of geographic subdivision, one may sometimes catch even substantial judicial subspecialization among the immediate subordinates of a governor, the norm is the all-purpose officer serving in the field.

The connection between tax gathering and judging is not confined to purely imperial situations. Much the same phenomenon is to be found in feudal monarchies. The English Exchequer described in chapter 2 is an obvious example, but in Tokugawa, Japan, as well, a good rule of thumb is that whoever is responsible for supervising the rice tax is also a judge.[40] Feudal systems like empires make liberal use of the all-purpose local administrator. And far more important than the fact that feudal magnates enjoyed the rights of the high justice and the low was that their bailiffs, who were primarily local agricultural administrators and tax collectors, also presided over the local baronial court.

As we shall see in chapter 2, English common law judges begin as royal administrators who dispensed the king's justice in the course of doing the rest of the king's business. And that great rival of the common law courts, the courts of equity, are the courts of the chief administrative official and tax collector of the realm, the chancellor. The justices of the peace were simultaneously judicial and administrative officers.[41]

We also encounter this affinity between judging and administration in the town magistrates, who are in many ways the equivalent of the general-purpose administrators of the countryside. From imperial Japan to colonial Massachusetts and medieval France, wherever a body of local notables has been vested with the authority to direct municipal affairs, it will be found with authority to do local judging. Indeed, the title "magistrate" has become an almost purely judicial one in the United States, although clearly the magistrates of colonial America, like those of medieval Europe, were all-purpose urban authorities.[42] Indeed, precisely because judging is traditionally an integral part of the local governor's tasks, in England and America we sometimes get the reversal of titles, as in those midwestern American states where county administrators bear the title "judge." The Roman praetors, whom we have seen play such a large role in early Roman litigation, were general city magistrates.

We can attribute this congruence of judging and administration to a number of factors. First of all, to return to our triad, it is as natural for two disputing parties to turn to a government official in places where there is a government as it is for two tribesmen to turn to the owner of many pigs where there is not. The local governor is a big man and thus "available" for judging. Like the owner of many pigs, the governor may import interests of his own into the resolution of the dispute, but also like the pig owner, he may counterbalance this drawback by his greater resources for eliciting the consent of or coercing the reluctant party. Second, endless disputes about the whole web of obligations owed by the locals to their lords, churches, sovereigns, and chiefs inevitably arise in the course of bringing the demands of the higher to the lower, which is the core of feudal and imperial administration. Moreover, as the growth of the Exchequer courts shows, these disputes grow outward from conflicts between man and distant master to conflicts between local man and local man. "I cannot pay my taxes because I loaned my neighbor money which he refuses to pay back. Get my money back and I will pay my tax." In these instances the administrator will find the settlement of disputes a routine part of his job. There is usually no one else to do the judging chores, and if he doesn't do them, he cannot get his job done.

Third, the mandarin or district officer is there to exert a certain measure of social control. Because the imposition of norms as a means of settling a dispute between two individuals is one mode of exercising social control, he will seize on it along with all the others.

COURTS AND THE REGIME

Perhaps the most important factor in explaining the historical congruence of judging and administering is to be found in a far broader aspect of the administrator's responsibility for social control. The origin of judicial systems in many parts of the world is to be found in conquest.[43] This is obviously true for imperial judicial systems such as those of Rome, China, and the black empires of central Africa such as the Barotse. As we shall see in chapter 2, it is also clearly true for the common law courts imposed over the old moot and hundred folk courts by the Norman conquerors. Conquest created the British courts of colonial India and Africa as well as many other colonial court systems. The Supreme Court of the United States and the lower federal courts insofar as they operate on the old Confederacy are courts of conquerors. Even where courts are not directly imposed by force of arms, they will often be identified with the political regime or with distant rather than local authority.

Conquerors use courts as one of their many instruments for holding and controlling conquered territories. And more generally, governing authorities seek to maintain or increase their legitimacy through the courts. Thus a major function of courts in many societies is a particular form of social control, the recruiting of support for the regime.

When conquerors impose courts, often we discover a form of "extraterritoriality." The new courts serve to resolve conflicts between one conquering cadre and another or between a conqueror and a native when the native courts cannot be trusted to do the job. The claim to Roman citizenship was in part a claim to Roman courts and Roman procedure even in those portions of the empire where indigenous courts functioned. At their inception English common law courts were resorted to on the civil side almost entirely by Norman overlords in their relations with one another. The King's Peace enforced by those courts was largely a body of rules designed to protect Normans from Saxons. The clerical courts of the Roman Catholic Church, which are so important in the whole development of Continental judicial systems, are one of the foremost examples of such extraterritorial courts.

Aside from this extraterritorial value of newly imposed courts, the conqueror is soon likely to discover a number of other advantages they may yield. A scattered population living largely by customary and local law may be governed more efficiently by central authorities if a unified body of law is introduced. Moreover the conqueror often finds that rule is facilitated by reaching some working relationship with the indigenous notables and delegating considerable authority to them in exchange for their support. As a result of the interaction of these two considerations, an imposed body of law is typically particular laws and customs that have previously governed the notables transformed into a body of uniform law designated to govern everyone. In short, the conqueror melds his own and indigenous upper class law, universalizes it, and imposes it over the local and particular rules that have previously been the body of law of the peasantry and smallholders. The Normans combine their own law with that evolved by Saxon notables in their relations with one another to create a body of law that is essentially landowners' law. They impose that law over the existing plethora of local customary law and make it common to all of England. We shall see in chapter 2 that English law and courts evolved as part of the attempt of a conquering regime to create centralized and uniform rule over all its domains. Some centuries later the descendants of these conquerors conquered another domain. They combined their own law with Brahmin law, imposed it over local custom and caste rules and made it the law common to all of India.[44]

Thus a major function of courts in many societies is to assist in holding the countryside. They provide an extraterritorial court to adjust relations among the occupying cadres according to their own rules. They also provide a uniform body of national law in order to facilitate central administration and cement the alliance between conquerors and local notables.

There is yet another strand to this development. One mode of consolidating the legitimacy of an imposed regime is to provide more and better government services than its predecessor. Newly imposed courts might provide not only the advantages just indicated but speedier, fairer, more just resolutions of conflicts within the indigenous population. New courts might compete with indigenous modes of conflict resolution. To the extent that they won the competition, they would aid the central authorities in breaking into the cake of local custom and bringing government influence down into the villages. Judicial services, like medical services, are a way into the countryside. Such new courts would provide a body of more specific, uniform, and flexible law that would appeal to those locals inhibited by the old customary law.[45] They would also provide an "independent" judge freer of local dominant interests than the village elders or the folk courts. Thus what we often mean by an independent judiciary is one that serves upper class and nationalizing interests rather than dominant local interests and thus one more satisfactory to persons trying to break through the web of local interests.[46] We shall trace this kind of phenomenon quite specifically in chapter 2 in describing the growth of English common law courts. In spite of a certain antipathy to litigation in Chinese imperial administration, chapter 4 will show that local administrators also used the availability of judicial services as a way of learning more about the countryside and exerting government influence often in alliance with the local gentry.

Given these considerations, the congruence between administering and judging is hardly surprising, for judging, like administering, may be principally designed to hold and exploit the countryside for the central regime. Indeed for roughly the same reasons, courts may appeal to those who wish to resist, revolt against or maintain their independence from central regimes. Thus the Cao Dai in Viet Nam built up its own court system as part of its sect building. Access to better judicial services than were provided by the French was one of the benefits offered to members.[47]

SOCIAL CONTROL, LEGISLATION, AND CONFLICT RESOLUTION

The relation of the social control function to the prototype of courts must be seen, however, in a far broader context than the special case of the newly imposed courts of conquering regimes, even though the special case accounts for a large proportion of court systems. To do so it is convenient to move from the substitution of office for consent to the substitution of legislation for disputant-originated rules of decision.

The substitution of law for the immediate consent of the parties to a particular rule is to be found widely in the dispute settlement as well as the social control aspect of judicial work. Indeed, while it would be overly ambitious to propose a general evolutionary hypothesis, laws of social control seem frequently to arise out of recurrent dispute-settlement situations. Criminal law is the most obvious form of social control through law. Yet simple societies rarely distinguish private from criminal law. The moot and more generally the popular witnessing of and participation in judicial proceedings often seem to express the understanding of communal societies that, where social units are small, any dispute between two members has immediate consequences for the whole. The whole therefore judges, and judges not only with an eye to conflict resolution, but to its own more general well-being. This understanding may also be expressed in the conception of the crime of witchcraft, which is often seen as an interpersonal dispute carried to a level of intensity dangerous to the community.[48] Banishment, a popular form of remedy in relatively simple societies, is obviously a simple mode of conflict resolution through the physical separation of the parties. But it is also a simple mode of social control by getting rid of a troublemaker. And more deeply, its rationale is frequently the fear that harboring a wrongdoer will bring the wrath of the gods on the community as a whole.[49]

At English common law, criminal law was not clearly separated from tort until the seventeenth century. Tort law represented the extension of judicial conflict resolution services by the crown to individual disputants where one man had injured another. Yet throughout the medieval period, many of these same personal injuries, such as assault, were recognized as breaches of the King's Peace. A single judicial proceeding might result in the levy of money damages to be paid to the injured party and a fine to be paid to the crown. Of course even today, in both common and Roman law systems, a single act may give rise to both criminal and civil proceedings.[50] In the earliest Roman law, all of the offenses that we would today label criminal were treated as civil injuries subject to private conflict resolution by judges selected by the parties. Roman criminal courts with preselected juries were first created for the peculiarly political crime of malfeasance in public office and only gradually acquired general criminal jurisdiction.[51]

Even when we look at property and tort—the central pillars of interpersonal conflict resolution—we discover important impositions of social control through bodies of law apparently designed essentially to serve only the private interests of the parties. In tort law the "reasonable man," and his equivalent in the civil law of delict, is a vehicle for importing into personal disputes general social standards of how men should act. If one does not act in accord with the general social norms defining reasonable conduct, the court will award damages to one's opponent. Anglo-American property law is essential feudal in origin and thus is marked by the intimate mixture of rights reserved against one's equals and inferiors and obligations owed one's superiors which characterizes feudal law. Even to the extent that modern Continental property law claims to be purified of its own feudal experience, it harks back to a classic Roman law of property that specifically subjects the personal use of property to the interests of the state.[52]

At the point at which the judge is expected to apply general preexisting law in the settlement of disputes, that law becomes an element of social control. That law must come from somewhere. Whether its origin is in custom, or in the systematizing of earlier judgments, or in the fiat of the rulers, or in some legitimated process of legislation, its very nature as a general rule applicable to future situations imports some element of social concern beyond the particular concerns of the particular disputants. The Marxists tell us that laws always embody the interests of the ruling classes. Certainly even those rules consciously designed to meet only the interests of prospective disputants cannot be totally neutral in the sense of embodying no general social vision of right and wrong or appropriate and inappropriate conduct. Even societies that profess no conscious desire to impose specific social norms in the process of resolving interpersonal disputes will in fact resolve those disputes on the basis of whether the parties have acted "as we always do things" or, alternatively, have "bloodied the arrows" or "spoiled the tjar."

Thus so long as a judge acts to impose preexisting rules on the disputants, he is importing an element of social control. Or to put the matter differently, he is importing a third set of interests, whatever interests are embodied in those rules, to be adjudicated along with interests of the two parties. In this sense the prototype's elements of judicial independence and judgment according to preexisting rules are always in conflict. For the preexisting rules almost invariably embody some public interest over and above and in contradistinction to the interests of the two parties. To the extent that the judge employs preexisting rules not shaped by the parties themselves, he acts not independently but as a servant of the regime, imposing its interests on the parties to the litigation. Chapter 2 is designed to illustrate this point at length.

PUBLIC REGULATION

When we reach the criminal law itself, and the other bodies of law that openly purport to impose the interests of the regime on individuals and groups, the vision of the triad becomes even more difficult to maintain, particularly where judicial office exists. If the judge is himself an officer of the crown, and the dispute is in the form of the *Crown* v. *Doe,* in what sense do we have a triad as opposed to a simple inquisition? We have noted that judging is a concomitant of sovereignty or at least political authority. When the whole tribe, or its representative jury, or the village elders meet to judge a transgression against the people or the community, in what sense do we have a triad? Yet over the whole range of our experience we observe acts that are defined as offenses against the collectivity judged by the collectivity itself or by "judges" who are supposed to be the representatives of the collectivity.

Thus even if we could preserve the notion of the completely independent third in the realm of "pure" conflict resolution, assuming such a realm existed, we could not do so in the realm of social control because of the very nature of judicial office and proceedings in that realm. Moreover, in that realm the legal rules applied to a litigation that in form is a dispute between one party—the community—and a second party—the alleged transgressor—are rules that consciously and openly were created by and for one of the parties. Thus to return to our prototype, the very facts that (3) the proceedings are adversary and (2) apply preexisting legal norms ensure that we will *not* have (1) an independent judge. For even in those few societies that seek to insulate the judge from the rest of government, he is expected to administer the criminal law, that is, to impose the will of the regime on a party being prosecuted by the regime. With extremely great care to the various rituals of independence and impartiality, some criminal courts may succeed in maintaining the appearance of thirdness. However, few of the defendants in contemporary Western criminal courts are likely to perceive their judges as anything other than officers of the regime seeking to control them.[53] The criminal defendant has not chosen his judge. Indeed, he would avoid the courtroom entirely if he could. But more important, the burglar correctly perceives that the judge is there as a social controller to enforce the law against burglary. He is not a neutral third who has no more attachment to the state's interest in preventing burglary than to the burglar's interest in pursuing his profession. It is not that the burglar does not grant legitimacy to the law against burglary. While they may excuse their own conduct in various ways, most burglars would acknowledge that their ought to be a law against burglary. It is precisely because they perceive the law to be legitimate and the judge obligated to enforce it that they know he is not a neutral third but a friend of the prosecution. So to put the matter somewhat differently, when the government or the people are one of the parties to a dispute, the triadic structure is necessarily weakened when the judge is either an officer of the government or is the people themselves.

While this weakening of the triad is clearest in criminal law, it is also fairly evident in all bodies of "public" law, that is, law setting out the relations between governor and governed. Those societies that engage in the greatest separation of powers or specialization of judicial function approach nearest to a perception of judicial independence. At least the private party engaged in a dispute with one segment of government is judged by an officer of another segment. But, as we have already seen, it is a far more typical governing arrangement to subsume judicial under administrative tasks than to create a judicial specialization. Moreover it is typical of Continental legal systems and their offspring to handle a substantial proportion of public law litigation in "administrative courts," which are less clearly differentiated from the administrative agencies than are the regular courts of the same systems.[54] Even in the United States and Commonwealth countries, where constitutional separation of powers is most complete, a curious paradox arises because of the very inclination to separate. We encounter a common pattern in which the courts of the central government are relatively independent of the rest of that government, a federal system exists, and the highest court of the central government referees constitutional disputes between the central government and the federal units. In this situation the central court is frequently and often rightly perceived not as an independent third but as an arm of the central government imposing central control on the federal units. Particularly when the central court is imposing the will of a national majority over that of a local majority, as in many of the United States Supreme Court's race and religion decisions, the local majority sees the court not as an independent adjudicator but rather as the imposer of national uniformity over local diversity.[55]

We have argued that the substitution of office and law for consent gravely impairs the basic triadic logic of courts in the sphere of conflict resolution and even more particularly when courts are primarily engaged in social control. Another way of putting this is that precisely because we vest social control as well as conflict resolution in courts, their triadic position is impaired. For in most legal systems the litigants are aware that the judge is concerned not only with refereeing their two sets of interests but with imposing a third set of interests on them both.

## Courts as Lawmakers

When we move from the conflict resolution and social control tasks of courts to their lawmaking tasks, the triad may be even further weakened. Nearly all contemporary students of courts agree that courts do engage in at least supplementary and interstitial lawmaking, filling in the details of the statutory or customary law.[56] In several major legal systems courts go far beyond interstitial lawmaking. The common law of the Anglo-American legal system is largely judge-made. Whether we should speak of the *jus gentium* and other praetorian law of imperial Rome as judge-made depends on whether we choose to call the praetors judges or administrators. Similarly, Jewish and Islamic law contain large components of judge-made law if we choose to call judicial the legal pronouncements of religious officials who frequently performed in triadic contexts.[57] Moreover, the affinities and overlappings between judicial lawmaking and administrative rule making are so great that they can be only artifically separated. When administrators do judging, it is often impossible to distinguish between "case law" and administrative law, as for instance in the mass of *harigami*, which formed an important portion of traditional Japanese law.[58] Even in modern Roman law systems, where theoretically the lawmaking power of courts is severely limited, substantial and systematically articulated bodies of law have been judicially constructed from very slight statutory foundations.[59] Chapter 3 focuses on judicial lawmaking in the Roman law systems of Western Europe.

Much of the thrust of the judicial behavior literature[60] has been toward showing that there has been a high correlation between judges' political attitudes and their decisions for and against certain categories of litigants. This literature further suggests that these judicial attitudes fall into the same relatively coherent ideological patterns found in the national political culture. Considerably less success has been encountered in linking these patterns of political attitudes to the personal backgrounds of the judges, their modes of appointment, or the social and political structures in which they operate. Nevertheless, the brute fact of judicial discretion, even within systems of highly articulated statutory and constitutional law, has been more than sufficiently demonstrated. In short, while the development of a political psychology of judging may be still at an early stage, the behavioral literature has fairly convincingly demonstrated that many judges are not entirely "neutral" thirds but instead bring to the triad distinct public policy preferences, which they seek to implement through their decisions.

Aside from actual empirical discovery of widespread judicial lawmaking, it is clear that such lawmaking is logically required wherever law is substituted for consent in the triadic resolution of conflict. For if the third person must resolve conflict, and if he must do so by preexisting law, then he must "discover" the preexisting law. Because no human society has ever sought to set down an absolutely complete and particularized body of preexisting law designed exactly to meet every potential conflict, judicial "discovery" must often of necessity be judicial lawmaking.

In addition to the simple fact and logical necessity of judicial lawmaking, it is clear that many societies, including even those that seek to separate judicial from administrative and legislative office, quite deliberately vest major lawmaking functions in courts. In common law countries numerous instances may be found in which legislatures have given courts new jurisdictions without giving them new substantive statutory law for those jurisdictions. Alternatively, they may have written statutes whose key operative words are common law terms of art that incorporate past and invite future judicial lawmaking. In the United States the statutory creation of a federal labor contract jurisdiction without the provision of any substantive federal law of contracts and the Sherman Anti-Trust Act's condemnation of conspiracies in "restraint of trade" are obvious examples. In France the creation of an elaborate hierarchy of administrative courts with extensive jurisdiction combined with a singularly cryptic body of statutory administrative law was surely an invitation to administrative judges to make their own law—an invitation that they have accepted.[61]

Two basic judicial lawmaking situations exist. The judges may make law in the sense that a generalized political authority does triadic conflict resolution, administers and enforces various social norms, and announces new norms without clearly differentiating among the three. Thus in Llewellyn's and Hoebel's famous example of Cheyenne lawmaking, the "soldiers," a group whose principal task is to supervise the tribe's collective buffalo-hunting operation, are confronted by an incidental task of conflict resolution. In this context they announce that from now on no one should borrow another's horse without asking permission.[62] In short, frequently when we speak of judicial lawmaking, we are really observing the phenomenon of merged judicial, administrative, and legislative lawmaking powers in a single political authority which we have already noted is far more common than judicial separation.

The second basic judicial lawmaking situation is one in which a separated and specialized judiciary nevertheless makes law. We have just noted that in theory, in fact, and in the consensus of scholarly observers,[63] all such courts do engage in lawmaking.

Both of these lawmaking situations arise from political economy in the most fundamental sense of that term. Most societies cannot afford or do not choose to allocate sufficient resources to provide three men or three institutions to do the job of governing that can be done by one. The general governor, whether he be king, chief, popular assembly, or district officer, will do the lawmaking and the judging because he has enough resources to do all the governing.

Even when a society does choose to nourish a number of governing bodies, including one or more primarily devoted to triadic conflict resolution, two other interlocking elements of political economy come to the fore. Separate courts are a very expensive commodity. Once in existence there will be strong and continuous pressure to pile additional tasks on them, to get one's money's worth out of them, so to speak. In the United States a strong constitutional tradition of separation of powers has allowed the Supreme Court to fend off some unwanted additional tasks. But that very same tradition has served as a basis for the Court acquiring enormous lawmaking powers. In the United States today federal and state courts are drawing school district lines, administering prisons, supervising railroads, prescribing personnel procedures for police departments, altering the time schedules and design features of vast construction projects, determining patterns of urban development, and preserving the seacoasts.[64] And one basic reason they are doing these things is that where there are tasks to be done, it will frequently appear quicker and cheaper to assign them to an existing government agency than to create a new one. Thus even in the context of a strong ideological commitment to separation of powers, courts will pick up many lawmaking and administrative tasks simply because they are there.

Because there is a general tendency to economize by piling tasks on existing institutions, any expensive institution of government can be expected to have multiple functions. This phenomenon appears in preliterate, feudal, mercantile, and industrial societies. Multiple-function government institutions also have a second political economic advantage. Sometimes consciously and sometimes not, they create governmental redundancies that have significant survival value for the political system. In no society is politics marked by totally rational sequences or even certainty of outcome. In all governing systems, key links intermittently fail. Thus the existence of many alternative channels for accomplishing any given task of government may be an important guarantee of even minimal political efficiency. If the police cannot quell the riot, perhaps the army can. If the city government cannot provide vocational education, perhaps the state can. If the legislature will not respond to the needs of racial minorities, perhaps the executive will.

The earlier enthusiasm of students of organization for rationalizing administration through an extreme form of the division of labor, in which each unit did do and could do only one thing, has faded. The messiness of most governments, with their multiple overlapping and competing agencies, has certain advantages after all.[65] Governmental redundancy is not only an advantage in the sense that a new agency can be found to take over from a failing one. As proponents of mixed government and the division of powers have argued from ancient times, multiple government agencies may also serve as a salutary check on one another. But what has often been less clear is that agencies cannot check one another unless each is capable of performing at least some of the vital functions of the other. If each agency of government is so specialized that it cannot do anything but one preset operation in the total process of government, the assembly line that results will give each agency an absolute veto over the operations of government. For if any one withdraws, the product cannot be completed. In theory, perhaps, skillful bargaining with elaborate side payments among the veto wielders could produce both internal checks and a functioning government. In practice, the more each participant can meet other participants' threats of absolute veto by moving to perform the tasks of the threatener, the more likely we are to achieve the functioning moderation that seems to be the aim of the proponents of mixed government.

Thus it is precisely in those governments in which the independence of the judiciary is stressed, because of a desire to check and balance, that the judiciary is likely to acquire substantial lawmaking and administering capabilities. In such governments the existence of checks and balances means numerous roadblocks along any policymaking avenue, so that a great premium is placed on exploring alternative avenues or detours. In those same governments, agencies pushed to watch and check one another necessarily acquire one another's capabilities. Thus the ultimate strategy for anyone wishing to get something out of government is to treat all agencies as multiple purpose, shopping among them until any one or any combination of them will yield what is desired.[66] Americans, for instance, have learned that if the Congress won't give them what they want, the president may, and if he will not, perhaps the Supreme Court will.

### JUDICIAL INDEPENDENCE AND JUDICIAL LAWMAKING

In a great many nations judicial independence is conceived not in terms of a tripartite constitution with checks and balances but simply in terms of a professional judiciary sufficiently insulated from other governmental influences to operate within its own sphere under the rule of law. The courts of Great Britain and czarist Russia would show the range of this sort of independence. It may be found all the way from liberal constitutional systems emphasizing responsible but centralized political authority to pure autocracies. Obviously some political systems that seek to concentrate political authority will find that the triad is an extremely useful tool of conflict resolution. Such systems will then encounter the dynamics of the triad that we have already encountered. They may be willing to pay the costs to centralization of creating a relatively independent judicial authority in order to reap the benefits of increased capacity for conflict resolution.

Precisely because they want such triads for routine conflict resolution among private citizens while seeking to keep political power away from the judges, such regimes necessarily encounter difficulties with their judiciaries. For we have already seen that in the course of doing conflict resolutions, either under preexisting legal rules or otherwise, courts will make law. To express the same thing differently, they will exercise political power. When this inevitable phenomenon is encountered, both autocratic and constitutional regimes of centralized political authority can respond in one of four ways. First, they can yield and in the process become less centralized. Second, they can systematically withdraw from the legally defined competence of the judiciary all matters of political interest to themselves. Third, they may intervene at will to pull particular cases out of the courts and into their own hands. Fourth, they can create systems of judicial recruitment, training, organization, and promotion that ensure that the judge will be relatively neutral as between two purely private parties but will be the absolutely faithful servant of the regime on all legal matters touching its interests.

Various mixes of all four of these solutions are to be found in Western legal systems. England and most Continental countries have deviated sufficiently from theories of parliamentary sovereignty to allow considerable autonomy to their courts.[67] Nevertheless, the intersection of courts and powerful bureaucracies in these countries is particularly instructive and illustrative of tactic two. Let us suppose that courts actually sought to serve as triadic conflict resolvers between administrative agencies and aggrieved individuals. Let us also suppose that they sought to do so according to the prototype set out at the beginning of this discussion. Then an independent judge, applying the preexisting law in an adversary setting would seek to decide whether the bureaucracy or the individual citizen should triumph in a dispute. Such court proceedings would inevitably operate to substitute judicial fact-finding and lawmaking for administrative fact-finding and lawmaking. For bureaucracies typically operate under rather broad and vague statutory mandates and either uncertain or changing fact situations. Thus they are inevitably themselves supplementary lawmakers. Just as inevitably, then, when courts seek to resolve conflicts by the application of "preexisting" legal rules where an administrative agency is one of the parties, they must either accept the agency's supplementary lawmaking or do their own. But the agency's own lawmaking is likely to be highly particularized and deeply embedded in the very decision being disputed by the other litigant. Thus if, on the one hand, the court accepts the agency's lawmaking, in many instances it will also automatically be finding for it and against the other litigant. It is rather as if, in the ancient Roman situation, instead of the two disputants having to agree on the legal rule to govern their dispute, one disputant was authorized to impose a rule of his choosing on the other. If, on the other hand, the court does its own supplementary lawmaking, it has become willy nilly a sharer in the political power of the regime.

As we shall see in chapter 2, the British solution to this paradox has essentially been tactic two, that is, to selectively but systematically withdraw large areas of conflict from judicial resolution. British administrative law is principally a series of doctrines that command courts to defer to bureaucratic lawmaking and thus to render themselves incapable of providing a neutral and independent resolution of most conflicts that might arise between government and citizens. As we shall see in chapter 3 the French solution has essentially been tactic four. The French have created a corps of administrative judges who form an integral part of the bureaucracy itself, sharing its values and experiences. In addition the government exercises strong influence over the selection, training, promotion, and assignment of the regular judiciary in order to assure its loyalty to political authority. Finally, French "public law" itself instructs judges to favor the interests of the state over those of individuals when conflicts between the two arise. At the Revolution of 1905, the czarist regime, apparently embarrassed by the highly independent and professional judiciary it had been nurturing for many years, adopted tactic three. It promptly set up special courts to bring revolutionaries to Siberia and the scaffold. These courts plucked what cases they liked from the regular criminal processes. Tactic three is also a favorite of military juntas that impose themselves atop going civil regimes, one of whose features is a relatively independent judiciary. While the regular courts function, courts martial take those few cases of special concern to the regime.

Read in one way, the prevalence of these four tactics is testimony to the real independence of judiciaries. In many nations at many times judges have been sufficiently their own masters to require even highly centralized regimes to adopt special tactics to avoid sharing power with them. Even in highly centralized regimes, judicial lawmaking is a reality that must be dealt with, just as it is in regimes that deliberately assign substantial lawmaking authority to the judiciary.

If judges then are inevitably lawmakers, what happens to our prototype of independence, preexisting legal rules, adversary proceedings, and dichotomous solutions, and more particularly, what happens to the substitution of legislation for legal rules consented to by the parties? In the first place, lawmaking and judicial independence are fundamentally incompatible. No regime is likely to allow significant political power to be wielded by an isolated judicial corps free of political restraints. To the extent that courts make law, judges will be incorporated into the governing coalition, the ruling elite, the responsible representatives of the people, or however else the political regime may be expressed. In most societies this presents no problem at all because judging is only one of the many tasks of the governing cadre. In societies that seek to create independent judiciaries, however, this reintegration will nonetheless occur, even at substantial costs to the proclaimed goal of judicial independence.

We will encounter numerous examples of this reintegration in chapter 2, which deals with English judicial independence. In the United States there has been a long debate over elected versus appointed judiciaries, with the key question being the extent to which judges ought to be subordinated to the democratic political regime. This debate is ultimately unresolvable because it involves two conflicting goals: one, that triadic conflict resolvers be independent; two, that lawmakers be responsible to the people. Indeed, it is because judging inevitably involves lawmaking and social control as well as conflict resolution that the tendency of judging to be closely associated with sovereignty or ultimate political authority, noted early in this discussion, is to be found in all societies.

Clearly, where judicial lawmaking occurs, adversary proceedings are something of a facade. If the judge is consciously seeking to formulate general rules for future application, his considerations must range far beyond the immediate clash of interests of the two parties. That is the message of the "Brandeis brief," with its parade of "legislative" facts, that is, facts about the general social conditions as opposed to the immediate facts of the dispute. Such briefs are open acknowledgment by bench and bar that the parties are essentially an example or sample of the social reality to be legislated upon rather than disputants whose conflict is to be resolved. Even where judicial lawmaking is less conscious or more surreptitious, the creation of general rules necessarily involves looking well beyond the two parties. Typically, the construction of such rules proceeds by appealing to custom, reasonableness, common sense, business necessity, fairness, or some other similar covers for considerations of general social utility. We shall see in chapter 3 that doctrine created by academic legal scholars plays a crucial role in the decision of judges in Roman law countries. This role is evidence of the extent to which such judges are making their decisions on the basis of general considerations of logic and social utility rather than simply trying to resolve the immediate conflict before them.

### CASE-BY-CASE LAWMAKING AND THE PROTOTYPE

Most obviously, case-by-case judicial lawmaking violates the prototype's demand for preexisting legal rules. There has recently been considerable interest in prospective overruling.[68] This interest has been coupled with calls for more rule making and less case-by-case lawmaking by administrative agencies. At the base of both movements has been the feeling that a party should not be told that his past actions have been legally incorrect because of a legal rule that has been discovered subsequent to his actions. Indeed, the legal rule is typically discovered in the very process of deciding whether his past actions were correct or not. This uneasiness has arisen primarily in constitutional and regulatory agency adjudication. It is in these areas of American law that case-by-case lawmaking is most dramatically evident and thus where the prototype of courts is most clearly challenged. Yet the basic tension between lawmaking and the prototype exists in many other areas of law as well and in many nations. Chapter 3 will pursue in detail the tension between the pretense of Western European legal systems that all law is embodied in the codes enacted by the legislature and the reality that much of the law lies in "the doctrine" and "the jurisprudence," that is, the law gradually built up by scholars and judges. That similar problems arise in the Moslem world will be seen in chapter 5.

Indeed it is difficult to understand why the prototype has been so popular among Anglo-American commentators. For the common law system openly proclaims that its principal virtue is lawmaking through case-by-case adjudication. Then the resolution of conflict proceeds, not by preexisting rules, but by rules discovered in the very process of resolving the conflict. Thus there is an important element of retroactivity in the common law style of lawmaking. The individual disputant does not know what rule will govern his actions until after he has acted. The rule is announced in the course of the litigation subsequent to his act.

Generally, common law systems tend to cover their deviation from the prototype of preexisting norms by two rationales. The first is a familiar one. Common law is essentially the ordinances of right reason indwelling in the race, or at least in the legal profession. New legal decisions only discover or draw forth the principle that has existed all along. Although a yearning for such principles still permeates the common law ideology, no one any longer believes that judicial lawmakers simply discover and apply the ancient legal principle. The second, or "gray area," rationale is more realistic. In effect it admits that judges make new law for current cases, but stresses the incremental nature of such decision making. There is a large body of well-settled statutory and case law. There are also some gray areas in which the law is not yet clearly settled and in which new case law is reasonably to be expected. The individual enters the gray area at his own risk. That is, where he commits acts that are at the edges of preexisting law, he consciously takes the chance that when the new law is announced it will run against him. This rationale is most likely to arise in precisely those cases in which new legal rules are announced that could not have been easily anticipated and that turn out to be highly unfavorable to one of the parties. Indeed, quite typically such a new rule is announced precisely because the judge wishes to extend the law to discourage future conduct of the sort engaged in by one of the parties. In the course of doing so, however, the initial conduct is penalized just as if there had been a law against it before it occurred.

Common law judicial lawmaking is only the most dramatic example of the more general phenomenon. So long as societies entrust courts with case-by-case lawmaking powers, and nearly all societies do, then conflict resolution cannot proceed solely by reference to preexisting legal rules. And where conflict resolution does not proceed by preexisting rules or, alternatively, by rules mutually consented to by the parties, then the loser of a case may well perceive himself to have been legislated against rather than impartially resolved. This fundamental deviation form the prototype is unavoidable. Judicial lawmaking necessarily creates a fundamental tension between courts and their basic social logic.

### The Logic of Courts

To briefly summarize then. The basic social logic, or perceived legitimacy, of courts rests on the mutual consent of two persons in conflict to refer that conflict to a third for resolution. This basic logic is threatened by the substitution of office and law for mutual consent, both because one of the two parties may perceive the third as the ally of his enemy and because a third interest, that of the regime, is introduced. Even within the realm of judicial conflict resolutions, no rigid prototype of court is applicable to the real world. Along one dimension we find a continuum of go-between—mediator, arbitrator, judge—in which most of those officials we normally label judges engage in a great deal of mediation and arbitration. Along another dimension we discover that most triadic conflict resolvers are deeply embedded in the general political machinery of their regimes and that the administrator or general big man as judge is far more typical than the holder of a separable judicial office. When we move from courts as conflict resolvers to courts as social controllers, their social logic and their independence is even further undercut. For in this realm, while proceeding in the guise of triadic conflict resolver, courts clearly operate to impose outside interests on the parties. Finally, in the realm of judicial lawmaking, courts move furthest from their social logic and the conventional prototype because the rules they apply in the resolution of conflicts between two parties are neither directly consented to by the parties nor "preexisting." Instead they are created by the third in the course of the conflict resolution itself. Thus, while the triadic mode of conflict resolution is nearly universal, courts remain problematical in the sense that considerable tension invariably exists between their fundamental claims to legitimacy and their actual operations.

### Trial Courts and Appellate Courts—Fact-finding

So far we have not differentiated between trial and appellate courts, but it is useful to do so for certain purposes. Both trial and appellate courts make law. Both trial and appellate courts find facts. This latter point requires some clarification, given the normal American practice. It is often said that appellate courts are to hear questions of law but not questions of fact, which are to be left to the trial court. A similar practice obtains in many other common law jurisdictions. However, side by side with this appellate division of fact and law, we find many other legal systems that use or have used trial de novo at the standard mode of appeal. Where appeal is by trial de novo, the appellate court simply hears the whole case all over again.[69] Trial de novo is found in most nonliterate societies, no doubt in large part because of the difficulty of preserving trial court findings of fact to serve as a basis for appellate decision.

One of the principal differences in the development of the English common law courts (see chap. 2) and the Roman law courts of Western Europe (see chap. 3) lies in the realm of appellate fact-finding. The basic instrument of appeal developed in England was the writ of error. Issued by an appellate court, it ordered that the "record" of the trial court be sent to it to be examined for error. In English trials the evidence was almost entirely oral or lay in the personal knowledge of the jurors. For jurors were originally summoned not to hear the facts but because they themselves knew the facts. Thus the written record of an English trial court would contain almost no factual material. It would be limited largely to the legal claims of the two parties and the findings of law made by the court. It might contain the conclusions of fact made by the court, but not the evidence on which they were based. At least until the eighteenth century, English trial courts rarely issued long written opinions. Indeed Anglo-American trial courts still feel no particular compulsion to do so and frequently do not. Thus the record on appeal often consisted of very cryptic entries of what legal claim had been made, which parties won and what remedy had been given. An English appeals court had little choice but to confine itself to spotting errors of law in the record. It could not have spotted errors of fact even if it wanted to, since it had none of the evidence before it.

Romanist procedures, on the other hand, emphasized the compilation by lower-level judges of a complete written record and analysis of all the evidence. There rarely was a trial in the English sense of everyone appearing at one time in a court room, telling their stories, and immediately receiving a verdict. Instead, a case proceeded by the gradual accumulation of papers in successive waves. The stack of papers literally became the case. If there was an appeal from the decision of the trial court, the whole file went up to the appeals court. The appellate court in effect decided the whole case all over again.

A number of causes for these differences in scope of appeal may be suggested. The introduction of the jury in England, discussed in chapter 2, is no doubt crucial. An appellate court cannot review what went on in the minds of the jurors. And, unlike professional judges, jurors cannot be expected to submit written records of their fact-finding.

The English preference for verbal presentation of evidence preceded the introduction of the jury, however, and so is probably an independent cause of the difference. It is, of course, impossible for an appellate court to review verbal evidence unless it holds the whole trial all over again. Modern Anglo-American courts may have a transcript of the oral evidence. Nevertheless, where oral evidence is the rule, an appellate court feels less capable of making factual judgments than the trial court which actually heard and saw the witnesses. Romanist procedures used a system of written questions and answers exchanged between the two parties as the mode of gathering evidence. Low-level judicial officers then shaped up the file of these questions and answers and supporting documents and presented them to the trial court judge. Exactly the same file could be presented to an appellate court. So Romanist appellate judges did not feel they were any further from the parties, the witnesses and the evidence than the trial court they were reviewing.

Also, as we shall shortly see, appeal is essentially a device for exercising centralized supervision over local judicial officers. The Continental pattern was one of scattered trial courts supervised by more centralized appellate bodies. Appeal by trial de novo greatly strengthens the supervisory powers of the centralized appellate courts over their scattered subordinates. Dawson argues that the appeals mechanism was one of the principal devices used by Continental regimes to impose a uniform and centralized Roman law on local courts in place of the localized, customary law they had been employing in the medieval period. As we shall see in chapter 2, the English centralized the trial courts themselves and so had less need of a strong appellate mechanism to enforce the will of the central government on the trial judges.

Finally, although it is not clear whether we are dealing here with a cause or an effect, the English system of appeal requires far less governmental resources than the Romanist one. The Continental system, with its emphasis on a complete written record, requires a huge number of judicial officials to collect, correlate and analyze the huge pile of papers that become the case. A system of appeal that involves reexamining the whole file requires an enormous number of appellate judicial man hours. It took hours for a French appellate judge to read his "records"; minutes for an English judge. The limited appeal constituted by the writ of error is part of an overall English pattern of attempting to run a government cheaply and with as few government personnel as possible. Trial de novo on appeal is part of a Continental pattern that tolerated and even encouraged the growth of large governmental bureaucracies, judicial and otherwise.[70]

The differing consequences of limiting appeal to questions of law and employing trial de novo are important to the balance of power between trial and appellate courts. Trial de novo, of course, gives an appellate court far more general supervisory power. It sees the whole rather than only a small part of what the trial court has been doing. Moreover, where appeal is by trial de novo, the appellate court issues a final order binding on the parties. Where appeal is on questions of law only, the procedure is different. After the appeals court makes a binding declaration of law, it sends the case back to the trial court for retrial or a new decision consonant with the legal rule announced by the appeals court. Thus the trial court still has the final say. Given the complex interaction of law and fact, in many instances a trial court again can find in favor of the same party who won the first trial. The trial court can always argue that a proper analysis of the facts shows that, even under the new rule of law announced by the appeals court, the party who won the first time is legally right and the winning appellant legally wrong. Of course such a decision may result in another appeal. It is not unheard of in the United States to have three or four rounds of this sort.

Many legal systems are quite aware of these balance of power problems. The U.S. Supreme Court must "remand" cases to state courts for final decision when it finds that the state court has made an error of constitutional law. This is an important curb on Supreme Court power. The Court has responded with the doctrine of "constitutional fact" through which it empowers itself to do final fact-finding of certain facts essential to a determination of whether the state has acted constitutionally. Thus, even on remand, state courts are frequently blocked from remanipulating their fact-finding so as to reinstate their initial holdings.

Many European countries use review limited to questions of law in certain spheres, particularly in connection with special constitutional courts or "courts of cassation." As we shall see in chapter 3, France, Italy, and Germany all have special courts to deal only with the question of whether a particular statute is constitutional or a particular administrative regulation in accord with its governing statutes. Such courts usually operate separately from but parallel to a set of regular appellate courts that use trial de novo. Since these special courts decide only special questions of law, they usually operate by remand to the trial courts. Often in Europe, however, we encounter statutory or constitutional provisions that require that the remand go to a different trial court rather than the one that originally handled the case. If the appellate court reverses the trial courts a second time in the same case, it may usually go on to make a final judgment itself.

In their nineteenth-century judicial reforms, the English recognized the weaknesses of the writ of error as a form of appellate procedure and sought to introduce trial de novo on appeal. The reforms were subsequently greatly whittled back but still remain in part. These developments are traced in chapter 2. The most important impact of the writ of error has been in the United States, which has strongly preserved the English tradition. American appellate courts have often greatly expanded the concept of "the record" so as to allow themselves to see more of what went on at trial. In theory at least, however, they still limit themselves largely to questions of law, leaving questions of fact to the trial court. And, as we shall see in a moment, while often breached in practice, this theoretical limitation still has important consequences.

In advanced societies, trial de novo frequently does not take the form of a complete rehearing of oral testimony, but instead involves appellate court review of the trial court record and then its own independent findings of fact. In the United States, trial de novo is usually a device for bringing cases from minor courts of incomplete jurisdiction and incomplete judicial status into higher courts of general jurisdiction and completely judicialized procedures. For instance in Massachusetts, a defendant in minor felonies may choose to appear in the municipal courts, whose jurisdiction and sentencing powers are limited, whose judges need not be lawyers, and where prosecution is typically handled by the police rather than by a professional prosecutor. Should he be convicted, he may appeal for trial de novo to the Superior Court, which is a fully professional trial court of general criminal jurisdiction.

Trial de novo would therefore appear to be something more than a necessity forced on preliterate societies. This becomes even more clear when we note the extreme reluctance of non–de novo appellate courts to confine themselves to pure issues of law. In the United States the distinction between questions of fact and questions of law which is supposed to be the key to the limits of appellate jurisdiction, is a notoriously slippery one. It is so slippery that a whole new category, "mixed questions of fact and law," has been invented. In reality that category defines the huge number of instances in which appellate courts have refused to accept trial court findings of fact and substituted their own fact-finding under the guise of law finding. As we have noted, the Supreme Court has long held that it will make its own findings of "constitutional fact." But constitutional facts are often the same routine facts that the trial court has already decided. For instance, let us suppose a trial court has determined that a given speech did incite a riot and so convicts a speaker of incitement to riot. The Supreme Court will, under the constitutional fact doctrine, redetermine exactly the same factual question. For it will decide the constitutional issue of whether the speech constituted such a clear and present danger of serious social evil that its repression might be justified in the face of the First Amendment's guarantees of free speech.

This pull of appellate courts toward the facts can also be seen in the endless proliferation in the United States, Great Britain, and on the Continent of statutes, rules, and practices about how much evidence a trial court or administrative agency must have to support its decisions. Typically there has been pressure from the legislature or the courts themselves to keep appellate courts from substituting their own fact-finding for that of the decision maker who hears the evidence in the first instance. Two basic rationales underlie this pressure. One is that the first-instance trier actually sees and hears the witnesses, examines the physical evidence, and is simply closer in space and time to the disputed events than the appeals court that sees only a printed record. The second, particularly important where administrative agencies are the first-instance trier, is that the agencies are more competent to find facts in the highly specialized areas of their expertise than are appeals courts staffed by nonspecialist judges. This pressure manifests itself in various rules requiring appellate courts to pay various degrees of deference to initial fact-finding by others. In the United States there are generally three grades of deference, although similar standards in different verbal formulations are to be found in other countries. Indeed the verbal formulations are far from uniform even in the United States. The strictest standard of deference is the "no evidence" rule used by the Supreme Court in review of state court fact-finding and the "some evidence" rule involved frequently where courts are reviewing agency fact-finding. The Supreme Court announces that it will reverse state courts on the facts in criminal cases only when the state record contains "no evidence" supporting conviction. While in theory this would mean that the presence of even a single bit of evidence tending to show guilt would be sufficient to obviate review, in practice the court has sometimes found that what others would consider quite a bit of evidence turns out to be "no evidence." Similarly, courts frequently say that they will not reverse on factual grounds an agency's decisions in areas of its peculiar expertise unless the record is totally devoid of agency fact-finding supporting its decision. In other words so long as the agency can show some evidence in support of its decision, the court will not make its own judgment on where the preponderance of evidence lies.

The next lower standard of deference is the "substantial evidence" rule. In various verbal formulations and degrees of severity, this rule has become the most typical rule of judicial review of agency fact-finding throughout the Western world. The court will look to see if an administrative agency has developed a substantial body of evidence in support of its decision. If it has, the court will not weigh the evidence of one side against that on the other and substitute its own judgment for the agency's about where the preponderance of evidence lies.

The lowest standard of deference is a "preponderance of evidence" rule. Under such a rule appellate courts generally purport to give great weight to first-instance fact-finding but nonetheless strike their own final balance of the weight of evidence on each side. Of course legislatures may seek to prevent court review of agency fact-finding altogether by providing that their decisions are final and unreviewable. As we shall see in chapter 2, courts tend to resist such limitations on their review power.

But why does this whole body of jurisprudence arise in legal systems that employ the general rule that appellate courts should not redetermine facts? Obviously, because there is such a strong thrust in appellate courts toward fact-finding that it cannot be contained by the general rule. And that thrust occurs because, while the principal job of appellate courts is lawmaking, they continuously seek to reiterate their connection with the basis of all judicial legitimacy, conflict resolution. So long as appellate courts do their lawmaking under the guise of doing substantial justice between man and man in particular cases—and they must do this if they are to be perceived as and supported as courts—they will keep clawing their way back toward the facts. For disputes about the facts are at the root of a large proportion of the conflicts to be resolved.

This point is well illustrated by the evolution of "jury instructions" in the United States where, as we have seen, the tradition of the writ of error and the employment of juries severely limits review. Trial courts need not write lengthy opinions. The jury's deliberations are oral and secret and thus cannot be reviewed at all. The appellate court may conduct only an extremely limited review of the trial transcript because it is almost entirely devoted to the presentation of factual evidence and trial court findings of fact are not appealable. About the only thing in the record that is reviewable by an appellate court is the instructions given by the judge to the jury. These instructions are technically the judge's explanation of the relevant law to the jury. In reality they tend to be a review of both the facts and law by the judge indicating what verdict the jury ought to bring in if it believes one or the other of the two versions of facts offered by the parties. Thus criticism of the instruction becomes the vehicle for appellate court intervention against the trial court's findings of both fact and law, even though technically appeal is limited to issues of law. Nearly everything in the instruction is a "mixed question of fact and law" subject to review.

Instructions thus become a crucial intersection between trial court and appellate court power. As a result they tend to become a highly complex and technical legal ritual in which the trial judge seeks to protect himself against appellate reversal by carefully quoting various verbal formulae that previous appellate opinions have announced to be the proper ones. A conscientious trial judge, therefore, tends to write instructions that bounce back and forth between legal statements so technical that they can be understood only by those who know the appellate precedents and simple explanations designed for jurors. What began as a message from trial judge to jury has become a defense by trial judge against appellate judge.

At the very opposite pole of appellate fact-finding lies the distinction between judicial and legislative fact. In theory courts are supposed to confine themselves to the particular facts of the particular case. And because they are supposed to follow adversary proceedings, they are supposed to limit themselves to consideration of the facts presented by the two parties rather than ranging broadly over social data in a way permissible to legislatures drafting new laws. These limitations, rooted as they are in the conflict resolution aspect of judicial activity, work in a rough and ready way for trial courts. Where appellate court lawmaking is involved, they hardly work at all. Whether it be dressed in the language of American sociological jurisprudence, Continental free decision making, or a tribal chief's common sense concern with preserving his authority, it is clear that where an appellate body seeks to formulate a legal rule, it must consider the fit of that rule to the society at large, not just to the two contending parties. In most societies the arguments presented to courts have either presumed or injected a great deal of general knowledge of the operation of the society. Courts usually hold that even the adversary model does not require them to be blind to what any fool can plainly see just because neither party got it into evidence. Doctrines like judicial notice have allowed either one of the parties or the judge himself to assume widely know social facts without proving them.

In the United States the "Brandeis brief," first invented for the special purpose of defending state regulatory statutes against constitutional attack, has now blossomed forth in nearly every instance in which an appellate court is in reality being asked to make new law. Today's brief on an environmental, desegregation, apportionment, or welfare issue frequently contains exactly the same data in exactly the same format as would a presentation to a congressional committee. The United States no doubt represents the extreme case. But on narrower fronts, for instance in the willingness of English and Continental courts to hear evidence on general commercial practices, most courts find some way of touching base with general social reality. Of course this is as true of trial as appellate courts, but the issue of just what range of facts a court may hear arises most dramatically at appellate levels. For appeals court lawmaking in rivalry to legislatures is much clearer than that of trial courts.

In spite of all these obvious connections of appellate courts to facts, it is still possible to focus on the trial as one of society's basic devices for finding facts.[71] Just how good trial proceedings are as a fact-finding device is a perennial question but also a misleading one if put too generally. It must always be remembered that the basic aim of a trial is to resolve a conflict or impose social controls, not to find the facts. Much of what may appear to be unsatisfactory as pure fact-finding, if we were applying general scientific canons for empirical inquiry, may be quite satisfactory in the specific context of trials.

The early stages of the English legal system and many tribal legal systems employed trial by ordeal, oath, combat, or divination. Explanation of these forms of trial in quasi-scientific terms is not totally incorrect. No doubt reference of factual issues to the Divinity, who was thought to be omnisciently willing to intervene in ordeals and combats in behalf of the person wronged, was a form of striving after accurate and complete fact-finding. And various physiological rationales for ordeal, such as that lying produces a dry mouth incapable of tolerating hot pebbles, are also no doubt partially correct. Above all it is clear that reference of a factual dispute to the gods or to ordeal will lead many parties who believe in the efficacy of these modes of inquiry, and who know they have misrepresented the facts, to change their stories or withdraw from the litigation.

Quite apart from these attempts to bring primitive modes of fact-finding into accord with modern notions of empirical inquiry, however, oaths and ordeals can be seen as serving the specific purpose of trials even where they were not the most reliable form of inquiry. In the context of conflict resolution, the major virtue of a trial is that it provides a definitive point of termination to the conflict. The conclusion of a trial allows the disputants to stop trying to get even with one another. In this sense it is more important that a termination be provided than that a just solution be reached. For the endless continuation of a dispute often creates psychological, social, and/or economic costs that neither the parties nor the society is prepared to bear. The oath or ordeal provided both a catharsis and a dramatic climax which assisted in providing termination. Instead of leaving factual issues dangling, they were decided once and for all.

Even legal systems that seem to rely heavily on supernatural modes of factual inquiry are likely to employ them only as the culmination of more commonplace methods of inquiry. In most such systems the litigants are permitted first to tell their own stories and/or bring witnesses. Members of the community may also be heard. Thus something like a trial in the sense of a factual inquiry typically takes place before the trial in the sense of the oath, ordeal, or combat. Not always, but typically, the real power of the court is its discretion in assigning the ultimate burden of proof to one or the other of the two parties. In some systems of trial procedure, for instance when the ultimate proof is a simple sworn oath, as it is in the classic law of Islam described in chapter 5, whoever gets the burden is very likely to win the case. In others, for instance when the ultimate proof is carrying live coals without being burned, whoever gets the burden almost surely loses. So long as the court assigns the burden, however, it can do so in such a way as to favor the party whom the weight of empirical evidence gathered at the preliminary stage seems to favor. That is why we encounter one society in which a man is in the wrong if a hot rock burns his hand, and another in which he is in the wrong if it does not. Trial seems to do substantial justice in both. Preliminary factual inquiry, plus the discretion to assign the supernatural burden of proof, plus the perceived definitiveness of such modes of truth-finding may provide a mode of fact-finding roughly as accurate and far more likely to lead to the essential termination of conflict than would a simple factual inquiry alone.

The universal history of the rules of evidence is far too complex a subject to review here. As we emerge from dependence on supernatural assistance, the central problem of judicial fact-finding is the problem of certainty. Testimony under oath is often the transitional stage. For the oath is in one sense an ordeal inviting divine intervention and in another an attempt to ensure more reliable human testimony. The medieval English practice of oath helping is instructive. The oath helpers were not witnesses who supported a disputant's assertion of fact from their own knowledge of the fact. They were persons who testified to the general reputation for veracity of the witness. They stood forth to share his oath and the risk of divine retribution, which was the lot of the false swearer. Oath helpers were unlikely to be forthcoming if the disputant's story rang false to the community.

Once confidence of divine intervention in routine trials is reduced, problems of credibility and weight of evidence arise. Few human societies have found probabilistic treatment of evidence morally satisfying. This is one of the many reasons so many triadic conflict resolvers resort to mediation of one sort or another. For mediation obviates the need to establish an agreed version of the facts. Most trial courts, of course, pretend to a certainty that they know is not there. If a real need for absolute certainty is felt by courts, the results may be untoward. It is probable that the Continental reliance on torture of the accused in part derived from the reluctance of judges to convict on any other basis than confession, which was one of the few certain ways to establish the facts of a crime.

Where fact-finding is done in the context of conflict resolution, reliance is typically placed on the stories told by the two disputants. The use of witnesses and physical evidence comes late in the development of legal procedures and is usually sporadic and incomplete. In part this is because the gathering of such evidence is expensive and time consuming. Thus even in advanced industrial societies, small claims courts aimed at quick, cheap disposition will usually operate on little more than the disputants' testimony. In part the reluctance to hear "outside" evidence rests on the fear of manufactured or falsified evidence, which is understandable where courts must rely on evidence brought in by the parties rather than developed by their own investigations. At least the judge may directly observe the demeanor of the party giving testimony. The well-known contrast between English and French legal developments that we have already touched upon illustrates this point. Until at least the eighteenth century, English courts were so reluctant to accept anything other than direct parol (spoken) evidence that they were severely hampered in resolving many kinds of disputes, particularly commercial ones in which ledgers, bills of lading, and the like were often crucial. French courts, on the other hand, followed Romanist procedure, which involved almost no parol evidence and relied almost exclusively on written interrogatories and responses and the examination of documents. But the Royal Courts of England consisted of a mere handful of judges, while medieval France developed a huge judicial bureaucracy to gather, digest, and evaluate evidence.

In the seventeenth century notions of probability or relative certainty seem to develop side by side in theology, science, and law.[72] In Western societies a trial gradually comes to be seen as an empirical investigation designed to determine the weight of evidence on each side rather than as an attempt to discover the absolute truth. This progression from the search for absolute truth by divine intervention up to modern notions of balance of evidence should not be taken, however, as a necessary or universal phenomenon. Ethnographic materials show us some tribal judges who seek to assert definitive fact-finding capacity while others openly admit to weighing or balancing the evidence and picking the more convincing story.

With notions of weighing evidence, however, Western law develops a new, policy-oriented discretion similar to the earlier discretion involved in assigning the "trial" or "proof" to one or another of the litigants. In civil cases, where conflict resolution is the dominant mode, most legal systems hold the burden of proof even, the victory going to the party with the preponderance of evidence. Where social control is the dominant mode, as in criminal law, all sorts of shifts in the balance of proof may be made for policy reasons. To an extent these shifts may even predate the development of notions of probabilistic proof. For instance in medieval England, where treason and certain other crimes that the regime particularly wished to crush were involved, the defendant was forbidden to make a statement under oath, thus cutting him off from the best mode of establishing the certainty of his story.

Presumptions, burdens of proof, and per se rules are the standard form for manipulating factual issues to achieve policy goals. The easiest example is the presumption of innocence and the burden to prove beyond a reasonable doubt in modern Anglo-American criminal law. Just as the medieval English law made it more difficult for certain defendants to prove their innocence, so modern law makes it more difficult for the state to prove their guilt. The presumption of innocence is not some fixed truth but a declaration of social policy. For various reasons we prefer to make it easier for the criminal accused than for the state.

Where social control is involved, however, there are numerous instances in which it appears preferable to shift the burden of proof in the other direction. The per se rules frequently encountered in American labor and antitrust law are good examples. When a court says that a tieing agreement is a conspiracy in restraint of trade per se, it is simply relieving the government of the burden of providing that the accused's actual conduct did in fact constitute such a conspiracy. Courts and legislatures can make very fine adjustments in burden of proof, for instance, by making a presumption rebuttable or irrebuttable. Modern developments of "absolute liability" or "liability without fault" are a major example of shifting burdens of proof for reasons of social policy. The fundamental rule in both common and Roman law systems for many centuries was that if one person injured another purposely or through negligence he or she must pay damages to the person injured. But where there was no intent to injure and no negligence, there was no liability to pay damages. Increasingly, however, in the twentieth century, legal systems assign absolute liability to compensate for injuries whether or not there was evil intent or negligence. The story of how this was done in France is told in chapter 3. This absolute liability is often introduced because in the conditions of modern society it becomes too hard to prove negligence, or at least just how negligent each of the parties was.

"No fault" collision insurance assigns absolute liability to the insurance company no matter how much or how little the driver was at fault. No fault laws are passed in part because we have learned that trials are a cumbersome, costly, and ultimately unsuccessful way of discovering which driver was in fact ultimately at fault.

Similarly we are increasingly making manufacturers absolutely liable for the injuries caused by their products. In part this is an attempt to make manufacturers as careful as possible in their production processes. In part, however, it is a recognition that in modern, mass production, assembly line technologies, it is often impossible to prove precisely how and where the manufacturer was negligent. If the steering wheel of your new car comes off in your hands, it is evident in a common sense way that the automaker was negligent. But it may be very difficult to legally prove exactly which worker at exactly what place on the assembly line committed precisely that act of negligence which caused the wheel to come off. The tendency, therefore, has been to relieve the injured party of meeting the whole burden of proof of negligence. That burden was easier to meet in a simpler society where it was easier to know exactly who had done what.

Behind this politics of fact-finding lies the fundamental reality that courts are far from perfect fact finders. On the one hand, those who have contravened social controls are often in an excellent position to conceal the facts of their misdeeds from courts, particularly when they are themselves organizations of great resources like corporations or unions, or cabals of treasonous barons. On the other hand, many of those who fall afoul of social controls have so few resources that they can hardly be expected to develop the necessary facts for their own defense. Thus the adjustment of the fact-finding incapacities of courts to the relative power of those subjected to social controls is itself a significant aspect of social control and ultimately of political authority.

## The Uses of Appeal

As we noted earlier, one of the principal virtues of a trial is that it provides an official termination to conflict, relieving the disputants of the necessity of further reciprocal assertions or retributions. But too much finality may be disturbing to the losing member of the triad. One of the functions of a "right of appeal" may be to provide a psychological outlet and a social cover for the loser at trial.[73] For appeal allows the loser to continue to assert his rightness in the abstract without attacking the legitimacy of the legal system or refusing to obey the trial court. Indeed the loser's displeasure is funnelled into a further assertion of the legitimacy of the legal system. Appealing to a higher court entails the acknowledgment of its legitimacy.

We also noted earlier that the principal problem of the triadic form of conflict resolution was keeping the loser from perceiving the final situation as "two against one." Appeals mechanisms are devices for telling the loser that if he believes that it did turn out two against one, he may try another triadic figure. Perhaps just as important, the availability of appeal allows the loser to accept his loss without having to acknowledge it publicly. The purpose of a trial is to effect a termination of conflict. But too abrupt a termination may be counterproductive of true conflict resolution. Appeal, whether actually exercised, threatened, or only held in reserve, avoids adding insult to injury. The loser can leave the courtroom with his head high talking of appeal and then accept his loss, slowly, privately, and passively by failing to make an appeal. We often see appeal principally as a mode of ensuring against the venality, prejudice, and/or ignorance of trial court judges and of soothing the ruffled feelings of the loser. Appeal does indeed serve there functions, but it does so by the imposition of hierarchical controls on trial court behavior. A great deal of interest to political scientists lurks in that hierarchical element.

We have already noted that in a predominant share of the governing systems that have existed in the world, judging is either a facet of administration, or is closely aligned with it. It is a commonplace of administrative lore that no matter what the theory, Weberian hierarchies do not give the top or center adequate control over rank and file administrators in the field. Such control will not occur unless a number of alternative channels of information are available that can be cross-checked at or near the top. The best-known modern example is obviously the Soviet Union, with its trade union, government, party, control commission, and police hierarchies superimposed on one another. When administrators hold courts, appeal becomes such a mechanism of control. A "right" of appeal is a mechanism providing an independent flow of information to the top on the field performance of administrative subordinates.

It is not only an independent flow, but one highly complementary to the normal administrative reporting. Such reporting usually takes the form of summarization. Each field administrator handles hundreds of thousands of bits of information about local affairs and his own performance. Let us suppose that each passed everything he knew along to his superiors. Each superior supervises a number of subordinates. Each would be flooded with millions of bits of information—far more than he could handle. So normally each field administrator passes to his superior only a summary of the information he has developed. And each superior passes on only a summary of those summaries to his superior. In the process much information is necessarily lost. And not unnaturally, what tend to get lost most easily are those instances in which the subordinate has done badly. The superior never sees the full details of any specific things his subordinates have done. The summaries he sees tend to emphasize his subordinates' successes and leave out the failures. ("Last year this office handled over three thousand claims of which 91 percent were settled within forty-eight hours.")

The appeals process cuts across this summarization because the unit of appeal is a single case, in all its details, rather than a summary of overall performance. It is not a single instance chosen by an administrator to illustrate his success, but an instance chosen by a consumer of administration who feels that the administrator has failed. Finally, not only is the appeals case a detailed sample of administrative work product, but it is a partially random sample. The distribution of cases appealed is not determined by either the goals of the administrative subordinate or his superior but by the nonadministrative motivations of individual litigants. Let us suppose that a chief engineer wishes to check the performance of his auto assembly line. His normal mechanism is to check the statistics reported by his foremen on the number of engines mounted, doors attached, and so on, including the final figures on cars produced. Or alternatively, he could look at every hundredth car. Appeal would allow him to check in yet another way. The customer who got the "lemon" would bring the car in and insist that the chief engineer take it all apart to see exactly what things had been done wrong on the line.

Thus, on the one hand, while appeal is a partially random sample, it is one loaded toward administrative failure. It will not be every fifth car or every green car that is sampled, but some of the worst cars and very, very few of the best. On the other hand, the administrative superior may impose some patterning by making it known what kinds of appeal are most likely to be successful. We have already seen that English appeals courts at one time said they would listen to appeals on questions of law but not of fact. Thus they got to see cases in which trial courts had made mistakes of law, but not those where the court had done bad fact-finding. Field administrators can also partially control the pattern of appeals. In chapter 4 we shall see that a Chinese local magistrate who did not wish his superiors to know about his performance in a particular dispute could pressure the parties to settle by mediation. A mediated settlement could not be appealed.

At the opposite extreme, it is possible to run an appeals system that takes 100 percent or at least a very full sample. In Tokagawa, Japan, every opinion of a trial court was prepared as only a draft of an opinion by the higher authorities. Each draft went forward and came into legal force only after the higher authorities had approved it. In this system, then, all cases are appealed. Most American states provide one appeal in criminal cases as a matter of right. The common practice of the defense bar in many of those states is routinely to file an appeal for every losing defendant. Some states have mandatory first appeals for all cases in which the punishment is severe. These state systems approach 100 percent appeal. Whenever a central government seems to be attempting 100 percent sampling, however, the reality will usually turn out to be otherwise. Thus in states where a first appeal is routine, the intermediate appellate court that hears such appeals will usually deny 90 percent of them in one-line orders that show that they were given only a cursory glance. The appellate court will decide the other 10 percent. And of those only a very few will move on to a further appeal to the state supreme court.

Of course, where there is a separate judicial hierarchy, appeal is typically the central mode of supervision by higher courts over lower, and reversal on appeal a central form of administrative sanction. In such instances the need for multiple channels of information and control leads the top to demand other institutions in addition to appeal, such as judicial conferences, centralized personnel systems, and administrative reporting, to increase their control over their subordinates.

The insistence, so frequently encountered, that the chain of appeal eventually arrive at the chief, the king, or the capital, instead of stopping at some intermediate level, is difficult to explain except in terms of centralized political control. If the only function of appeal were to ensure against corruptness or arbitrariness on the part of the trial judge, then appeal to anyone even a single step higher in the scale of authority would be sufficient. In the American states we have just discussed, for instance, appeals could all stop at intermediate appellate courts. Why should any go on to a state supreme court? Its justices are really no more capable of righting the injustices done to the loser in the trial court than are the appeals court judges who first heard the appeal. The top insists on being the ultimate level of appeal because it serves its purposes, not those of a losing disputant.

Of course, just as one of the functions of any appeal may be to reduce the psychic shock to losers, so the right to "take the case all the way to the Supreme Court" provides even greater catharsis for the loser whether he employs it only rhetorically or actually does it. Yet even at this personal level, and quite apart from the question of hierarchical control, the top is likely to see advantages in preserving a right of ultimate appeal. Earlier we noted that the extension of judicial services outward and downward is a device for wedding the countryside to the regime. So the preservation of appeal to the chief–king–emperor–capital is a device for keeping the strings of legitimacy tied directly between the ruled and the person of the ruler or the highest institutions of government. In the imperial Chinese legal system that will be examined in chapter 4, cases involving capital punishment were automatically appealed from local courts through intermediate appeals courts and ultimately to the emperor himself. The accused was shipped along with his appeal up the appeals ladder. When the death sentence was ultimately commuted, the commutation was ceremonially delivered to the prisoner in the capital and depicted as the personal mercy of the emperor. When the death penalty was confirmed, the prisoner was shipped back down the appeals ladder. He was dispatched on the local execution ground of the trial court that had convicted him initially. No clearer declaration of the political purposes of appeal could be made.

Conversely, the ability to reach down occasionally into the most particular affairs of the countryside provides an important means of reminding the rank and file that the rulers are everywhere, that no one may use his insignificance or his embeddedness in the mass to hide from central authority. Thus the personal ruler, be he Zulu war chief or medieval monarch, rarely totally gives up his personal participation in appeals. Nor do modern central governments often provide that there be only a single appeal from trial court to regional appeals court without any opportunity to go on to a central appeals court.

Thus appellate institutions are more fundamentally related to the political purposes of central regimes than to the doing of individual justice. That this is true is evidenced by the nearly universal existence of appellate mechanisms in politically developed societies, even those whose governments place little or no value on individual rights. In chapter 5 we shall examine the absence of appeal in Islamic law as a test of this hypothesis about the relation of appeal to centralization of political authority.

Even if judges did nothing but conflict resolution, appeal would be an important political mechanism both for increasing the level of central control over administrative subordinates and for ensuring the authority and legitimacy of rulers. When we enter the realms of social control and law-making, the multiple functions of appeal are even more apparent. When trial courts or first-instance judging by administrators is used as a mode of social control, appeal is a mechanism for central coordination of local control. The "questions of law" passed on to the appeals courts are in reality requests for uniform rules of social conduct and indicators of what range of case-by-case deviation from those rules is permissible by first-line controllers.

A partial breakdown of this supervisory mechanism is largely responsible for the wave of discontent with American criminal courts. In most Western criminal law systems there can be no appeal after a plea of guilty. Something over 90 percent of American criminal cases are settled by a guilty plea or its equivalent, frequently as a result of specific or tacit plea bargaining. As we have noted, appeals courts do not normally consider questions of fact. In the United States "disposition," or sentencing, that is, the decision about what to do with the person of the convicted criminal, is not normally reviewable by appellate courts.

These three factors combine to create a major anomaly, at least within the Western political and administrative tradition. The basic business of American criminal courts is not the triadic resolution of disputes cast in the form of the *People* v. *John Doe*. And this is quite apart from the point that casting criminal law enforcement in this ritual form of conflict between individual and the state is a transparent fiction. Most American trial courts rarely bother even with the ritual of trial. Their time is spent disposing of the bodies of those who have pleaded guilty. Thus they are clearly administrators distributing the scarce sanctioning and rehabilitative resources of society among a mass of "applicants." In this sense trial courts have ceased to be courts.

This absorption of "courts" in administrative tasks is not particularly surprising or alarming in view of the natural affinities between judging and administration that we have repeatedly noted. The anomaly arises precisely because we persist in formally viewing these administrative tasks as judicial. As a result we get an enormous volume of particularized administrative discretion without any of the hierarchical supervision we normally exercise over low-level administrators. In short, what trial courts really do, sentence, is not subject to appellate court review. And because trial courts are *courts* in a political system that endorses judicial independence, they are not subject to any other form of hierarchical supervision. Thus they are one of the few agencies of government in which rank-and-file operators are subject to almost no supervision at all in the wielding of enormous discretion. Imagine the loss in legitimacy that any bureaucratic agency would suffer if the clients were told that the clerks at the windows had broad discretion and their decisions were not reviewable by their superiors.

This American situation is an example of the need to focus clearly on appeal as a mode of hierarchical political management, as well as a guarantee of fairness to the accused, if we are to understand the actual operation of real political systems.

In this context social control and lawmaking are usually intimately connected. Appeal is not simply a device for ensuring a certain uniformity in the operations of rank-and-file social controllers. It also ensures that they are following rules or laws or policies of social control acceptable to the regime. Indeed, appeal is a key mechanism in injecting centralized social control into the conflict resolution activities of courts. For appeal is the channel through which the central political authority assures itself that its rank-and-file conflict resolvers are applying legal rules that resolve conflicts in the desired directions. Earlier we noted that the substitution of legislated law for rules created by the mutual consent of the parties introduced a third set of interests into two-party litigation, whatever interests were embodied in the legislation. At least in large and complex societies, trial courts are too many and too localized to articulate this third set satisfactorily. Appellate courts are more suitable.

Tort serves as a good example. When social policy is stable, trial courts will finally dispose of most tort cases. The "reasonable man" doctrine applied by juries will impose sanctions on those who deviate from commonly accepted standards of conduct. The parties will see their conflict as existing within fairly clearly preestablished rules enunciated in the pattern of previous cases. It will be resolved by a judgment of their peers about who was at fault or more at fault. However, when new social and economic policies are to be introduced, appellate courts will become active, enunciating new tort doctrines, or theories, and creating or plugging exceptions to existing rules. Thus, during the rapid industrialization of the United States in the nineteenth century, when allocating the costs of industrial accidents became an important economic issue, the high courts of the states created or expanded the contributory negligence and fellow-servant rules and the doctrine of assumed risk. Trial courts still resolved conflicts between employer and injured worker and controlled deviations from accepted standards of proper industrial conduct. But they did so within a set of overarching doctrines that injected the national interests in industrial growth as a counterweight to the interests of injured workers.[74] We have already noted the role jury instructions can play in the relations between trial and appellate courts. When appellate courts are striving to impose centrally determined uniform policies, such instructions will serve as a battleground where, no matter what he says to the jury, the trial judge is threatened with reversal if he does not achieve outcomes satisfactory to the central authorities.

On the broadest scale, of course, constitutional review by the highest appeals courts in federal systems has been a principal device of centralized policymaking. A good example is school desegregation in the United States. And appeal has been used in highly centralized political systems such as that in France as one of numerous routine mechanisms for controlling and coordinating government agents in the field. Appeals courts can and do act in this capacity whether they are themselves doing a great deal of lawmaking or acting as enforcers of law made by others. An interesting variant is the sending of trial judges on "circuit" from the capitol or the insistence that suitors travel to the capitol for trial—both important tactics of the medieval English monarchs for centralizing political authority, as we shall see in chapter 2. It is because England had this special overlay of national trial courts, above the essentially local county and baronial courts, that a large proportion of English common law has been made by what are technically trial courts, while most of American judicial lawmaking occurs in appeals courts. Far more typical are the arrangements of the nineteenth- and twentieth-century European-based empires, all of which provided for appeal either to a high court sitting in the metropolis or a territorial high court employing metropolitan law and/or staffed by judges trained as imperial servants. The British system of appeal to the Privy Council is the best-known example.

Quite obviously, if there is any judicial lawmaking within a territorially dispersed system of courts, then a pyramid of appeal is necessary in order to assure that any central body of law is relatively uniformly administered throughout its domain. For instance, in spite of its onerous constitutional duties, the United States Supreme Court devotes about 40 percent of its opinions to creating uniform interpretations of federal statutes among the intermediate federal courts of appeal. In a unitary (as opposed to federal) non–common-law state, in which courts do not enjoy the power to declare laws unconstitutional and in which intermediate appellate courts exist, about the only legal rationale possible for the existence of a high court of appeal is the need for uniformity of statutory interpretation. Indeed, that does seem to be the major legal task of most Continental high courts described in chapter 3.

Earlier we noted that even if all courts did was conflict resolution, appeal would serve the regime's purposes of hierarchical control by providing a sample of low level administrative performance. When we focus on the lawmaking activities of courts, we can see that appeal is a mechanism that sorts out unresolved issues of public policy and moves them toward the top for decision. In some cases the questions of law appealed from trial courts represent instances in which the trial court has deviated from the uniform national rule and will be brought back into line by an appeals court. In others the question of law arises because there is no national rule and the appeals court is being asked to make one. This is why appeals courts inevitably become lawmaking bodies even in legal systems that denigrate judicial lawmaking.

To emphasize this function, however, is to assert that most high courts of appeal are barely courts at all. That is, while in form they may be engaged in finally resolving one particular dispute between two particular litigants, their principal role may be to provide uniform rules of law. Naturally such rules must be based on considerations far broader than the concerns of the two litigants, essentially on considerations of public policy that may have little to do with the particular litigation. At worst the litigants are irrelevant; at best they are examples or samples of the general problems to be solved.

Political scientists and lawyers concerned with the legitimacy of courts have tended to concentrate on appellate courts. Appellate courts are the furthest removed from the basic social logic of courts. As a result courts appear far more problematic to scholars than they do to the citizenry. Nevertheless, the study of appellate courts makes clear that courts always exist in a state of tension between their basic source of legitimacy as consensual triadic resolvers of conflict and their position as government agencies imposing law on the citizenry. To put this matter somewhat differently, the social legitimacy of courts as a universal social device for conflict resolution and the political legitimacy of courts as a particular segment of a particular political regime are sometimes additive and mutually supportive and sometimes quite the contrary.

### Popular Courts

Early in this discussion we noted a certain natural affinity between judging and administration, or that judging is normally one of the functions of ruling elites or simply "big men." The extended discussion of appeal tends to emphasize further the elite element. Therefore it might be well to conclude this discussions of courts with some discussion of the popular element in judging. It is doubtful, however, that very many societies experienced much pure popular judging. The Greek jury and its Roman derivative, chosen by lot under procedures that ensured the representation of all the generic components of the society, probably came the closest in form to complete democracy. But these juries typically operated in highly politicized contexts, subject to constraints and manipulations that reflected a far from democratic basic political structure. They may have represented a popular element in Greek and Roman governance, but they are far from a pure form of judging by the people.

The folkmoot, in which judgment is theoretically rendered by the whole people, is encountered in a number of societies. Whatever patterns of social and political hierarchy existed in the society at large no doubt were reflected at the moot as well. The folkmoot is often said to be the basic judicial institution of the ancient Germanic tribes and thus of the Anglo-Saxons. There are Roman reports of such moots in the forests of Germany. Apparently they were periodic meetings of the whole tribe in which all sorts of tribal decisions, including judicial ones, were made by acclamation. As we shall see in chapter 2, there is no actual evidence that the Anglo-Saxons ever held moots. The first English courts we know of have a popular element that is often said to derive from the moot, but may have other origins. Far more common than the moot as such is judging by the chief or the chief and his advisors, or the elders, *surrounded by* a participant audience of the people. This form of popular participation is not limited to tribal societies. As we shall see in chapter 4, imperial Chinese judges were required to hold open trials and attend to the sentiments of the audience. Probably the German moot was really of this sort. The audience may participate in a number of ways. First, it may be an important channel of fact-finding. Either individually or collectively, and by specific testimony or general demeanor, the people may convey to the judges information on specific facts, local customs and usages, and on the good character of litigants and witnesses. Second, they may provide important levels of judicial enforcement. Their presence may be a strong incentive to the litigants to behave properly before the courts. They will remember its judgment when the losing litigant seeks to forget it. And they may provide social pressure toward obedience to the court's decree. Most important, they are likely to provide strong pressure toward consensual behavior, superficial or real, on the part of the litigants. Even when judges cannot arrive at a mediatory settlement, truly satisfying both parties, the presence of the people may elicit a "good citizen" or "good sport" consent from the loser. Subsequently, the people may hold him to that consent on pain of loss of his moral reputation. Third, the popular audience may serve as the receptacle for the received legal tradition or a sounding board for the invention of new legal rules. In practice no distinction is likely to be made between traditional and new rules—the judges simply make trial enunciations of the "law" and see how they play to the audience. Finally, by its participation, the audience attests to the legitimacy of the judges—that they are perceived as holding judicial office. Popular participation links the court to the affective and effective world of local affairs, a particularly important function if the judges are themselves envoys from a distant central regime.

The popular element in English and Western European legal traditions that we have really substantial evidence for is the suitors' court. The English hundred, shire, and manor courts of this sort will be described in chapter 2. Where such courts exist, all persons of a certain social status, usually adult free men, are obliged to attend periodic sessions of their court. These "suitors" are the judges who hear cases and render verdicts, although some outside official may preside. While in theory all those qualified to be suitors must attend, in reality attendence was such a burden that the poorest suitors were not required to do so and the best off evaded their responsibilities. It is probable that most suitors' courts actually consisted of a relatively small share of the total body of locals who were theoretically "court-worthy." They would tend to be of the most respectable, middling sort. The larger the territory covered by the court, the greater the expense of travelling to and attending its meetings. So suitors' courts of more than very local jurisdiction would tend to be courts of gentry or notables.

Suitors' courts are found as local, feudal, and national institutions. Sometimes there was a purely local, customary obligation to attend a traditional local meeting. Sometimes there was an obligation on the part of subjects to attend their king's courts, and sometimes there was an obligation on the part of a vassal to attend his lord's courts. The presiding officer might be a local notable selected by the suitors themselves, a royal officer, the lord's bailiff, or indeed the lord himself. Typically, the suitors would apply local, customary law since as laymen they would know no other. Suitors' courts might be truly popular in the sense of reflecting local popular understanding of law. Or they might be popular facades behind which the king or lord worked his will by intimidating the suitors.

The origins of the English jury are obscure. What we do know is that such juries were at first a coercive device imposed on the people by a central regime bent on increasing its control over the countryside. The English kings required that a certain number of persons in each locale come together periodically to report to a king's officer which of the king's laws lately had been broken by which of the local residents. This was the grand jury. The jury thus began as a form of collective responsibility for reporting crime. Such systems are encountered in many societies as a form of "popular participation" that the people rarely care for very much. Both in medieval England and in imperial China, for instance, we encounter systems in which every ten or hundred or thousand persons or families, or every village, is collectively responsible for reporting criminals and vagabonds and whatever crimes they have committed to the central authorities. They may be punished for failure to discover and report crime or render up the criminal. As we shall see in chapter 2, the petit or trial jury first arose not to judge but to testify to certain facts which the king's judges needed to know in order to enforce royal legislation.

By the nineteenth century, the notion of the jury as a popular safeguard against the possible tyranny of royal prosecutors and judges was common in England. For instance the only basic "constitutional" protection of free speech in England to this day is Fox's Libel Act. It is a parliamentary statute requiring that prosecutions for "seditious libel," that is, criticism of the government, be heard by a jury. The introduction of both grand and petit juries in the United States was a result of this English experience. Yet it can be argued that, in reality, the grand jury has retained much of its original nature as an arm of government policy rather than a protection against it. Indeed, the grand jury has long since been abandoned in England and has been much criticized in the United States.

The petit jury, or something like it, has been introduced for criminal trials in many European countries. Sometimes, as in France, an actual jury is used with roughly the same role as an English or American jury. Often, however, European nations inject "lay assessors" instead of juries. Unlike the practice in the English-speaking world, Continental trial courts are usually presided over by a panel of judges rather than a single one. Thus, instead of using a jury, a popular element may be introduced by providing that one or more of the judges be laymen rather than professional judges.

This introduction of an essentially foreign element into Continental jurisprudence has resulted, as we shall see in chapter 2, in a rather uneasy court structure in most European countries. It is never quite possible to integrate criminal court proceedings fully into a unified court structure. The popular element introduced for criminal judging does not fit into the basic tradition of a professional judicial bureaucracy that dominates the judicial system as a whole.

Imperial powers sometimes employ mixed panels of metropolitan and native judges, in part to provide some element of local participation in government and in part to provide expertise on native law. Whenever a central legal system is attempting to absorb or make use of local, idiosyncratic, or specialized bodies of laws, customs, usages, or technologies, it may add representatives of the specialized communities to the regular judicial staff. Thus medieval courts both in England and on the Continent sometimes employed panels of merchants or craftsmen to assist in commercial and technological litigation. The privileged position of expert witnesses to offer the court "opinion" evidence is a similar device. Most witnesses may testify only to what they have personally seen or heard, but experts may give their opinions about matters within their particular expertise. The alternative is extraterritoriality or other forms of judicial enclaves, in which merchants, tribesmen, town dwellers, men of the sea, religious sects, and the like are allowed special courts partially or wholly divorced from the general judicial system.

In all these instances the need for special factual and/or legal expertise and the need to increase the legitimacy and penetrating power of the courts in resistant enclaves can be met simultaneously by provisions for community participation. Such participation, however, runs partially against the capacity of the court system to wed local elements to a central regime. It is often an intermediate stage that tends either to disappear as the national government becomes stronger or to be transmitted into a general democratic safeguard as the jury is in England.

A similar set of dynamics is encountered in the use of lay as opposed to professional judges.[75] The distinction only superficially rests on the absence or presence of formal legal training. Its real significance is in the relative independence from or incorporation into a government personnel system with its capacity for disciplining subordinates. The English justice of the peace system, the American use of nonlawyers as local magistrates, and the encouragement or toleration of village elder courts by many governments ruling over peasant populations are major examples of lay judging. Such courts provide a cheap means of thrusting law down into the local communities. The countryside rather than the regime pays the lion's share of the costs of the administration of justice, usually in the form of unpaid or low-paid time devoted to judging by local, prominent men. Against the cheapness of this device must be balanced the reduced capacity of the regime to control such judges as opposed to professional local judges at the lowest step on a career ladder, who must look to the central authorities for promotion. Thus in some instances, most notably that of the English justices of the peace, the institution of lay judging may be a successful device for exploiting the pool of judicial and administrative skills in the countryside. In others, however, it may be part of a deliberate refusal or failure of a central regime to push its legal controls and services down into that countryside.

We noted earlier that the union of judging and administration was far more common than their separation. The English justices of the peace constitute such a union of lay judging and lay administration. As we shall see in chapter 2, the English experimented with various combinations of centralized and local judging and administration. Basically, they opted for a highly centralized professional judiciary and bureaucracy. They supplemented it, however, by a system of local justices of the peace. These J.P.'s were typically local gentry, that is, landholders, who provided local law enforcement, administration of local government services and judging in minor criminal matters. Sitting in panels, as a court of quarter sessions, they handled somewhat more important criminal cases. After the early decline of the grand jury, the J.P.'s served as "presenting" officers for more serious crimes, which involved a combination of indicting and prosecuting. For centuries, quarter sessions was the basic instrument of local administration. Only late in the nineteenth century did the J.P.'s begin to lose much of their authority, both judicial and administrative. They long constituted one of the great institutional successes of British politics, but they were deemed successful largely because they were the faithful servants of the central government. They brought only a slight leavening of popular or lay participation to that government.

As we noted earlier, the other side of the coin of the capacity to control professional judges by controlling their career patterns may be the resistance of a professional judicial corps to government policies contrary to its conception of law and justice. One variant of lay judging, the "people's courts" of communist regimes, seems specifically designed to deal with this problem. As with many other communist institutions, this one varies markedly between the revolutionary stage and the stage of consolidation of the new regime. During the revolution, people's courts were little more than the borrowing of a familiar, legitimate form through which to identify local noncommunist populations with the destruction of the class enemy. Such courts require the people, as an egalitarian mass under the leadership of communist cadres, to participate directly in the murders and expropriations of the landlords and capitalists and to share in the distribution of the spoils. The people's courts serve as an integral part of the revolutionary process itself. Their ritualized violence breaks old social structures and loyalties, brings to the fore the most violent, malicious, and alienated, and openly fastens responsibility for revolutionary acts on the participants.

Once a communist regime is established, people's courts tend to split into three streams. The first, which confusingly often retains the official name "people's court," is in actuality a regular, professionally staffed, court system. In the Soviet Union, and throughout Eastern Europe, whatever the claims made, this regular court system is clearly identifiable in the education of its personnel, career patterns, procedures, and concept of judicial role with the preceding Roman law tradition. Indeed, these people's courts can be considered as simply the Eastern European branch of the family of Continental, civil law courts we will survey in chapter 3. While quite obviously much of the law they administer, particularly in the area of property, is not civil or Roman but communist law, their style and indeed much of their legal thinking is still within the Roman law tradition.

Of course, there are differences of degree. The Polish courts and law are most openly Roman law. The Soviet courts seek to stress their class character by such touches as the wearing of street clothes on the bench. By law Soviet judges are popularly elected and serve only limited terms. In reality there is a professional, civil service judiciary quite similar to that in Western Europe. Soviet trial courts generally employ a panel of two lay assessors and one professional judge to emphasize their popular character. Nevertheless professional, legally expert judges and procurators—that is, government attorneys—tend to dominate the regular judicial system. Almost all judges in the Soviet Union are members of the party. In this way the regime insures that even a professional judiciary "independent and subordinate only to law," as the Soviet constitution and judicial statutes put it, is properly in tune with the goals and values of the communist government.[76]

The second stream is a large variety of "comradely courts," block committees, tenants councils, factory committees, and so on. These are genuine peoples' courts in the sense that they are gatherings of the people who live on a certain street or in a certain building or work in a certain place. Generally they confine themselves to the mediation of minor quarrels that arise between neighbors or fellow workers, or within families, guided by their sense of "socialist justice."[77]

The comradely courts have had their ups and downs in communist states, becoming more prominent when regimes have sought to stress revolutionary fervor and less so when the regimes have been emphasizing stability and "socialist legality." At those times when a communist regime has sought to return to full revolutionary status, as during the "Cultural Revolution" in China, the comradely or real peoples' courts may return to their origins as instruments of class violence and terror. So, at one extreme, these popular courts may be lynch mobs and, at the other, approach pure mediation.

These two extremes also mark the third judicial stream of communist states. The stream is composed of a series of special tribunals. At one extreme they include the tribunals of the secret police, which during periods of terror secretly consign people to death or the labor camps without inconvenient legal formalities. At the other extreme are arbitration tribunals which arbitrate disputes between state-owned industrial units that arise under the contracts they enter into with one another. Such arbitration is sometimes binding, but sometimes consists of mediation which may be followed by a suit in a regular court should the mediation fail.

At the times of their initial revolutions, communist regimes saw that professional courts of law would necessarily be courts staffed by prerevolutionary judges applying prerevolutionary law. They turned to peoples' courts precisely because they did not want the prototypic court with an independent judge applying preexisting legal rules. Indeed Soviet and Chinese communist regimes at first urged their peoples' judges to make liberal use of analogy to make new law in every case in which it was necessary to do so to punish the class enemy. While the Chinese persisted in this approach, most communist regimes retain only remnants of it. For they have discovered that an "independent" judiciary applying "preexisting legal rules" is no threat to the workers' state so long as certain conditions are met. The judges must be party members subject to party discipline. They must also be subject to the career discipline of the judicial bureaucracy. And the legal rules must be those made by the regime. Thus the peoples' courts of the first stream we described are popular courts only to the extent one subscribes to the claim that communist regimes are popular regimes.

No doubt peoples' courts have certain ideological advantages and are particularly appropriate to the system of massive mutual surveillance encouraged by communist regimes. Modern noncommunist societies, however, have also proliferated small claims courts, domestic relations and juvenile tribunals, industrial and commercial arbitration panels, housing courts, counseling services, and administrative boards that handle a great deal of conflict resolution and social control through quasi-judicial proceedings but without professional judges or outside of the normal forms of litigation. Peoples' courts, often in conjunction with peoples' "militia," can perform many similar functions.

CONCLUSION

If we ground our notion of courts in the triadic structure of conflict resolution, a wide range of social phenomena are courtlike, many of which are not specifically political unless we choose to label all situations of conflict political. However, once we encounter the substitution of judicial office and law for spontaneous consent, the intermix of conflict resolution, social control, and lawmaking in most courts, and the frequent integration of judging with administrative or general political authority, a substantial share of courts and judges seems to be engaging in politics. Like most other major political institutions, courts tend to be loaded with multiple political functions, ranging under various circumstances from bolstering the legitimacy of the political regime to allocating scarce economic resources or setting major social policies.

In the succeeding chapters of this book, we shall examine the courts of England, Western Europe, imperial China, and Islam, in each instance attempting to relate them to the political regimes of which they form a part. In the process a great many of the points made in this chapter will be amplified and illustrated. Each chapter picks up a central theme introduced in this one. In each instance I have chosen those comparative and historical materials that seemed best suited to falsify the propositions I have advanced. Thus my suspicions about the notion of judicial independence have been placed against the background of the judicial system that is generally regarded as the most independent—the English. My questioning of the prototype's insistence on preexisting legal rules has been put in the context of that legal system which is commonly supposed to best exemplify the subordination of the judge to statutory law—the code law systems of Western Europe. My insistence on the inevitable mixture of judging and mediation is tested against the legal system most often reputed to be totally dominated by mediation—that of imperial China. My argument that appeal is universal because of its political utility is pursued in relation to the one major legal system that does not generally employ appeal—that of traditional Islam.

# 2 ENGLISH COURTS AND JUDICIAL INDEPENDENCE

### Introduction

In chapter 1 we traced the substitution of office and law for consent that characterizes at least a segment of most developed legal systems. A judicial official chosen by government is substituted for the selection of the triadic figure by the two conflicting parties themselves. As a result the losing party can no longer be persuaded that the trial did not break down into two against one by reminding him that he himself chose the third person. Consequently, the legal system will find it useful to endow the third party with some special attributes designed to content the loser.

In this sense the notion of an "independent judiciary," which is central to the conventional prototype of courts, is simply an elaborate rationalization for the substitution of coercion for consent. The state now imposes a judge on the parties. The judge is openly and admittedly a state official. It is repeatedly asserted, nonetheless, that he is "independent." The myth of judicial independence is designed to mollify the loser. He is told that he must not view the triad as two against one because, by the very nature of judicial office, the third person is neutral and independent of both the parties and debarred from forming a coalition with either one.

The functional utility of the myth of judicial independence is so great that we find it widespread among the various past and present legal systems of the world. It is particularly associated, however, with the evolution of Anglo-American judiciaries. It is also an important element in Continental jurisprudence, but assertions of judicial independence have never been as clear or simple-minded there as they have been in the English-speaking world. Particularly among American and English authorities, "judicial independence" has been less a rigorously defined concept than a generalization of Anglo-American experience.[1] Consequently an examination of the actual institutional development of Anglo-American courts should tell us a good deal about the reality of that judicial independence which is one of the four essential features of the conventional prototype of a court.

### Judicial Independence and Political Centralization

Before turning to the details of the British data, some preliminary definitional remarks are in order. We are not going to discover that there is no such thing as English judicial independence. As a central category for understanding English historical experience, however, the notion of judicial independence leads to overemphasis and misinterpretation of some facets of historical experience and an almost conscious refusal to deal directly with others. Above all, viewing the historical evolution of British judicial institutions as a kind of teleological and ultimately successful quest for judicial independence is too simple. It leads us to neglect the key fact that most of the phenomena we come to call judicial independence, or see as the roots of judicial independence, are closely associated historically with a long-term English tendency toward extreme political centralization. That tendency is at least potentially antithetical to meaningful judicial independence. This interplay between judicial independence and political centralization is the crucial theme of this chapter. Observation of this interplay will teach us one important thing. Whatever conventional observers have meant by an independent judiciary in the Anglo-American context, they could not have meant some simple, clearly delineated sphere of pure or complete independence for judges. For such spheres have existed only fleetingly in Anglo-American experience. Instead, what we customarily label judicial independence has typically involved paradox, conflict, ambiguity, and unresolved tensions.

For instance, whatever judicial independence might mean in the English context, it certainly could not mean political independence. The theory of the British constitution has always been one of complete, absolute, and unified sovereignty.[2] No one has ever suggested that the judges were exempted from this sovereignty. In practice unified sovereignty was softened initially by the conception that it was the king in council or in Parliament rather than the king alone who wielded sovereignty. Later the system of popular elections and two-party competition limited in practice the theoretically unlimited political power of Parliament. The belief that Englishmen had certain fundamental rights also somewhat limited notions of sovereignty. So did the concept of rule of law that we shall examine shortly. But none of these deviations from the strict theory of sovereignty ever resulted in more than momentary assertions that the courts wielded an independent political authority unsubordinated to the king in Parliament. In theory, in practice, and in constitutional structure and procedure, the British courts have always been firmly placed under the king in Parliament. Their powers and jurisdiction, indeed their very existence, have been determined by the king's commission and/or parliamentary statute. The Parliament is the ultimate and unchallengable maker of the law they apply. Yet those who stress judicial independence as a basic characteristic of courts rarely stop to remind us that British judges are in theory and practice firmly subordinated to their political masters who wield the sovereign authority of Parliament.

Of course, it may be that the notion of judicial independence involved in the conventional prototype of courts does not really involve political independence but only independence vis à vis the two conflicting parties, or impartiality. It might be argued that so long as the English judge was not dependent on either of the two parties, it would be irrelevant to his triadic role that he was a political dependent of the sovereign. However, as we have already seen, such an argument is valid only in certain limited circumstances. It applies when the judge is guided by a rule of law created solely by the parties themselves. It also applies when the two parties belong to the same legal class so that the legal rule being applied appears to be equally favorable to both. Where the judge is a political dependent of the government and is employing a legal rule created by that government, he is not independent of or impartial toward both the parties in those instances where the policy embodied in the law favors the class to which one of them belongs. As a dependent of the government and its law, the judge becomes a dependent of whichever party the law favors.

While the historical English experience we are about to review may show the growth of an independent judiciary in the sense of an impartial judiciary protected from the direct fear or favor of the particular parties, such a finding will not relieve us of the ambiguities inherent in calling a politically dependent judiciary "independent." Even viewing independence as a synonym for impartiality, we may be encountering an English judiciary that is impartial in particular but not in general. It may be immune to the particular threats or blandishments of particular litigants, but partial in general to those classes of litigants favored by the law it applies.

### THE RULE OF LAW

Closely related to this kind of impartiality in particular is the English notion of rule of law. We shall find deeply embedded in English experience the doctrine that although the sovereign is the sole source of law, even the sovereign is bound by the law once it is enacted and until it is modified or repealed. Thus, while the sovereign could intervene at any time to change the general law that the courts were applying, he ought not to interfere in particular cases to compel results contrary to existing law.[3] Here again the courts are totally dependent on the sovereign for their legal authority, independent of him for the decision in particular cases but dependent in general in the sense of applying the law he has provided.

### FUNCTIONAL SPECIALIZATION

One of the central building blocks of conventional notions of English judicial independence is the functional specialization of courts. Unlike the imperial Chinese system examined in chapter 4, England does possess distinct institutions and personnels devoted more or less exclusively to the job of judging. The historical data will make clear, however, that this functional specialization is slow in coming to English law, never completed, and now probably receding. Moreover, functional specialization per se ought not to be confused with independence. Many tightly controlled, hierarchical organizations contain highly specialized subordinate components. For instance, the artillery and engineering units of an army may be highly specialized while nevertheless strictly subordinated to its high command. Functional specialization is not a sufficient and perhaps not even a necessary condition to judicial independence. But it is easily mistaken for such independence.

COMMON LAW AND COMMON LAWYERS

More important than functional specialization itself for the growth of English notions of judicial independence was the growth of a special body of judicially made law and a legal profession in sole possession of the mysteries of that law. Here again the actual historical data will show that the law of England is not quite so exclusively judge-made as is conventionally supposed nor is the legal profession quite so monopolistic in its possession of knowledge of that law. Nevertheless, that much of the law applied by English courts was created by them rather than passed to them by the sovereign was an important practical deviation from the theory of exclusive and unified sovereignty vested in the king in Parliament. The data will show that, at certain times and in certain substantive areas, the courts were substantially free to make their own law and were then, to an extent, politically independent. The data will also show, however, that this political independence existed at the suffrance of, and in between massive interventions by, the sovereign law-making authorities. Nevertheless, the judge-applied common law obscured the fundamental subordination of English courts to the sovereign. It became easier for Englishmen than for Continental Europeans to think of their courts as independent. For Europeans saw their courts as taking the law they applied exclusively from the statutes made by emperors, kings, and legislatures.

Perhaps even more important was the common law's contribution to the growth of an independent legal profession.[4] That profession grew as an essentially private guild, and one to which the judges at times were more intimately connected than they were to the government. Both the growth of the profession and this intimate connection were fostered by the fact that the common lawyers built a body of law so complex and illogical that no one but its creators could understand it. As that law grew, it became essential that the judges be appointed from and maintain close contacts with the practitioners, for only such judges could even pretend to understand the law they were supposed to apply. Here again it was easier for the English than for Continentals to see their courts as independent because their judges appeared to be members of a private and autonomous professional guild rather than officers of a hierarchical government bureaucracy.

### LAISSEZ-FAIRE AND JUDICIAL INDEPENDENCE

The English notion of judicial independence is opposed to the basic theory of sovereignty espoused in the British constitution and incompatible with the reality that English judges apply law made by the king in Parliament. That notion of independence has been greatly fostered, however, by the fact that over long periods of English history the judges have appeared to apply law made by themselves rather than the sovereign. English judicial independence is essentially composed of three motifs: the rule of law, the functional specialization of the judiciary, and the autonomy of the legal profession. As we shall soon see, these motifs represent important realities of English history. They do yield a model of judicial independence that is roughly true for eighteenth- and nineteenth-century English and American courts. Indeed, when we speak of judicial independence, we are basically writing large and treating as final culmination or eternal verity this eighteenth- and nineteenth-century experience.

That experience was, however, somewhat peculiar, particularly in its tendency to separate "private" from "public" law. By the nineteenth century most legal thinkers had concluded that in the very limited sphere in which the state had direct interests of its own, it should pass statutes favorable to itself which judges would enforce as loyal servants of the state. In other spheres, particularly in that of commercial activity, the state would serve only as the referee and protector of private enterprise. Private law would be derived from and reflect the actual practices of the business community and provide a natural channel for the regularization and enforcement of customary commercial relations. Thus, in this laisse-faire moment of legal history, the unresolvable conflict between judge as applier of law made by the state in its own interest and judge as "independent" resolver of bilateral conflict was bridged. For in the vast central bodies of private law the state was conceived as having no interest other than facilitating the affairs of the litigants. The moment did not last, and the bridge has not lasted. In the twentieth century we are again concerned with the special interests or, if you like, the public interests of the state and their embodiment in all facets of law. Consequently judges again become enforcers of public policy as well as referees of private disputes throughout the whole range of legal relationships including those we used to call "private."[5] Now with these preliminary problems of perspective disposed of, let us turn to the historical materials.[6]

## The Courts of the Imperial Conqueror

Anglo-Saxon England enjoyed a fairly well-developed legal and judicial system based initially on the Germanic tradition of the folkmoot in which trials were held before the assembled tribesmen who gave judgment. The English had hundred and shire courts attended by "suitors," that is, the men of the district, who gave judgment largely according to the local customary law. Whatever its origins, the hundred court had become simply the lowest level territorial trial court and the shire court a somewhat higher court both in terms of the importance of the cases and the social status of the suitors.

When the Norman Duke William conquered England in 1066, he acquired a going legal system. The Norman conquest was not a great movement of peoples into a new land but a gloriously successful foray by a small body of armed adventurers and their soldiery. William was glad to preserve the English legal system along with most of its other basic economic, social, and political arrangements. Indeed he had little choice, for he did not have the Norman manpower to do much more than impose his followers at the top of whatever authority structures already existed. Normans displaced Saxons as tenants in chief to the king, that is, as the largest landholders in a quasi-feudal system where Normans held land directly of the king and Saxons held land of Normans. Normans served as household officials to the king. Initially about the only changes in the legal system were a few special laws designed to protect the conquering cadres, such as that providing a special procedure of investigation, trial, and punishment when a Norman had been killed.[7]

William and his successors may have been roving adventurers, but they had ceased to be mere freebooters. They fiercely and singlemindedly fought to centralize political power in their English realm at the same time as they pursued Continental adventures that ended in the loss of their French territories and their quite unwilling conversion into English monarchs. Their first approach is precisely the one we expect of imperial conquerors. They appointed all-purpose district officers, each one doing all the administrative and judicial business of his own territory. The shires and the sheriffs had existed before the conquest. Normans were now appointed to the posts, and there were many signs that they would turn into all-powerful provincial governors reporting to the capital.[8]

In the judicial sphere, however, the sheriff was limited by the inherited court system. Judgment in the shire court was rendered by the suitors, that is, the local landholders and town representatives. The sheriff only presided. The Normans accepted this tradition. The extent to which sheriffs turned their presiding powers into domination of the shire courts' decision is not known and probably varied greatly from time to time and shire to shire.[9]

This slight check upon the sheriff's power was of relatively little significance. The sheriff was the king's delegate wielding the full sovereignty of the crown at the local level. The little band of Norman adventurers did not bear up well under success. Quarreling broke out between the royal successors of William and his lieutenants. With the land granted them by William, they had converted themselves from military subordinates into the barons of the realm. Each of the barons tended to dominate some portion of the countryside. As the barons became more powerful, they tended to garner the position of sheriff in their locale for themselves or their friends. From the king's viewpoint the sheriffs ceased to be a mode of extending royal power into the countryside and instead became an element in the centrifugal powers of the barons. Accordingly, after a period in which some sheriffs came close to the status of autonomous provincial governor, their powers were sharply reduced.[10] They continued to preside over the shire courts and undertake important responsibilities in connection with some of the king's writs, but they became specialized local officials rather than all-purpose local governors.[11]

William the Conqueror's initial solution to the problem of holding the conquered territories, that of parcelling them out to his friends and lieutenants as landholders and sheriffs, had failed. From being the king's local governing delegates, the barons had become his local rivals. Judicial institutions had played a part in this failure.

Whether or not Norman England is to be characterized accurately as "feudal" or only as containing elements of feudalism is an issue to be avoided by nonspecialists. It is clear, however, that in granting lands to the Norman conquerors and their successors, the crown often granted, among many other franchises, rights, powers, and sources of income, the capacity to hold a court for the landholder's tenants. These were feudal courts in the sense that they typically "belonged" to the landholder in connection with and by virtue of his landholding, that the landholder or his steward presided in them, that he took their profits, that they had jurisdiction over his tenants because they were his tenants, and that they dealt principally with disputes between tenant and tenant or between the landholder and his tenant. Whether in theory the landholding magnates were granted complete judicial powers by the crown or only the profits, that is, fees and fines levied by the courts, is uncertain. It probably made no practical difference. The lord's court applied local customary law. The tenants themselves acted as both the witnesses testifying to and the judges applying the custom. The extent to which a given lord or his bailiff dominated his attending tenants and manipulated their judgments no doubt varied from time to time and place to place depending on numerous factors, the least of which was the exact nature of his judicial grant from the king.[12]

The existence of these local feudal courts controlled by the barons, together with local hundred and shire courts also largely dominated by local magnates, was one element in the struggle between local powers and the crown.

THE EYRE SYSTEM

The royal problem was to exercise royal control over the various local areas of England by some means other than delegating the king's authority to local "subordinates." For those subordinates had turned into the baronial enemies of the king. The royal solution was the "eyre" system.[13] Instead of long-term delegation of royal authority to a lord permanently connected to a single territory, there would be a temporary delegation to a king's officer. This royal dependent normally resided with the king, travelled once on his "eyre" through the designated territory exercising his delegated authority, and then surrendered his authority upon his return to the king's household. Even though granted sweeping powers, the royal delegate could not become an independent territorial magnate and rival to the king because his only real base was in the king's household, from whence he came and to whence he must return.

While it had its inevitable historical forerunners, the eyre system reached its peak in the reigns of Henry II and Henry III. Its adoption meant that the conquered English empire would not be ruled on the district officer model, but along even more totally centralized lines. This development had an enormous impact on the evolution of English judicial institutions.

The justice in eyre, as he came to be called, does remind us of the district officer in a number of ways, however. He was at first a single, all-purpose, and thus extremely cheap instrument of imperial rule. As he travelled from town to town within the designated shire or shires, he exercied the king's commission to collect the taxes, collect fines, audit local accounts, inspect public works, keep the peace, suppress crime, resolve disputes, and in general insure that everyone performed the services and paid the monies owed the king.

The justice in eyre was in a sense conceived as a surrogate for the king's own progress through his domains. As we shall see shortly, on such progresses the king exercised the full judicial powers that were a component of his sovereignty. The justice in eyre did the same. Thus he could hold the king's court at each stopping place along his circuit. He presided over sittings of the shire court. Armed directly with the king's justice, he probably took a more active part in its decisions than the sheriff typically did. Indeed, when he presided, it is not clear whether the court remained the shire court or became a king's court in which the king's judge had full decisional powers. At first the justice in eyre heard whatever cases coincidentally were ready for trial at the time of his visit. As the eyre settled into regular visits to a particular shire every two to eight years, local authorities and litigants began to save up cases for its decision.

As the business of the eyre grew and holders of eyre commissions began to be sent out in groups, there probably arose some division of function, with some commissioners specializing more or less in tax and accounting matters and others in litigation. But in general and at its height the eyre constituted essentially an administrative solution to an administrative problem. It brilliantly resolved the crucial problem of all conquest-based empires, how to bring central political authority to bear on the countryside cheaply and without creating local centers of power capable of resisting central authority. Most empires solve this problem by thinly spreading administrative cadres over the countryside, rotating them frequently, and/or otherwise insuring that they do not develop strong local ties, and subjecting them to rigorous hierarchical discipline. We shall see such a pattern later in looking at China. The English solution was to send members of the central authority itself, that is, the king's own household, on quick tours through the countryside. In the course of these tours they gathered the information needed by the central regime, imposed its power on the local authority, and then returned to the bosom of the central authority itself. Thus the king did not have to finance a corps of territorial administrators separate from his household staff. More important, he did not have to worry about such administrators becoming locally independent because they went from under his thumb temporarily to do their field administration and then quickly came back under his thumb again.

Of course, this brilliant solution depended in large part on the small size of the English portion of the Norman emperor's domains. And it also depended on the existence of traditional hundred and shire institutions, the sheriffs, and the feudal authority of local landholders to do the day-to-day business of government between visitations. Whatever its prerequisites, the eyre system was one of the key building blocks in a highly centralized English political and administrative system. And that led to one of the most centralized judicial systems to be encountered in any nation-state or empire. The eyre system meant that the most powerful judges in the realm appeared as traveling representatives of a central judicial authority. They were not local subordinates of a central judicial authority tied to it by lines of hierarchical control, that is, appeals procedures. Instead, they were literally pieces of a central judiciary on temporary trips through the countryside.

## CENTRALIZED ADMINISTRATIVE AND JUDICIAL BODIES

The eyre system was not the only means of sending concentrated central authority through the countryside, instead of dispersing it by way of a district officer. The king himself took his government, that is, his household, on tour. Medieval monarchs customarily progressed through the countryside. It was easier to go to the food and drink and the game than to have them brought to a permanent court. As the sovereign, the king was the font of justice obligated to hear all complaints and right all wrongs. At the same time, the theoretically absolute sovereignty of medieval monarchs was usually hedged by the custom that the king act in council after receiving the advice of his great men. The Norman kings of England heard cases personally but usually in council.[14] Moreover, among the king's administrative officers and councillors were several, most particularly the chancellor and the justiciar, who acquired special responsibility for legal matters. Since the Norman kings were frequently absent from England conducting their wars in France, these officers began to wield administrative and judicial authority in the king's absence.[15]

We cannot say exactly when England first had a royal judge per se. The councillors assisting the king when he heard his subject's pleas for redress of injuries were, among other things, judges in a sense. When the king was out of the realm, the council began to hear such pleas in his absence. The justiciar and the chancellor seemed to play a particularly important part in the judicial aspects of the council's business. So even in the twelfth century we can speak of a king's court or curia, but the curia was the forerunner of later legislative and administrative, as well as judicial, institutions.

### THE BENCH

The first really distinctly judicial court arose out of the king's habit of doing personal justice as he traveled through the countryside. It became quite inconvenient for suitors to troop along after the king on his progress, waiting for him to settle their cases. One of the provisions of the Magna Carta, that great bill of complaints against King John, was that a permanent place be designated for the hearing of "common pleas." Common pleas were disputes between private persons not touching directly on the interests of the king. Not even the rebellious barons would have suggested that the king be required to allow crown pleas directly involving his own interests to be heard outside his presence.

The provision of the Magna Carta appears to be designed to make permanent an arrangement that had already been used sporadically. The early Norman kings had sometimes left some of their officers home to hear cases when the king set off on his travels. Commissioned to hear cases at Westminister in the king's absence, these officers were referred to as the bench and considered a branch of the curia, the rest of which was traveling with the king.[16] When the king was out of England, the whole curia tended to stay at Westminister, where most of their number would join in hearing cases. And when the king was present, he would hear cases, too. But the very existence of the bench settled very early that the king's court could decide cases without the king's presence. The personal justice of the king had become the institutional justice of the king's court.

### The Curia and the Major Crown Officers

By the end of the fourteenth century the eyre system had virtually disappeared, displaced by the growth of a centralized, institutionalized bureaucracy at the capital. At first the justices in eyre had been quite literally whichever of the king's friends and lieutenants, and thus noblemen, he commissioned to tour the countryside. Usually they were the same noblemen who sat by right in the curia. In the course of the crown's struggle with the barons, the Norman kings found that they would be better served by elevating lesser noblemen and commoners than by seeking crown officers from among the very barons who were opposing the crown. The later justices in eyre were more and more often men of relatively humble origins who were making careers as servants of the king. The large curia in which the great nobles sat by right continued to exist. The business of government, however, was increasingly done by a smaller version of the curia, a kind of inner cabinet. It was largely staffed by men who had been made great as a result of their having been chosen by the king to hold public officer rather than men who held public office because they were great hereditary landowners.[17]

The result was a quasi-professional group of government officials sitting permanently at the capital and building up professional bureaucracies of clerks and lesser officials who could maintain centralized pools of information, such as tax rolls. During the fifteenth century all of England could be ruled from London. From our point of view, what is striking about this developing centralized bureaucracy of the fifteenth and sixteenth centuries is that nearly every part of it wielded judicial authority.

First of all, the larger and smaller versions of the curia itself heard cases in the presence of the king and in his absence. The greatest administrative officer of the realm was the chancellor, who was keeper of the king's seal. Petitions for the king's favor passed into Chancery, and orders by the king under his seal passed out of Chancery. The Chancery thus was the center of most of the crown's business. Chancery was the source of the writs that initiated and defined the nature of actions in the common law courts that we will examine shortly. But the chancellor also maintained a separate jurisdiction to right wrongs for which the common law writs were not

suitable.[18] The Exchequer, which was the king's tax collection and accounting agency, had become a separate department from Chancery, and it,
too, heard cases.[19] It had become cumbersome to do all government business under the king's great seal held by the chancellor. So the king had
developed a second and personal or "privy" seal for the dispatch of lesser
government business. The keeper of that seal, the lord privy seal, quickly
developed judicial functions.[20]

### COMMON PLEAS AND KING'S BENCH

At the same time as these administrative-judicial agencies grew, two
functionally specialized courts unattached to administrative officers grew
out of the older bench and the court that followed the king. One was
Common Pleas; the other, King's Bench. As the names imply, the former
principally devoted itself to litigation between private parties and the latter
to matters in which the crown had an interest. In reality, however, both
courts heard a wide range of causes that in strict theory, if there had been
one, would have belonged to the other.[21]

### Centralized Collegiality

At first, however, there was little concern for establishing jurisdictional boundaries between all these "courts." For in this early period an
essentially collegial stamp was placed on British government which it wears
to this day in the form of cabinet rule. Even at a very early period some of
these courts had some judges who held no other office. But many crown
officers could sit upon many courts. The chancellor, for instance, heard
Chancery cases personally, almost invariably attended those curia sessions
devoted to settling litigation, and appeared at King's Bench and Common
Pleas when he had a mind. Common Pleas separated only gradually from
the court that followed the king, which consisted of his general advisors.[22]
When King's Bench was first created, it was hardly differentiated from the
council and was "expressly subordinated to the magnates and wiser men to
whom difficult cases were to be referred."[23]

The generally collegial character of Engilsh administration left a
strong mark on English courts. The high courts were typically multijudge
courts. Their personnel shifted somewhat from day to day as various
administrative-judicial officers shifted from job to job to meet the changing
press of government business. Moreover, the judges of one court would
customarily call in the judges of another when they needed help on a problem that seemed to require outside expertise. Both Chancery and Exchequer
freely called in Common Pleas and King's Bench judges to assist when some
troublesome point of common law arose in one of their cases.

This collegiality and the extreme centralization of courts also created a rather peculiar English appellate structure. Appeal from Common Pleas lay to King's Bench although in other respects both were first-instance national trial courts sitting at the capital, and many of the same judges sat in both. Appeal from King's Bench and from a number of other courts lay to the Court of Exchequer Chamber, which was essentially a meeting of all the judges who sat in all the central courts.[24] Thus, the English system of appeal substituted a centralized college of judges for a hierarchy of appeals courts. There was no need for a hierarchy of appeals courts to facilitate centralized control over dispersed trial courts because the trial courts were themselves centralized.

### JURIES AND CENTRALIZATION

We have already noted that this London bureaucracy of which the judges were an integral part had largely replaced the eyre system of administration during the fourteenth century. But the judicial aspects of the eyre were transferred to a new of circuit-riding judges. The Assize of Clarendon of 1166 had provided a new royal procedure for protecting the property interests of those in possession (seisin) of land. As we shall note shortly, a local jury was the essential feature of this new procedure. Moreover, the Grand Assize, for proving the better title as opposed to simply the seisin of land also employed a jury.[25] Thus in land cases judges had to travel to the juries. The king began to commission persons to travel in the shires and conduct the new procedures. Typically it was judges of King's Bench and Common Pleas who held these assize commissions, but sometimes they were granted to other king's officers as well. With the usual economy of the crown, the assize justices soon began to be empowered to hear other sorts of cases, particularly criminal cases, which had earlier been heard by justices in eyre under commissions of gaol delivery.[26]

The jury procedure proved extremely popular and gradually was extended to many kinds of litigation. This development posed a serious threat to judicial centralization because the essential virtue of the jury was its localness, that is, its personal knowledge of local events and conditions. The local jurors could hardly be compelled to travel to London to assist King's Bench and Common Pleas. Thus, the use of juries implied the creation of territorial trial courts.

The central courts protected themselves by devising the system of *nisi prius*. Suits initiated in Westminster at King's Bench or Common Pleas, and later at Exchequer, were pled up to the point at which the issue emerged that was ultimately to go to the jury. At that point instead of summoning a jury to London from the locale where the case arose, the case was turned over to the justice of assize traveling in that locale, and he presided over the jury portion of the trial. The ultimate control of the courts in the capital was assured by a provision that only those assize judges who were King's Bench or Common Pleas judges, king's sergeants, or barons of the Exchequer (if learned in law) could hear cases at *nisi prius*. The *nisi prius* system was begun in the latter part of the thirteenth century and extended to a very wide range of cases in the course of the fourteenth.[27]

The creation of circuit-riding justices of assize exercising *nisi prius*, as well as many other jurisdictions both criminal and civil, allowed England to develop and maintain probably the most centralized trial court system of any major nation in history.[28] The justices of assize and *nisi prius* judges were largely drawn from the body of central court judges or from the sergeants, that is, the elite corps of legal professionals who were intimately linked to the central courts. The eyes of all litigants remained fixed on Westminister, which dictated the procedural and substantive aspects of law because *nisi prius* cases had to be brought initially in a central court and a judge sitting *nisi prius* was considered to be representing that court. King's Bench and Common Pleas defined the extent of *nisi pruis* jurisdiction, and in difficult cases the *nisi prius* judge might adjourn the case back to the court from whence it came. Since the *nisi prius* judge was taken to be a representative of the court where the case was initiated, appeal lay to whatever court heard appeals from the initiating court. We find, too, the universal clue to centralizing motives: judges of assize could not hear cases in the counties where they were born or where they resided.

Thus assize with *nisi prius* was a way of getting central court trial services out into the countryside without creating local judicial institutions and without inspiring the local clamor for such institutions that would have resulted if all litigants and jurors had had to travel to London.

### Centralized Law

The creation of a body of powerful central courts with tentacles running into the countryside was one side of the development of English judicial centralization. The other was the development of a highly centralized body of law—centralized in the sense that it was made in the capital and applied uniformly over the whole countryside. Just as the Norman conquerors had acquired a going body of courts, the hundred and shire courts, so they had acquired a going body of law. While the Anglo-Saxon kings had imposed some measure of uniformity, that law was essentially local and customary and thus fragmented. The northern and eastern portions of England, which had been conquered earlier by the Danes, knew many legal practices substantially different from those in the south and west. Moreover, every town, borough, shire, hundred, estate, manor, port, and fair might have its own legal customs on matters ranging from proof of land transfer to adoption of children.[29]

Conquerors have usually found such localized legal diversity inconvenient. They find it far easier to administer uniform national rules than to keep track of local peculiarities. Moreover, following a conquest, customary law that lies largely in the memories of the conquered local inhabitants has a strange way of always favoring the old tenant against the new landlord, the taxpayer against the tax collector, and so on. In England, local law was often the vehicle for local "liberties," that is, claims of customary barriers to the complete sovereignty of the crown.

So, to put the matter negatively, the conquerors wished to sweep away Anglo-Saxon restraints on Norman rule. But there is a positive side as well. One of the most important aspects of the social control practiced by courts is that of wedding the populace to the regime, of strengthening the people's perception of the regime's legitimacy and their sense of loyalty to it. A major mode of exercising such control is the provision of official dispute settlement and other legal services better than those available elsewhere. The conquerors of England set out to show that the justice of the new king could be superior to that of the hundred and shire courts. As more and more hundred courts came into the possession of private landholders, as the feudal courts of landholders flourished, and as shire courts came to be dominated by local magnates, the king's justice was not only an alternative to Anglo-Saxon custom but to the landlord's courts.

There were a number of natural advantages that the king's courts could offer simply because they were central courts. Those individuals and classes of persons who found themselves disadvantaged by local customary law or the constellation of local political forces would naturally prefer a court located as far as possible from the local scene. Tenants involved in disputes with their landlords might well prefer to have their cases decided in courts other than those presided over or dominated by the landlord. Persons who are the officers of the central government or those with special ties to it may prefer its justice. Normans would prefer a Norman king's justice to that of an Anglo-Saxon local court.

In addition to these natural advantages, the Norman kings quickly provided a very important series of artificial ones. The first and most important of these was that the King's courts used a new body of law, the common law. The hundreds, shire, and feudal courts applied a law that, because it was customary, local, and unwritten, was highly uncertain and difficult to learn for any but long-time local residents. And because it was customary, the sanction behind it was essentially local opinion. In contrast, the common law developed as a uniform, national law, partially written and partly resident in the minds of a few hundred easily consulted lawyers in the capital, and directly backed by the authority of the crown. For many litigants such a law was simpler, more certain, and more easily enforceable than the web of local customs. Moreover, in contrast to the customary law, the common law could be rapidly changed to meet the changing needs of litigants.

### THE WRITS

The common law developed as a series of writs.[30] Initially a writ was simply a written order by the king to some person or persons. A prospective litigant desiring the king's justice requested an order from the king directed to the person who had injured him. It commanded that person either to provide a remedy for the injury he had done or to appear before the king or some officer designated by the king to explain why he had not done so. Thus, the writ began as a request from a subject that the king personally intervene to right a wrong he had suffered. The potential of such a device for recruiting political support and loyalty to the regime is obvious.

Requests for writs were naturally channeled through the chancellor who, as keeper of the king's seal, was the supervisor of most of the paperwork that flowed in and out of the royal household. What began as a series of personal and particularized requests soon settled into a kind of catalogue of standard forms.[31] For soon too many people were asking for the king's justice to allow each of them to ask in his own particular way. If one wanted the king's justice, one looked through the series of standardized forms for requesting royal assistance until one found the form with the wording best fitted to the facts of the particular dispute and the remedy desired. Then one filled in the blanks and submitted the form through the chancellor to the king. Here, for example, is one form of the writ of right.

> [Name of the king] to [name of the tenant in chief] greeting. We command you that without delay you hold right to [name of petitioner to the king], of [number of acres] of land with the appurtenance in [place where land is located], which he claims to hold of you by the free service of one penny yearly in lieu of all services, of which [name of defendant] deforces him, and unless you so do let the sheriff of [name of the county in which the land is located] do it, that we no longer hear complaint thereof for defect of right.

Because of the form in which it is written, a prospective litigant could not use this writ to recover anything but land. He could not use it to get back a horse for instance, that someone had taken from him. And he could only use it if he had freehold title, not if he only leased the land from someone else. And he could use it only if he had been "deforced" from the land, that is, if he had been in possession and been forced off. He could not use it, for instance, if he had just bought the land and the seller refused to turn the land over to him after receiving the purchase price. In any or all of these circumstances he would have to look for some other writ.

At first all writs were requests for special intervention by the crown, and a special fee had to be paid. As repetition of a particular type of request led to the establishment of a standard form, that form of writ would issue "as of course," that is, routinely without a special fee. Thus the writs, which began as special interventions of the king, as a kind of extraordinary royal justice, became the common law as they became a set of standard forms of action through which persons who met certain legal criteria could routinely bring their cases into the king's court. We have noted that this shift from extraordinary to ordinary justice comes when a writ begins to issue "as of course." The second major aspect of routinization occurs when the writ becomes "returnable." Nearly all of the standard writs came to contain a final sentence commanding that, if the defendant were not willing to grant to the plaintiff immediately the remedy described in the writ, the defendant must appear before a certain court of the king on a certain date and bring the writ with him. Thus, the writ became not only a description of what legal rights the king would protect under what circumstances, but the means by which the plaintiff got the defendant into court.

At first, the chancellor invented new writs, that is, standard forms, as he saw fit. But by the fourteenth century new writs were usually the product of the king in Parliament. As the common law courts developed, they began to develop new forms of action by extending or relaxing the wording of existing writs to cover a wider range of fact situations. For instance the writ of trespass contained the words *vi et armis* and so, strictly speaking, was applicable only to injuries to persons or property when breach of the peace had occurred. Common law courts began to allow trespass actions without allegations of breach of the peace, for instance, when an injury was the result of negligence rather than deliberate assault. These actions were called trespass on the case.[32]

Thus the common law makers could and did create new law both in response to and in the hope of attracting requests from prospective litigants. The common law courts directed the eyes and thus the loyalties of the litigants more and more toward the capital. They provided new forms of action that suited litigants better than those of the local courts.[33] In the England of that day there were two central types of conflict. The first was conflict over land ownership. The second was conflict arising over the injury of one man's person or property by another. The writ of trespass dealt with the latter problem. Through trespass on the case it was constantly extended and modified to meet new injury situations until it became a relatively complete law of torts. The writ of right handled land problems. It was designed quite specifically to attract litigants who either had failed or anticipated failing to get their land back through litigation in their lord's feudal court, for it directed the relevant lord to get the land back into the hands of the plaintiff and ordered the sheriff to act if the lord did not.

### NOVEL DISSEIZIN

The principal contribution of royal courts to the resolution of land conflict, however, was the assize of novel disseizin.[34] To understand it we must make a brief excursion into the substance of English land law. In theory the king was the only absolute "owner" of the land. He granted the land to tenants in chief. Each tenant in chief regranted portions of his grant to tenants, who might regrant portions of what they received to subtenants and so on. Thus each piece of land was subjected to a series of feudal tenures. Under such a system of tenures, no individual had an absolute title to land good against the claims of everyone else. The issue was never who has title to Greenacres. It was always does A or B have a better title to Greenacres. In one action A might show he had a better right to possession than B because A had a valid grant from tenant in chief X and B had no such grant. But in another action tenant in chief X might show that he had a better right to possession than A, because A had not done the feudal services that his grant from X required as a condition of continued possession. And in another action, the king might show that he had a better right to possession than tenant in chief X because X was a minor and the king had a right of wardship over minor tenants in chief which permitted him to take possession of their lands until they reached majority.

This system of relative tenures was rendered even more complex because there were numbers of different kinds of tenure, such as knight service and copyhold. Some tenures were for a certain number of years, others for life. Others were held indefinitely by religious bodies and still others were held in trust, that is, held by one person with the profits of the land going to another. Furthermore, a person in possession by any of these tenures might lease to another. Some forms of tenure allowed the tenure holder to sell (alienate) his tenure while others did not. Furthermore, some tenures and interests in land could be freely "devised," that is, left by will to any heir. Others were entailed and upon the death of the tenure holder could pass only to his eldest son.

The potential for dispute over what we would call land ownership was very great in England. Anyone living on a given piece of land might be confronted at any moment by a claimant with a better right or at least one who claimed to have a better right.[35] This situation was even further aggravated by the unsettled conditions of twelfth- and thirteenth-century England in which many barons had private armies. Might tended to make right in the countryside. Many persons were ejected from their land by brute force.

Because of the complexity of feudal tenures, seisin became a crucial concept of land law.[36] The person in actual physical possesion of the land was seised of it. Given the uncertainties of the times, there was a strong desire on the part of those seised to be protected in peaceful possession, a desire that seemed to correspond with the needs of public policy and those of a conqueror anxious to stabilize his domains.

The Assize of Novel Disseizin is customarily traced to the Assize of Clarendon of 1166, that is, it is one of the statutory writs made by the king in Parliament. An action under the assize was reduced to two simple questions. First, had the bringer of the assize (the demandant) been in possession (had seisin) of the land in question as of a certain recent date (usually the date of the last progress of the king through the shire in which the land was located). Second, had the current possessor ejected the demandant from the land since that date (committed novel disseizin). If the answer to both questions was yes, the demandant got a royal order putting him back in possession.

Novel disseizin was a simple way of protecting peacful and continuous possession. The possessor did not have to go through the time-consuming, complex tracings and proofs of the elaborate chains of tenurial relations that would prove he had the better right—while someone who had grabbed his land got the enjoyment of it. If he had been in possession, he got it back immediately. Any subsequent challenge to the ultimate legitimacy of his tenure, which might well take years, was fought out while he remained in possession and enjoyed the profits.

Through novel disseizin the crown pursued its own policy of stabilizing a conquered countryside, while also providing an enormously desirable service to landholders. Novel disseizin largely displaced the protection to tenants previously offered by lords' courts. It protected immediate possession. The writs of right protected the ultimate feudal tenure behind possession. Another set of crown writs, the writs of entry, protected landed inheritance. Between them they tended to transfer most land disputes, and land was the central concern of medieval England, from local to central courts, basically to Common Pleas.

Novel disseizin and the writs of entry illustrate the creation of new substantive law as a means of attracting the loyalty of the countryside. They are even more important as illustrations of the offering of a new and more rational procedure to attract popular support. There had been four traditional modes of proof in English lawsuits.[37] Proof by witness involved both sides bringing in witnesses who under oath swore to the truth of their claims. Whoever had the most witnesses won. Trial by compurgation or oath involved the defendant taking an oath denying the charges. He won if he used the proper verbal formula and brought in enough persons to swear that they believed that he swore truly. The Normans brought with them to England trial by battle, in which the litigants or their champions fought, the winner winning the lawsuit. Finally there was trial by ordeal, in which one of the parties carried red hot iron or put his hand in boiling water or was submerged in water. If he was not burned or if he sank in the water, he won.

All of these forms of proof reflected what "trial" itself originally meant in England. To put one's factual claims to trial meant submitting them to God. Oaths, ordeals, and combats all brought divine intervention to bear. For no one would risk his soul by swearing falsely, and God would insure that the just man won the battle or passed the ordeal.

The need for divine intervention existed because fact-finding was too hard for humans. For instance, the maze of grants, regrants, leases, inheritances, and so on that would establish whether A or B had the better ultimate title to Greenacres would have to be proven out of numerous documents that were not centrally registered, were in the possession of many different persons (most of them not party to the suit), and were often lost, damaged, or easily forged. Ultimately title rested on events that had occurred years earlier among persons often long deceased, of failing memory, or under great incentive to lie. Only God could know the facts.

The Assize of Novel Disseizin revolutionized trial in England. Instead of courting divine intervention, it simply called twelve men of the vicinity together and asked them to decide. It could adopt such a simple solution because it asked only two simple factual questions: whether A had been in possession as of a certain recent date and whether B had subsequently taken possession. This writ, combined with the writs of entry, enabled "one with recent and known facts on his side to recover the land without putting the right in issue and so without giving the wrongful holder the option of battle."[38]

The assize, that is, the jury specified as the mode of trial in the Assize of Novel Disseizin, was such a popular conflict resolution service that it soon became the typical mode of proof in the king's courts.[39] At first the assize had decided only the two questions central to novel disseizin. If other questions of fact arose in the same case, they were subjected to the older methods of proof. Soon, however, there grew a tendency to submit the whole case to the body of twelve men, which began to be called a jury. The new writs of the thirteenth century such as trespass and its many offshoots required jury trials. And the custom grew in the king's courts of the litigants "putting themselves upon the country," that is, submitting the issue to a jury, whenever a factual issue arose. By the fifteenth century the jury had become the standard judicial instrument for finding facts in both criminal and civil cases.

The use of juries by the king's courts not only provided a far more rational and predictable mode of resolving factual issues than was available in the older courts, but it also allowed the king's courts to compete with local courts in the one area where the local courts seemed to enjoy a great advantage. That advantage was, of course, that local institutions always have better access to facts than central institutions. Such an advantage would seem to be crucial in judicial rivalries, because in litigation facts are more often at issue than law. Against the local knowledge of the suitors, witnesses, and oath takers of the hunderd, shire, and feudal courts, the crown now counterpoised the trial jury. And as we have already noted, the system of sending the judges who administered the Assize of Novel Disseizin on circuit and the *nisi prius* system meant that a local jury could be used conveniently by a central court.

Novel disseizin and trespass have been used here to illustrate the process by which the central regime invented and extended forms of action more attractive to many classes of litigants than those available in local courts. Those examples will suffice without going on to survey the dozen or so other major writs developed between the twelfth and the sixteenth century.

### EQUITY

The writ system was an incomplete system of justice. The writs originated as special and personal interventions of the king into a legal realm that was essentially customary and in the hands of a relatively complete system of hundred and shire courts. There was no occasion to develop a "code" of writs covering all legal disputes. But as part of its drive for centralization, the Norman regime and its successors did seek to offer a more complete line of judicial services through institutions other than the writbound common law courts.

The best-known of these is the system of equity. We have already seen that the chancellor, as keeper of the great seal, was the principal administrative officer of the realm. In the Norman period he was usually a churchman. He came to be thought of as in some sense "the conscience of the king." As the writs became fixed, persons continued to direct requests for special crown justice to the chancellor. Out of this combination of circumstances there arose the chancellor's equity jurisdiction.[40] If no common law writ appeared to meet the needs of a prospective litigant, he might go instead to equity, which supplemented or complemented common law in a number of ways. First, equity could do substantial justice in any fact situation or type of dispute including those that fell outside of the fixed framework of the various writs. Second, common law courts soon limited their remedies pretty largely to entry and possession of land and money damages. Equity would provide a wider range and more specific remedies. These included injunction, which is an order forbidding someone to harm another, and specific performance, an order requiring someone to do what he is legally obligated to do. Thus, at equity Roe might be ordered to deliver to Doe the horse that he had contracted to sell him rather than simply paying Doe common law damages. And Smith might be ordered not to cut down Jones's trees rather than only having to pay money damages after he destroyed them. Third, for reasons we will get to in a moment, an equity court was much more capable than a common law court of dealing with complicated commercial transactions, particularly those involving account books and securities. Fourth, common law was strict law. Whoever had a legal right defined by writ would win his common law suit even if he were morally in the wrong. And whoever had no such right, or technically violated the legal right of another, would lose even if he could show that substantial justice was on his side. In theory at least, equity looked to substantial justice. One requesting an equitable remedy had to come to the court with "clean hands." He could not seek enforcement of a legal right which he himself had obtained by trickery, coercion, or other unjust means. And in fashioning remedies, an equity court looked to the "balance of equities." It sought to arrive at a resolution which would meet the needs of the winner without excessive cost to the loser.

Because the chancellor and his subordinates were churchmen and basically employed in controlling and storing crown documents, Chancery courts developed written procedures, as opposed to the essentially oral procedures of common law. Documents at issue were filed with the court. This was one reason that Chancery tended to do better than common law courts at commercial matters until at least the seventeenth century. And Chancery would take both oral and written evidence of contracts not under seal[41] which would have been barred from common law proceedings. Particularly on its "common law side," Chancery developed the examination and cross-examination of witnesses both orally and by deposition and written interrogatories faster than did the common law courts.[42] It looked at the ledgers and documents that common law courts tended to distrust.

Decision was in the hands of the chancellor himself after his examination of the entire written record. Chancery did not normally use juries. Thus decisions were not made by laymen relying on their own personal knowledge of local affairs but by an expert administrator relying on systematic presentation of evidence by the two parties. When an issue of common law was involved, the chancellor could call on the common law judges for their advice. Thus, the Chancery court offered a mode of procedure, a mode of inquiring into the facts, and a final judge very different from those in the common law courts. It also provided a different body of remedies and release from the occasional injustices that would result from strict application of the letter of the law. It proved to be a highly popular court.

It need hardly be argued at length that it was a highly centralized one. Its subordinate personnel were firmly anchored in the capital. Equity actions could only be undertaken there. Its judge was one of the most important administrative and political figures of the central government. Its legitimacy rested on the status of the chancellor as a direct conduit of the king's justice.

### STAR CHAMBER AND BILLS

Even more intimately related to the person of the king and perhaps equally important in the scheme of judicial centralization was what became known as the Court of Star Chamber, which grew out of the king's council.

The Curia Regis, that is, the king's council of William the Conqueror's time, is the parent body of many of the political institutions of later English government, including the Privy Council, the Parliament, and the cabinet.[43] The king's council was not a fixed body, but a constitutional idea of advice. On those occassions when all the lords of the realm plus representatives from the towns and shires were called together to advise the king, the council was the medieval Parliament. On other occasions when the king was traveling, the council was the handful of advisors who traveled with him. When the king was in the capital, the council would consist of all the important administrative and judicial officers of the government.

As the business of the government increased, the council tended to split in a number of different ways. A smaller council of direct advisors to the king, which was in effect the policymaking executive committee of the government, tended to break off from the larger council, which had become too large and contained too many lesser officers to govern well. This smaller council became the Privy Council. Privy councillor became a rank or office awarded by the king to those whom he wanted to be central policymakers. But the administrative establishment sitting in London was growing. Its major administrative officers needed a device for coordinating the work of the dozens of major and minor departments, offices, councils, courts, and boards that made up the central government. Their meetings came to be known as the king's council in the Star Chamber.[44] Thus, although a strict, formal separation never occurred, the king had two councils. One was a small body of high policymakers who traveled with him. The other was a larger body of London-based administrative officers who met together to do the regular business of the central government.

Some or all of the privy councillors and indeed the king himself, often sat in Star Chamber. But so did many lesser government officials who did not hold the rank of privy councillor, including many of the judges of

King's Bench and Common Pleas. Of course the chancellor and the barons of Exchequer, who were themselves high judges, sat. So did other administrative officials with judicial functions such as the lord privy seal. And it will be remembered that the king had traditionally dispensed justice personally in his curia.

Indeed, Professor Harding[45] argues that too much emphasis has been placed on the writs and not enough upon bills as the vehicle for the formation of English law. From the time of the conquest, the king and his council, the chancellor, the Parliament, and many other king's officers had been the recipients of unending streams of requests (bills) for help from people in trouble. These requests did not differentiate between executive, legislative, or judicial help. The writs were a device for turning many of these individual bills into standard, judicial forms. But bills continued to flow to the crown and its officers, some inspiring yet more writs and others leading to legislation or direct royal intervention. The concilliar courts— that is, the courts that wielded their judicial authority by virtue of being parts of the council—did not use writs. They did accept individual bills and responded to them by summoning the parties and issuing final orders after their inquiries. Thus they were the particular target of bills from persons who could not find an appropriate writ for their problem. Because writs had to be served by the sheriff, who was often deeply involved with a local faction, prospective litigants who belonged to other factions might prefer a bill to the council because then they could get into a court without having to depend on the help of the sheriff.

In what was probably a quite unanticipated development, as Star Chamber became institutionalized in the sixteenth century, its judicial business tended to overshadow its work of administrative coordination. No clear distinction was ever drawn between the two, jsut as no clear distinction was drawn between the Privy Council and Star Chamber. But Star Chamber became more and more a court which heard cases at regular, publicly attended, judicial sessions in the same term times as the other courts. In civil cases it used a procedure similar to that in Chancery involving the filing and evaluation of documents. On the criminal side it heard complaints from the attorney general and then proceeded by the ordinary rules of procedure used in King's Bench. However, Star Chamber tended to act in a more summary and expeditious way than the equity and common law courts. It frequently summoned and directly questioned the parties, using torture when appropirate. And given the high position of its judges, it could deal more easily than could the ordinary courts with powerful persons. Star Chamber inherited the sweeping jurisdiction of the medieval king's council. It could not deal with freehold, treason, or felony. Much of the earlier equitable jurisdiction of the counicl was now handled by Chancery and by the Court of Requests, which in theory was a committee of the Privy Council. And it tended to leave to the common law courts those cases it felt could be handled routinely. Otherwise it felt free to handle what cases it pleased.

Star Chamber took special responsibility for cases that concerned the state, but there were many varieties of these. Thus we find Star Chamber hearing many cases involving international trade although it sent many others to the Court of Admiralty. It heard many cases of fraud, forgery, and the like. It, along with the Court of High Commission, became the tribunal for cases of religious deviation.

Quite aside from these cases of state concern, Star Chamber heard a great many purely private litigations. Jurisdiction over some of these could be rationalized on the grounds that they presented anomalies difficult for the regular courts to handle or involved parties particularly linked to the king, such as holders of royal charters. But most were in Star Chamber simply because one of the parties wanted them there and the court was willing to hear them.

In the fifteenth century Star Chamber was a "court" staffed by a mixed body of central administrators and judges. It exercised a broad and general judicial power as part and parcel of its general administrative task of keeping the machinery of the government running and its broadly political task of insuring the peace and prosperity of the realm. It appears to have been a highly popular and successful court. An independent judiciary it certainly was not.

The absence of judicial independence in the king's council in Star Chamber is emphasized by the two great sixteenth-century branches of the council.[46] These were the Council of the North and the Council of Wales. Each was staffed with a mixture of great political magnates and administrative officers of the next lower rank. Each wielded full administrative and judicial powers over regions of the country particularly troublesome and particularly far from London. Neither differentiated its administrative from its judicial functions or personnel. Like imperial district officers, each council held the county, collected the taxes, kept the peace, and resolved private conflicts, all as integral parts of governing.

### English Courts and Law at the End of the Sixteenth Century

At this point in our brief outline of the development of courts from the eleventh through the sixteenth centuries, clearly centralization, not independence, is the major theme we can see emerging from English experience. The king's courts were replacing the suitors' and the lords' courts. The basic initial authority of the courts that came to be the most important in England was the personal judicial authority of the king. The judges of King's

Bench and Common Pleas were the king's officers, wielding the king's judicial powers, serving at the king's pleasure, and participating as subordinate officials in the general administrative and policymaking instruments of the regime such as Chancery and Star Chamber. The writs, which were the mode of entry to King's Bench and Common Pleas, were in form petitions to and orders from the king. The basic writs were created either by royal statute or the practice of his chief administrative officer, the chancellor. Moreover, much of the judicial power of the crown was wielded by central administrators as part of an undifferentiated mass of governing powers. Chancery, Exchequer, Star Chamber, Requests, Wards, Admiralty, the Stannaries, the councils of Wales and of the North all show the pattern that is the most typical when office is substituted for consent—triadic conflict resolution by administrators.

Other tendencies must be noted as well. They ought not, however, to be noted, as they customarily have been, as the seeds from which developed that judicial independence which was the true destiny of British courts. We ought to consider them for what they were at the time.

FUNCTIONAL SPECIALIZATION

As we noted earlier functional specialization is often confused with judicial independence. But we may well encounter a regime that develops specialized tax collectors, soldiers, record keepers, diplomats, and judges without allowing any particular autonomy to any of these subsets of the bureaucracy. The English regime of the thirteenth century through the sixteenth century was developing judicial specialization along two interlocking paths. First there is the emergence of some persons whose primary task is the handling of litigation.[47] Most prominent of course are the judges of King's Bench and Common Pleas. From the point in the thirteenth century at which it is provided that a court of common pleas must sit permanently at Westminister, we encounter judges of that court who are no longer all-purpose administrators or magnates who occasionally do judging. King's Bench follows soon after. Certainly in the fifteenth and sixteenth centuries the judges of Common Pleas and King's Bench are called and conceived of as Judges and are principally involved in triadic conflict resolution. Moreover most appeals from the decisions of these judges would end up being heard by the judges themselves, either as King's Bench hearing appeals from Common Pleas or all the judges together sitting as the Court of Exchequer Chamber. Yet final appeal lay to the House of Lords, which was of course not a specialized judicial body, but a general political one. The House, however, normally called in the judges to give their advice on appeals.

While the justices in eyre and those holding assize, gaol delivery, and *nisi prius* commissions had initially been drawn from the whole spectrum of the governing elite, increasingly such commissions were issued only to the judges of the common law courts. Yet these judges were king's officers, appointed by him and serving at his pleasure. Particularly when on assize circuit, they were often assigned secondary administrative duties. They were summoned by the chancellor to assist him, and they sat in that great mixed, administrative-judicial board, Star Chamber. As assize judges they continued to be charged with overseeing the general good governance of the countryside and served as a crucial link between the central government and the local justices of the peace.

Moreover, much of what in form appeared to be litigation or conflict resolution in the central common law courts was not so in reality. There is not space here even to sketch the development of English land law, but that development had some peculiar results for common law courts. We have noted at some length the tendency of judges to preserve strong elements of consensual mediation even within the litigation process. From the earliest times English judges viewed a mutually agreed settlement under the supervision of and recorded by the court as an ideal resolution of conflict.[48] The formal record of such a settlement was called a fine. One copy was retained by the court, and the other copies (called "feet") went to the parties. Since England had no general system of land registry, one good way of formally recording a transfer of land was to pretend a dispute about it and then settle the dispute by fine. The fine would leave a permanent written record of the transfer authenticated by a court.

Moreover, because of various rules of English land law, the conclusion of certain kinds of suit in certain ways would allow landholders to give, sell, lease, or devise interests in land to persons and under conditions that were legally forbidden if done directly by gift, sale, or will. The practice grew up of entering into purely fictional land suits shaped to yield a court decree that was in fact a judicially authorized and recorded transfer of land that would have been invalid without the decree.[49] Thus even when engaged in what appeared to be the judicially specialized task of deciding land litigation, the common law judges were frequently doing the essentially administrative task of maintaining land records. Probably only in the seventeenth century did Englishmen begin to feel that, because a royal judge was a judge, he was somehow less a subordinate of the king than other royal officials.

Specialization was clearest in, but not limited to, the great common law courts of King's Bench and Common Pleas. As we have seen, the most important departments of royal administration, Exchequer and Chancery, both acquired significant capacities for handling litigation. In theory, and initially in fact, final decisions in such litigation were rendered by the heads of these departments, the treasurer and the chancellor. In practice the chancellor continued to make final decisions in equity cases throughout this period. But both Exchequer and Chancery quickly developed relatively distinct branches with special staffs to handle their litigation business. In the fourteenth century the judicial side of Exchequer had become relatively distinct and the barons of Exchequer had become a special set of officers in charge of this litigation rather than simply general subordinates of the treasurer. Indeed, after a period of more or less specializing in revenue cases, in the sixteenth century the Court of Exchequer had developed fairly ambitious equity and common law jurisdicitons, and its barons were ranked with the common law judges.[50]

The judicial functions of the chancellor were at first inseparable from his functions as a chief officer of the crown and a major participant in the council. Indeed his decisions were usually viewed either as decisions of the council or common law decisions rendered by him in conjunction with the common law judges and in his capacity as a key administrator of the common law system of writs. Only beginning in the fifteenth century do we find a distinct Court of Chancery in which the chancellor makes his own decisions on his own authority and only in the sixteenth is its equitable business clearly defined.

This development of a distincltly judicial character for Chancery corresponds to its decline as an administrative center. Well into the seventeenth century some chancellors were powerful politicians and leaders of the government. And the Chancery never ceased to have a major administrative component. But major administrative power shifted to other officers and other departments. As it did, the Chancery became more and more primarily a court. Its major functionaries, the masters and the clerks, were more and more concerned with litigation. Finally the chancellor himself became primarily a judge. In the sixteenth century it became common for the crown to appoint leading common lawyers as chancellors. The last chancellor who was a major political leader rather than principally a judge was Lord Shaftesbury, who served in 1672–73, and his appointment was viewed as a dubious anomoly. From the sixteenth century onward the chancellor was assisted in his judicial functions by a master of the rolls appointed by the crown. Again originally an administrative officer, he subsequently became a second judge of the court. There were eleven other chancery masters who gradually shifted from primarily administrative to primarily judicial duties, particularly hearing the preliminary stages of cases and preparing the huge files of documents eventually submitted to the chancellor or master of rolls for final decision.[51]

In Chancery we have a great department of government that inextricably mixes political, administrative, and judicial business until well into the sixteenth and even the seventeenth century but eventually becomes primarily a court.

Star Chamber retains its mixed administrative and judicial functions throughout the period we have been looking at. The only hint of judicial specialization that appears is that some of the common law judges will invariably be in attendance at Star Chamber proceedings that involve issues of common law.

Along this narrow dimension of specialized judicial offices or institutions, the picture is not terribly clear at the beginning of the seventeenth century. Those who sit on King's Bench and Common Pleas are clearly seen as judges. Chancery and Star Chamber are doing so much judicial business that they are usually conceived of as courts. But even to the extent that judging is viewed as a special function, there is as yet little notion that it is to be done by persons or in institutions that devote themselves exclusively to that function.

### THE AUTONOMY OF COMMON LAW AND COMMON LAWYERS

There are, however, other dimensions besides the narrowly institutional one. The most important of these is the interlocking autonomies of the law and the legal profession that we find developing before the seventeenth century in the English legal system. The foundation of English law as a bundle of special writs, each limited to special fact situations and legal issues and each with its own procedures, almost inevitably meant that common law would be complex law. In an attempt to get the narrowly drawn writs to cover new fact and law situations, they were extended by judicially created analogies, fictions, and liberal interpretations. Moreover the writs were basically procedural in character. Substantive legal rules had to be worked out for each in the course of litigation.[52] Since such substantive rules were tied to the particular writ for which they were developed, no general body of legal rules or legal theory emerged. The writ system meant that English law would be a series of discrete causes of action, each surrounded by its own judicial lore, statutory interventions, and customary modes of professional practice. Thus the common law become a complex body of traditional practices that no one pretended could be reduced to a set of rational principles comprehensible to those not steeped in the tradition.

At least until the eighteenth century the central concern of English law was the land. And English land law became so complex that no one truly understood it, not even the lawyers and judges who employed it.[53] It became a set of complex verbal formulas full of evasions, fictions, frauds, and purposeful ambiguities and designed to create such a mass of complexity that no one could penetrate it to upset the intentions of the landholder.[54] This body of law owed something to statutory and judge-made law, but it consisted largely of evasions of such law created by "conveyancers," that is, the body of specialized lawyers who drew up wills and land transfer documents.[55] The conveyancers were so successful that soon only they understood the law they had made, and later no one, including them, understood the whole of it.

Thus English law in general and its core, the land law, in particular, became highly complex and riddled with strange words and formulas that only the law men could understand. It was not as a matter of courtesy that the common law judges were invited to Chancery, Exchequer, and Star Chamber when common law issues arose. It was because they were often the only ones of the king's officers who could understand them. The growth of a functional specialization of judging was in part the result of a growth in the complexity of law so great that only those initiated by a lifetime of its practice could deal with it. One interesting clue to this developing autonomy of law is the provision that only a baron of Exchequer who was "a man of the law" could sit on assize and at *nisi prius*.[56] At first assize commissions had been held by all sorts of king's officers, later only by judges and lawyers. The provision on Exchequer barons indicates both the development, albeit an incomplete one, of a judicial speciality in Exchequer and the growth of a law so complex that even a high officer of the crown could administer it only if he were also a legal specialist.

Closely connected with the growing autonomy of law was the growing autonomy of the English legal profession.[57] In an important sense what we mean by judicial independence in England is that judges were more closely linked to lawyers than to the government. By the reign of Edward I a legal profession is being formed. Because the courts from which it draws its business are highly centralized, it is highly centralized too. Those who plead cases in court are the sergeants. They have something of the character of a guild, living and doing business in a cluster of inns that become the Inns of Court. Apparently as early as the fourteenth century, law students begin to frequent the courts and the inns. If English law had been civil or Roman law, it would have been taught as an academic subject in the universities. But a system of law that was essentially a series of special procedures, that is the writs, could only be learned where the procedures were conducted and constantly modified, in the courts and the offices of the lawyers. The inns became corporate instructional institutions for the sergeants' guild.[58] The students attended court, ate dinner at the inns where they were exposed to the few common law books that existed, listened to the lawyers talk shop, listened to and participated in the argument of moot cases, and were crossquestioned by the lawyers. Eventually a more or less formal system of legal education evolved in which each student was expected to attend a certain number of readings and lectures, hear and participate in a certain number of moots, be subjected to oral examinations, and work for a time as an apprentice. All this was done under the supervision of the corporate officers of the inns, called the benchers. Eventually the title "sergeant" was reserved for the more distinguished of the pleaders, the rest being the barristers.

There was also another main division of the bar, the attorneys, of whom there were a number of varieties, most notably the conveyancers we have already noted. Attorneys did all the legal work for their clients except actually pleading cases in court, which was reserved for the barristers and sergeants. Eventually they were all called solicitors. Because they were not directly tied to the courts, they were to be found throughout England.

This connection of the barristers to the courts is crucial for our story. In the fourteenth century, appointment to King's Bench and Common Pleas was limited to sergeants who by then constituted a special order, promotion to which was in the hands of the crown. Thus there was a melding of the top of the legal profession with royal administration. The sergeants were private practitioners but also crown officers. Assize commissions, too, came to be reserved for judges and sergeants. In the sixteenth century the Court of Exchequer came to draw its judges only from among the sergeants. On difficult questions of law the crown might consult the whole body of judges and sergeants. The judges and sergeants as a body were the corporate keepers of the common law.

By the sixteenth century the crown had acknowledged that it must appoint all common law judges from the ranks of the sergeants. It somewhat evaded this rule by simply promoting to sergeant any barrister that the king contemplated appointing to a judgeship. But nonetheless the practice became firmly anchored that all judges would be drawn from among the barristers.[59] The judges were both officers of the crown and leaders of an independent profession that saw itself as the maker and guardian of the law—a law so complex that no nonlawyer could understand it.

It must be added that these developments occurred on the equity as well as the common law side. We have already noted that the chancellors were increasingly chosen from among the common lawyers. Moreover in the sixteenth and seventeenth centuries equity developed its own highly artificial, complex, and rigid rules and practices which could be mastered only by specialists at equity pleading. So here again the law became less and less the general province of government officials and more and more the preserve of the legal profession.

By the time of the Stuarts (1605–1702) a constellation of factors existed that in some peculiar sense can be called judicial independence. It consisted of the development of a highly complex body of law, an independent legal profession, and a degree of judicial specialization. Interlocked and mutually supporting, these factors provided some degree of judicial autonomy. How weak that autonomy was, however, came to be seen in the early part of the seventeenth century as the Stuart monarchs brough the nation to the civil war.

## The Seventeenth Century

The English Civil War and the Revolution of 1688 are crucial events in the growth of the idea of English judicial independence. For the the conventional wisdom is that it was the English Revolution that firmly established judicial independence by breaking the subordination of the judges to the crown. For this reason it is necessary for us to take a fairly careful look at actual developments in the seventeenth century.

### ROYAL FINANCIAL POLICY

The Tudor predecessors of the Stuarts had been busily engaged in strengthening the monarchy throughout the sixteenth century.[60] They recognized that a key to political power was wealth. English monarchs had three basic sources of revenue. The first was to call Parliament and ask for "supply."[61] But once called, the Parliament might make all sorts of political demands before passing the new taxes. The second was the acquisition, management, and sale of crown lands. The third source of crown revenues was a large, complex, and often obscure set of payments, fines, taxes, and duties owed the king either in his capacity of feudal overlord or as part of his prerogative powers. The king's prerogatives were an odd assortment of personal privileges, powers, and authorities which he was free to wield personally without the consent of Parliament.

The feudal and prerogative revenues rested on ancient law and custom. They were not seen as arbitrary exactions but as the exercise of the legal rights of the crown. For instance one of the chief sources of royal revenue was wardship. Under feudal tenure rules, when a tenant in chief of the kind died leaving as his heir a minor child, the child became the king's ward. The king received all the revenues of his ward's estates until the child reached adulthood. These wardships and their revenues were administered by the royal Court of Wards[62] because they were essentially matters of feudal land law.

The Stuarts sought to follow the lead of the Tudors in building the financial strength of the monarchy on the prerogative revenues. Indeed, they attempted to govern independently of Parliament by developing those revenues sufficiently so that they could manage without Parliamentary supply.

### THE CRISIS IN THE SOCIAL LOGIC OF STUART COURTS

Along dozens of paths the Stuart monarchs sought to extend and reactivate their ancient financial rights, often by rediscovering financial prerogatives that had lain dormant for hundreds of years or extending their claims to persons and property that previously had been ignored.[63] From the king's point of view, these were matters of thorough legal research. The king's lawyers looked at the ancient law to discover what was legally owed the king even though, through the obscurity of the law and the oversight of previous monarchs, the royal due might have long remained uncollected. From the point of view of much of the population the crown appeared to be attempting to collect new taxes without Parliamentary consent.

Stuart financial policy was of enormous significance to the status of English courts precisely because it took the form of the assertion of old legal rights rather than the imposition of new taxes. This form brought to the fore almost all of the factors that tend to undercut the basic social logic of courts.

First of all the typical political conflict between a Stuart monarch and the opponents of royal power took the form of a lawsuit. The king as one party asserted an ancient legal right and the prospective taxpayers as the other party asserted that the king's legal claims were incorrect. But this dispute goes to a king's judge for resolution. The tension created by the substitution of office for consent becomes clear. Englishmen had always known that the king's judges were the *king's* judges, administrative officers of the crown. But now all of the "two against one" potential of that fact suddenly came to the surface. The subject was challenging the king in the king's own court. How could he expect a truly triadic structure there?

The king's legal claims were researched and established by the administrative institutions of the crown, particularly the financial ones, the Council, Exchequer, Admiralty, Wards, and so forth. Yet these very administrative bodies that asserted the king's claims then became the courts that declared that they were legally correct. Exchequer as tax collector would one day levy a new tax and then, when the legality of the tax was challenged, sit as a court and uphold its own levy. Thus, because the judges were officers of the king, and administrative officers at that, the undercutting of the social logic of the triad that occurs when office is substituted for consent comes to the foreground of political consciousness in the Stuart period.

The tension created by the substitution of law for consent also comes to the fore. For the king is clothing his revenue claims in ancient crown rights, that is in preexisting legal rules. Challenges to the king's exactions had to be brought in courts that announced themselves bound by preexisting rules that favored the king. For instance, the Court of Exchequer Chamber (that is, all the judges meeting together) often sat to announce, even in advance of litigation, that a new assertion of prerogative by the crown was in accord with the ancient law. Under such circumstances challengers of royal claims could hardly see the judges as truly triadic figures.

The judges were servants of the law which they themselves asserted favored the king over his subjects.

The Stuart period was a dramatic illustration of the extent to which the policymaking role of courts can undercut their legitimacy as conflict resolvers. To Stuart subjects the courts were part and parcel of the crown apparatus for making and implementing its policies of independent revenue maximization and thus independence from Parliament. Stuart subjects could hardly be expected to trust the courts to resolve conflicts that arose out of the very policies that the judges were participating in making. Moreover, the social control and conflict resolution functions of courts openly came into conflict. Since the king's prerogative claims were assertions of legal rights, the opponents of those claims were hauled into court and found in violation of the law. The punishment was usually a fine. Thus the revenue policy and social control functions of the courts could be neatly combined since the king's treasury got the fine. For example, by 1640 Star Chamber had clearly become a revenue court, but its name was then and has always since been associated with one of the severest kinds of social control, the repression of political dissent. Clearly such a court had lost much of the social logic of courts.

In short the period from 1603 to 1640 was a sort of vast morality play in which the inherent contradiction between the English theory of sovereignty on the one hand and the notion of judicial independence on the other was dramatically presented. The general response of those Englishmen who opposed the Stuarts was not, at least initially, to attack the institution of courts, or even the concept of the judges as king's officers. At first, they attacked individual judges as corrupt and/or as giving the king bad legal advice. Then they moved on to attack certain courts. Such courts were accused of having invaded the lawmaking powers of Parliament, or having become cats' paws of the king's financial policies, or having become hopelessly oppressive, corrupt, and inefficient.

By the time the revolution broke out in open warfare in 1641, almost all of the principal king's judges then living had been indicted for treason by the Parliamentary forces. During the course of the revolution Star Chamber, Requests, the councils of the North and of Wales, and the Court of Wards were abolished. There were also serious proposals to abolish Chancery, but it survived.

CHANGING MASTERS

The period immediately preceding the revolution pitted the king and his judges on one side and the Parliament on the other. The revolutionaries did abolish some courts and attack others. As a result it is often assumed that the revolution must have broken the tie between the king and the judges and thus been the crucial step in the creation of an independent judiciary. The actual historical picture is more complex.

It is always dangerous to allege that any category of Englishmen was on one side or the other in the Civil War. Nearly every variety of Englishman was to be found on both the royal and Parliamentary sides. Yet by and large the common lawyers sided with Parliament.[64] The serving judges were crown appointees and necessarily Royalists. The revolution thus broke that autonomous bundle of common law–common lawyer–common law judge that had created a species of judicial autonomy in sixteenth-century England. It left the judges exposed in their roles as king's servants. The revolution also brought to the fore a set of radicals who wished to abolish the common law itself and substitute for it a simple set of biblically based laws.

The result was considerable ambiguity during the period of rule by Parliament and protector from 1640 to 1660. The common law segment of Parliament certainly did not want to abolish the common law and had willy-nilly to defend the common law courts against the radicals.[65] It is indicative that it was the rivals of the common law courts, Star Chamber and Chancery, that were most widely denounced in Parliament. The fundamental relation of the courts to the sovereign was not altered. Nor was the theory of a unified sovereignty to which the judges were subordinated altered. The bundle of common law–common lawyer–common law judge was firmly reestablished. From the seventeenth century onward, it is extremely unusual to find any but a prominent common lawyer appointed to any important judgeship, including the post of chancellor.

The end of the Protectorate and the return of the Stuart monarchy in 1660 saw the king's judges still indubitably the *king's* judges. They were still conceived to be administrative officers of the crown, and they were often employed as direct social controllers and policymakers for the crown. Until Queen Anne's reign, all the judges resigned at the death of the monarch. Charles II reinstituted the long abandoned practice of appointing judges at his pleasure rather than for good behavior. This practice was not forbidden until the Act of Settlement of 1702.[66]

Nevertheless, the seventeenth century did contribute to the growth of a certain species of judicial independence. It had demonstrated that judges too closely implicated in the day-to-day policies of an unpopular government would suffer. More important, it had emphasized the rule of law—that the government must live by the existing law not influence the judges to change the law day by day so as to decide each case in a way favorable to government policy.

This very concept of the rule of law, which is so important a building block in most theories of judicial independence, is at the root of the fundamental ambiguity of the revolution insofar as judicial independence is concerned. The revolution did not alter the theory of a single and complete sovereignty vested in the king in Parliament. It only made the Parliament the potentially dominant voice in the sovereign partnership. The sovereign was the lawmaker. The rule of law meant that the government must undertake new policies by passing new laws, not by breaking existing ones. The sum of Parliamentary sovereignty plus rule of law is not judicial independence but judicial subordination to Parliament. The great father of American constitutionalism John Locke, writing in the latter part of the seventeenth century, places the judges firmly in the executive branch bound to carry out the commands of the legislative branch.[67]

If there is one single case crucial to the whole problem of English judicial independence, it is that of Dr. Bonham, decided by Coke in 1610.[68] In the reign of James I, Coke and company had firmly rejected the claim that the king acting alone could make law. In Bonham's case Coke insisted that a statute contrary to common right and reason would be invalid at common law or, as he put it, be "controuled" by common law. In effect this was a claim that where the common law as proclaimed by the judges was in conflict with parliamentary statute, the statute would be void. If Coke's view had been accepted, the contradiction between judicial independence and judicial decision by preexisting legal rule and the contradiction between the English theory of sovereignty and judicial independence would have been partially eliminated. For the courts would have been independently giving preexisting rules to themselves. And unitary sovereignty would have been replaced by a divided sovereignty in which both courts and Parliament independently wielded lawmaking authority, albeit with the courts clearly superior to the Parliament in the event of conflict. Although accepted as late as 1701, Coke's view was fundamentally rejected in the longer run. With its rejection any claim to an unambivalent judicial independence for English courts must fail. That independence must again rest on the practical inability of the Parliament to penetrate the complexities of common law. For the Parliament retained its constitutional authority to do what it pleased with the common law and thus with the common law courts by passing new statutes changing the old common law.

In short, the English revolution did not clearly and immediately liberate the judges from their master the king. And its long-term effect was simply to transfer the courts from one master to another, from the king to the Parliament.

Signs of this transfer of ownership were readily apparent even during the seventeenth century. We have noted that the Court of Exchequer Chamber had become unpopular because of its quasi-lawmaking activities.

The seventeenth century clearly established the House of Lords as the ultimate appeals court for cases arising in England.[69] This direct hierarchical control by the Parliament itself over the English courts is a clear enough statement that the courts remain the servant of the sovereign. Only the nature of the sovereign is changing.

In the longer run a more important factor is that the change in the balance of political power between king and Parliament that occurred durign the seventeenth century meant that Parliament had to be called frequently and for relatively long sessions. As a result it could become a more vigorous and efficient lawmaking body. As it made more law, it increased its mastery over the courts that were bound by that law.

### The Eighteenth Century

Nevertheless the eighteenth century is in many ways the high point of English judicial independence. The growth of judicial functional specialization that we had observed in the sixteenth century and which continued during the seventeenth was based more on the growing complexity of common law than upon conscious administrative choice. On the one hand that complexity compelled administrative officers faced with occasional legal problems to call upon the judges for specialized advice. On the other it compelled administrative officers faced with streams of litigation (e.g., the chancellor) to devote ever increasing time and energy to their judging and thus gradually become primarily judicial officers. The eighteenth century was the period of final culmination of the unchallenged, self-congratulating, bizarre complexity of the common law. The best-known eighteenth-century legal commentator, Blackstone, spoke of the mysterious science of the law.[70] This complexity compelled a very high level of judicial specialization even though the specialists barely understood what they were doing much of the time.

In the seventeenth, eighteenth, and early nineteenth century, equity, which was supposed to do simple justice when the common law was inadequate, was taken over by chancellors trained in common law and turned into a highly technical set of rules. The complexity of equity proceedings, combined with the fact that there were only two equity judges, the chancellor himself and the master of the rolls, resulted in equity cases spinning on for years, typically either reaching no conclusion or concluding after the deaths of the original parties.[71]

The sixteenth century statute of uses had sought to reform and simplify real property law. In the seventeenth and eighteenth centuries the conveyancers reached such heights of elegant indirection and fictional transaction that the uncertain titles of the medieval period had become far more uncertain. Security of possession rested more upon the time and expense that would have been incurred by a challenger seeking to unravel the complex and multiple estates burdening any given piece of land than upon any clear title secured by basic law.[72]

In the course of the seventeenth and eighteenth centuries the common law courts also finally managed to manipulate some of their older writs, particularly assumpsit, so that they were able to deal more or less adequately with commerical contracts and other "mercantile specialities." Much of this capacity resulted from Lord Mansfield's borrowings from equity, Roman law, and the law merchant. But Mansfield's innovations were only partially accepted by his fellow judges and their successors.[73] As a result English commercial law remained something of a patchwork, often to be explained in terms of its historical evolution from the medieval writs rather than in terms of consistent legal principles.[74] Most of the smaller specialized courts, such as the admiralty courts and the successors to the church courts, had also sunk into an antiquarian maze of colorful formulas and empty but expensive ritual.

The disorderly nature and ad hoc, antiquarian quality of English law in this period was aggravated by tendencies in English legal education. The educational aspects of the great "university" of English law, the Inns of Court, while subject to occasional revival, largely had been reduced to ritual dinners. English lawyers were trained largely by the apprenticeship method.[75] With rare exceptions they learned nothing of general principles or even rationales for the rules they applied. Instead they simply learned to apply the formulas that their seniors applied, to whatever they applied them.

That bundle of (1) complex common law, (2) guild of common lawyers, and (3) common law judges, which we have earlier seen was at the core of what commentators choose to call judicial independence, reached its tightest and most resistant condition in the eighteenth century. No one could understand the law except the lawyers, who consituted a closed guild that co-opted new members by apprenticeship. The judges were chosen from and led the guild. The growing theory of parliamentary sovereignty meant little in the face of this reality. The judges were independent because they operated a system of law that was essential to the well-being of the nation but which no one but the lawyers could understand.

It would be a gross oversimplification to say that English judicial independence was solely a matter of functional specialization transposed into autonomy by the complexity of the law and the power of the legal profession. Other factors were at work as well. The constitutional developments of the seventeenth century had clearly aimed at the reduction of the powers of the crown and most particularly the prerogative powers, which had largely been eliminated by the Act of Settlement of 1702. This treaty between Parliament and the crown defined the constitutional position of the eighteenth-century monarchy. The prerogative and other personal powers of the king had always been closely connected with control over the judiciary. With their reduction, the king's judges remained the king's judges, but it was expected that he would wield little authority over them. In the seventeenth and eighteenth centuries judges were conceived of more and more as servants of the law rather than the king, particularly since the king was seen as having less and less independent governmental power. The Georgian monarchs enjoyed the services of a number of judges who were notorious cat's-paws of royal interest and authority, but even in their own day such judges were more infamous than famous.

After the abolition of Star Chamber, the Privy Council had retained appeals from overseas courts as its only judicial function. As we have noted, the chancellor had become primarily a judicial officer. The barons of Exchequer had become functionally specialized judges separated from the financial side of Exchequer. Moreover, in the eighteenth century the chief ministers of the king were gradually shaping themselves into what later became the cabinet. They constituted an executive committee which wielded the lawmaking and administrative powers of the government and did so as leaders of the Parliament rather than servants of the king. Judges no longer participated freely and ubiquitously in this new multimember executive body. They had ceased to give advisory opinions and to participate freely in meetings of the executive, which now got legal advice from its own law officers rather than from the judges.[76] Thus as the king grew weaker and the cabinet emerged, the judges lost most of their direct connection with the executive segment of government.

Moreover, beginning in the sixteenth century and flourishing in the seventeenth was a school of thought which saw trials as a weighing of uncertain evidence to arrive at the most probably correct version of the facts. The word "trial" itself shifted from its medieval meaning of a device for ascertaining facts without rational inquiry to exactly the opposite meaning, a scientific inquiry into the probable truth of various factual allegations or hypotheses. Such a mode of thought, of course, emphasized the nature of the judge as detached investigator, although his importance in this connection was substantially reduced because the jury remained the principal fact finder. The jury was now seen, however, not as finding facts from its own personal knowledge, but as using its common sense and knowledge of human character to decide which of the rival versions of the facts presented by the two parties was more probably correct. To assist the jury in focusing clearly on the factual issues, the courts developed rules of evidence. The judge who enforced these rules thus became in a sense the master investigator.[77]

All of these factors, from the impentrable complexity of the law, through the reduction of the prerogative powers and the growth of institutions of parliamentary government, and on to the notion of a trial as a scientific inquiry, fostered allegiance to the ideal of the rule of law. In the eighteenth century, it was surely not unknown for the king or the Parliament to interfere in the outcome of a particular lawsuit. Indeed through the appeals jurisdiction of the House of Lords, Parliament was specifically authorized to do so. But most eighteenth-century Englishmen would have viewed it not only as wrong but contrary to the constitution for the government to dictate the outcome of cases to the judges or to act outside the legal authority given to it by the statutes.

When we combine this theoretical commitment to the rule of law with the practical complexities of the common law in the eighteenth century, we can see why eighteenth-century Englishmen and Americans could assert a simple theory of judicial independence without noting the contradictions that lay behind it. The constitutional authority of the king had been cut back so far that the judges were no longer to be his servants. New notions of executive leadership resting in the leaders of Parliament rather than in the king's servants were only gradually emerging. As a result the judges, who were not parliamentary leaders, ceased to participate in executive decision making. Thus the judges became separated from the executive institutions of government. And once separated, rule of law notions urged that the judges not be subordinated to the day-to-day desires of the political executive. At the same time efforts at parliamentary law reform were as unsuccessful in the eighteenth as they had been in the sixteenth and seventeenth centuries.[78] It proved impossible to unravel the legal tangle created by, and thus the autonomy of, that bundle of common law–common lawyer –common law judge to which we have repeatedly referred. Eighteenth-century developments did not make clear what had really happened in the seventeenth century, namely, that the courts had changed masters from king to Parliament rather than becoming politically independent. For the eighteenth-century Parliament was unwilling and unable to assert its mastery. The nineteenth century tells a different story.

### The Nineteenth Century

In the nineteenth century two movements combined to destroy much of the autonomy that the English courts had enjoyed in the eighteenth. Jeremy Bentham was the legal philosopher most centrally associated with the first movement. He argued that the common law was a mass of contradictions and illogicalities whose complexities were designed only to enrich the lawyers. For Bentham the goal was a simple yet complete body of law that could be understood by laymen without the need for employing lawyers. Such a body of law could be rationally derived from two premises. The first was that men seek pleasure and flee from pain. The second was that government should rule for the greatest good of the greatest number. It would pass laws which granted pleasures for individual activity that contributed to the greatest good and assigned pains for activities that did not. Law was not a set of external principles or hallowed rights. It was an instrument which, through the assignment of pleasures and pains, would move people to engage in socially desirable activity.[79]

The second major movement was one toward the creation of democratic, representative government. Beginning with the great Reform Act of 1832, suffrage was broadened and the electoral system reformed so that Parliament came to reflect more closely the views and interests of the English population. At the same time the Parliament reorganized and clarified its own lawmaking powers and procedures. The result was a Parliament capable of passing substantial bodies of new legislation that more or less reflected dominant opinion in the population, or at least in the politically active middle and upper classes.[80]

The Benthamite urge to create a new and rational body of law and the parliamentary capacity to do so led to an enormous body of law reform. It will be remembered that demands for law reform had been fairly constant since at least the sixteenth century but that the common law–common lawyer–common law judge nexus had proven largely immune to such demands through the eighteenth century. In the nineteenth century reform succeeded. In substantive law, the most dramatic reform was in the most central area of common law obscurantism, land law. The reform of the land law was embodied in dozens of piecemeal, patchwork statutes each designed to overcome one or a few of the absurdities and inconveniences of the received body of common law without altering its fundamental practices. Yet their cumulative effective was to greatly simplify the law and render much of the ancient learning inapplicable.[81] There were many other areas of substantive law reform, but that of land law clearly shows the new dominance of Parliament over the judges in the creation of substantive law.

That dominance is shown even more clearly in procedure. In a series of statutes beginning in 1854 and culminating in the Judicature Act of 1873, the Parliament completed a fundamental reorganization of the courts and simplification of procedures.[82] Chancery, King's Bench, Common Pleas, Exchequer, and the courts of Probate, Admiralty, and Divorce were merged into one Supreme Court of Judicature, which was divided into the High Court of Justice and the Court of Appeal. The chancellor and the chancellor of the Exchequer lost their power to sit as trial judges. Judges of the High

Court were to be appointed from barristers of ten years' standing. The High Court received all the jurisdiction of its former components as well as the former jurisdictions of those holding commissions of assize and goal delivery. Equity and common law jurisdictions, procedures, and remedies were merged. All the judges of the High Court could sit in any of its divisions. There were Chancery, King's Bench, and Probate, Admiralty and Divorce Divisions, which reflected the historical streams of equity, common law, and Roman law, but this compromise with the past only partially undercut the fundamental consolidation achieved. The assize system was continued with judges of the High Court and others given assize commissions in the exercise of which they were deemed to constitute a sitting of the High Court itself. Each High Court judge usually sat alone in the conduct of a trial.

The new Court of Appeal consisted of five judges appointed by the crown, the lord chancellor, master of rolls, lord chief justice of England (i.e., chief judge of the King's Bench Division), and the president (i.e., chief judge) of the Probate, Admiralty and Divorce division. It received the old equity appellate jurisdiction of the chancellor, the appellate jurisdiction of Exchequer Chamber and various other miscellaneous appellate jurisdictions. Appeal was now to be by a new trial (trial de novo) conducted by the Court of Appeal itself rather than by limited examination of the record of the trial court which had been the previous practice in England and remains so in the United States. The King's Bench Division retained its old appellate jurisdiction over various minor local courts. The House of Lords continued as a court of final appeal from decisions of the Court of Appeal, and the Privy Council as the final appeals body for overseas cases. But in both instances the appeals mechanisms were specialized and professionalized. Only those lords who had held high judicial officers or were barristers might sit to hear appeals, and they were bolstered by two lords of appeal in ordinary appointed to the House of Lords for life by the crown. It was envisioned that these "law lords" would also constitute the Judicial Committee of the Privy Council which wielded its appeals powers.

A new simplified code of procedure was adopted for the entire Supreme Court which provided general procedural rules for all actions as opposed to the old law which contained a special set of procedures for each of the writs. In the process much of the old learning of special pleading was rendered obsolete.

The nineteenth century elucidated the real developments of the seventeenth. Parliament had belatedly asserted the mastery over the judges that it had gained from the crown in the course of the revolution. It now determined the structure of the courts, their procedures, and the substantive law they were to apply. The impenetrability of the common law, which had been the true foundation of the autonomy of the judges, had been breached by parliamentary statutes. Parliament had finally demonstrated that it had the real authority to change the preexisting legal rules of the courts by actually carrying out a successful program of law reform.

Parliament did not achieve, or even attempt, the Benthamite program, however. The reforms of procedural and substantive law took the form of editing the common law materials rather than replacing them with a short, simple, rational code. Even after a severe pruning of obsolete learning, historical curiosity, and meaningless form, the common law definitely remained the domain of common lawyers, and a quite complex domain at that. The relapse of the High Court into three divisions reflecting the older structure of the courts indicated the tenacity of tradition. Most important in the midst of all the parliamentary victories, the common lawyers managed to infiltrate the final defenses of their master and seize control of the very top of the appeals hierarchy. For as we have seen, the law lords and the Judicial Committee of the Privy Council become functionally specialized judicial units of the legislative and executive branches, exercising their final appeals jurisdictions. And these specialized units were staffed exclusively with lawyers and bolstered by a new group of judges, the lords of appeal in ordinary.[83] Thus while the Parliament wielded ultimate authority over the courts through its ultimate and unlimited lawmaking powers, the day-to-day operation of the courts had finally become totally insulated from the intervention of the general government. The rule of law, in the sense of the inability of the government to influence the outcome of any individual case, had now reached its high point in English experience.

The nineteenth century is the forming period for the orthodoxy of both English and American legal thought. What Englishmen and Americans thought they saw in that century was the final culmination of judicial independence. If judicial independence means the functional specialization of courts plus the rule of law, they were correct. But that usage of the term tended to obscure certain developments, or rather the obscurity of certain developments led to a complacency about judicial independence that was reflected in the definition offered.

Parliament had after all broken into the main body of common law, the land law. By the end of the nineteenth century Parliament had begun to pour our volumes of new statutes in many areas of law and was indeed creating whole new areas of statutory laws where the common law had no place. Why was this wholesale overthrow of judicial autonomy not given first place in legal consciousness rather than those other factors highlighted by the conventional use of the phrase judicial independence?

First of all, because the common lawyers were used to statutes. They had always been recognized as an element of the law of England. So the lawyers were not immediately alarmed by the new statutes. Late nineteenth-century and early twentieth-century academic commentators desperately tried to ignore statutes or downgrade them into "sources of law" rather than law itself, which they pretended to see only in the decisions of the courts.[84] But the common lawyers themselves had little need of such sophisms. They had encountered statutes and successfully cocooned them within the common law for centuries. The new land statutes and many others were incremental changes rather than fundamental disruptions of common law. They too could be absorbed. It was not until well into the twentieth century that legal observers came to realize that a step-level change had occurred in the activity of legislatures late in the nineteenth, a change that would eventually lead to the dominance of statutory over common law in both England and America.

Second, as we noted earlier, laissez-faire ideology blinded contemporary observers to much of the change. Because in theory the government was supposed to remain neutral vis-à-vis competing economic interests, even the statutory reforms of such private law areas as land law were not seen as turning the judge into an imposer of state interests over the interests of the two conflicting private parties. The judge would indeed humbly obey the laws of Parliament, but those laws would require only that he act in a neutral and benevolent way toward the private disputants. Of course observers occasionally encountered statutes, such as the factory and mine safety acts, that clearly did try to place the weight of state interests on the side of one class of persons and in opposition to the other. They placed those statutes in some special category, such as business regulation, and continued to perceive neutrality in the vast central bodies of private law.

Third, the political stability of nineteenth-century England and its general success on the world scene led, both in England and America, to a worship of its basic institutions as the final evolutionary product of the freest and most enlightened society in the world. When one sees functionally specialized courts, the rule of law, *and* an essentially enlightened, benevolent, and democratic government, one is not very conscious of the potential conflict that exists between notions of parliamentary sovereignty and notions of judicial independence. Surely the greatest and wisest representative assembly in the whole history of the world would not threaten the independence of the judiciary.

### The Twentieth Century

The basic organization of the courts created by the nineteenth-century parliamentary reforms has persisted in the twentieth century with some minor changes.[85]

The High Court of Justice continues its three divisions of Kings (at the moment Queen's) Bench, Chancery, and Probate, Admiralty and Divorce (the latter has been renamed the "Family Division" although it retains its admiralty jurisdiction as before). Any judge of the High Court can sit in any division. The Court of Appeal now consists of eight justices of appeal, the lord chancellor, former lord chancellors, the lords of appeal in ordinary, the master of the rolls, the lord chief justice (i.e., the senior judge of Queen's Bench) and the president of the Family Division. Customarily the Court of Appeals in any given case will be three of the lord justices of appeal, plus perhaps the master of the rolls. The House of Lords retains its appeals jurisdiction, normally wielded by the nine lords of appeal in ordinary plus the lord chancellor.

The Court of Appeal hears appeals as of right on points of law arising in the county court involving more than about $50 or when the remedy is an injunction. It will hear other appeals if the judge of the county court gives permission. Appeal from the High Court to the Court of Appeal is now as of right on points of law but only by permission of the Court of Appeal on points of fact. Where the facts are at issue, the Court of Appeal may make its own decision on the basis of the trial transcript but may not take new testimony. Usually, however, when the High Court is reversed, the Court of Appeal directs it to retry the case rather than reaching a final decision itself. Appeal to the House of Lords is only on important points of law and may be had only when the Court of Appeal certifies the importance of the question or Lords itself permits the appeal.

The one great historical exception to the centralizing trend of the British courts was the establishment in the fourteenth century of the justices of the peace with their petty and quarter sessions.[86] These were and basically remain criminal courts. In spite of repeated demands for change from the seventeenth century onward, only the assize courts brought civil jurisdiction to the countryside. Beginning with legislation in 1846, county courts were established to take over much of the civil business of assize. There are now about 500 county courts grouped in more than fifty circuits. There is at least one circuit judge for each circuit. He or she holds each county court at least once a month. Each county court has a registrar who provides continuity of administration and hears minor cases. The county courts are limited by statute to hearing cases involving relatively small amounts of money. The hearing of serious cases remains centralized in the High Court.[87] On the civil side appeals from county courts go directly to the Court of Appeal in most instances. In some appeal is to the divisional court of Queen's Bench, Chancery, or Family. (Thus we get such awkward designations as "Divisional Court of the Queen's Bench Division," which means three to five judges of the Queen's Bench Division of the High Court sitting in exercise of the appeals jurisdiction of Queen's Bench).

On the criminal side the basic trial courts for low level offenses remain J.P.'s courts sitting without a jury. In larger cities J.P.'s have been replaced by stipendary magistrates. They are paid judges who are full-time solicitors or barristers and part-time judges. These courts not only try minor offenses but also carry on the functions that in the United States are called indicting and arraigning. That is, they decide whether there is sufficient evidence of a serious offense to hold the accused over for trial in a higher court. J.P.'s sit alone or in twos or threes. Stipendary magistrates sit alone. Two or more J.P.'s or one stipendary magistrate constitute a Court of Petty Sessions. In 1971 a statute created the new Crown Court, which took over the criminal jurisdiction of the traditional Courts of Quarter Session and the assizes, that is, jurisdiction over serious criminal cases. It is staffed by High Court judges, circuit (county court) judges, and recorders, that is, barristers who are appointed to part-time judicial duties. The judges of this court may sit singly or in banc and in certain instances J.P.'s are added to the Bench.[88] The Crown Court hears cases with a jury. Appeals from Petty Sessions go to Quarter Sessions or to the Divisional Court of Queen's Bench Division. Appeals from the Crown Court go to the criminal division of the Court of Appeals, which sits without a jury.

A major reform of the nineteenth century was to substitute trial de novo for writ of error as the procedure for appeal. Under the writ of error the appellate body only saw the record from below which included little more than the findings and the trial judge's holdings on points of law. Thus the writ of error procedure meant that, as has generally been true in the Unites States, appellate judges reviewed only findings of law not findings of fact. When appeal is by means of a whole new trial, appeals courts could, of course, redecide factual questions for themselves.

In the twentieth century the English have restricted trial de novo on appeal both by allowing appeal on questions of fact only by permission of either the trial or appellate court and by forbidding the appeals court to hear new evidence. The impact of the nineteenth-century reforms is still felt, however, in three important respects. It is not the bare record but the full trial transcript that goes up to the appellate court for review. Because appeal is still legally conceived of as trial de novo, the appellate court may substitute a different sentence for that imposed by the trial court or even convict the defendant of a different offense. And for the same reason the Court of Appeal need not order a retrial in the trial court if it reverses the trial court but may conclude the case itself.

Criminal appeals may proceed to the House of Lords only if certified by the attorney general as raising a point of law of "exceptional public importance," and only if the appeals court or Lords itself grants permission for the appeal.

With these minor twentieth-century modifications, the reformed courts of the nineteenth century have flourished and are generally held to be among the most independent in the world. They are functionally specialized, performing none but judicial tasks, and are almost entirely separated from the "government," that is, from the cabinet and Parliament. Only in the figure of the lord chancellor, who is a legal advisor to the government, a judge of the highest courts, and the possessor of wide judicial appointing and disciplinary powers, do we encounter a strong reminder that the king's judges are servants of the government. In practice, however, the lord chancellor rarely sits in the courts of which he is a member and, when he does, rarely appears to espouse the government's interests directly.

While there may be the same kind of back-room jockeying for judgeships as there often is for university professorships and other posts in the hands of the government, partisan political considerations have played little part in the appointment of judges during this century. Judges serve at good behavior and those of the High Court may be removed only by action of both houses of Parliament. Circuit court judges and recorders and J.P.'s may be removed for cause by the lord chancellor. In fact only one judge has been removed by government action since 1701. There is little or no evidence that the government has approached judges for the purpose of influencing the outcome of particular cases.[89]

The connection with an autonomous legal profession which is a principal component of judicial "independence" remains. All but the lowest rung of judicial appointments can be made only from among the barristers and many of the highest rungs require many years' service as a barrister or judge.

Save for the fact that the whole system of courts and its staffing depends entirely upon parliamentary statute and so could be changed at any time, one might well be justified in concluding that the English courts had reached that teleological goal of pure independence that a conventional reading of English legal history seeks.

The ambivalent and paradoxical aspect of that independence, however, becomes clear if we look at the growth of administrative law, which is the truly central phenomenon of twentieth-century English legal development.

### Administrative Law in Twentieth-Century England

In one sense the acceleration of parliamentary activity in the middle and late nineteenth century was a response to the Benthamite urge toward law reform and reationalization. Along other dimensions, however, it was a foreshadowing of the greatly expanded sphere of law and government in the twentieth-century English welfare and socialist state. By the turn of the century, and certainly by World War I, the accelerating rate of lawmaking was taking on a quite distinctive character. Most of the new laws were

arming the British executive with increasing authority and discretion. Just as
the British Constitution in general was being altered by a massive shift of
political authority from Parliament to cabinet,[90] so the whole legal structure
was shifting from one of law made in Parliament and enforced in court to
one of law made by administrators and enforced by administrators. Quite
clearly, from at least World War II onward, English administrators have
made far more law than English legislators and resolved far more legal
conflicts than English judges.

Of central importance in the growth of English administrative
power have been the phenomena known as "delegated legislation" and
"administrative tribunals." A very high proportion of parliamentary legislation does little more than state the purposes to be achieved in rather
sweeping language and then state with some precision the jursidictional
boundaries between the various government agencies involved. Most of
Parliament's authority to legislate the actual provisions of the statutory
scheme are then delegated to the specified agencies. These administrative
agencies then legislate in the form of various orders, circulars, plans, and
policy statements, the most prominent of which are Orders in Council.

Parliamentary statutes are also the sources of the two thousand or
more administrative tribunals that handle the bulk of the disputes that arise
between the administrative agencies and private citizens. They also handle
an increasingly high proportion of disputes between one citizen and
another, for instance, rent disputes between landlord and tenant. England is,
of course, a welfare state with the government taking a direct hand in most
facets of the feeding, housing, medical care, education, recreation, and basic
income levels of its citizens. It is a socialist state in which the government
owns or directly controls most of the major means of production and strictly
regulates the secondary economic activities it does not directly control. Thus
a very high proportion of the disputes in which any Englishman may find
himself involved are resolved by administrative tribunals rather than
courts.[91]

These developments have presented an enormous challenge to the
English courts and indeed to the whole notion of rule of law. In a famous,
but even then anachronistic, passage in *Law of the Constitution*, Dicey
argued that the rule of law required that government officers be answerable
for their actions in the regular courts under the regular procedures just as a
private person would be. He denounced administrative law and administrative courts as Continental manifestations forever foreign to English law. The
strain of opinion that Dicey represented was sufficiently dominant to prevent the creation in England of an explicit hierarchy of administrative courts
charged with insuring the legality of administrative actions.

While there are some fairly large holes in the scheme of judicial remedies, that scheme would appear to provide for extensive judicial control over administrative acts.[92] In certain sense it does, but the full picture can be seen only after examination of both the specific statutory limitations on these remedies and the general principles under which they are applied. Many parliamentary statutes provide a statutory remedy such as appeal to the minister. Such a provision may substantially reduce the availability of the courts to persons involved in disputes with administrative agencies. Modern statutes often contain finality or ouster clauses of various degrees of severity. The mildest of these provides that some administrative decision made under the act shall be final. Others provide that after a brief period, often six weeks, a government action "shall not . . . be questioned in any legal proceedings whatsoever."[93] Moreover a great many statutes provide that the government may act "if the Minister is satisfied" or "if it appears to the Minister" that a particular fact situation exists. This "subjective" standard will generally exclude a judicial challenge to administrative fact-finding since the question is not whether the administrative authorities made a wrong finding of fact or drew the wrong inferences from the primary facts but only whether they could have had reason to believe that their conclusions of fact were correct.[94] The courts have frequently provided the narrowest possible interpretations of these statutory limitations on their powers. Governed as they are, however, by the theory of parliamentary sovereignty, they have never denied the authority of Parliament to limit their jurisdiction by such provisions.

It is when we turn to the general principles of English administrative law that we can see most clearly that, no matter what the temporary victories of the nineteenth century, the English courts did not become independent in the seventeenth but merely exchanged a royal master for a parliamentary one. Indeed they have fundamentally returned to the pre-seventeenth-century position. For the judges are again the faithful servants of the crown although the crown is now the cabinet and the bureaucracy rather than the king.

THE POWER TO GOVERN WRONGLY

The first principle of English administrative law is that the power to govern comprehends the power to make mistakes. So long as an administrative officer or tribunal is acting within the scope of its statutory authority or within its jurisdiction, the correctness or incorrectness of its decisions may not normally be brought into questions in judicial proceedings. The proper remedy for misgovernment is ministerial responsibility. The cabinet member ultimately responsible for the government program or decision is answerable to his fellow cabinet members and to Parliament and so need not be answerable to the courts unless appeal is provided by statute.[95]

### REVIEW AND APPEAL

Relatively few statutes provide for appeal from the decisions of the ministries themselves, although appeal often does lie from decisions of administrative tribunals. Much of whatever judicial supervision of administration there is takes place in the form of review rather than appeal. A reviewing court may not look to the merits of the decision. Even should it reverse the administrative authority, it merely returns the matter to that authority for further consideration rather than substituting its own judgment.[96]

In theory, with one major exception to be noted later, judicial review of administrative acts goes to only two questions: ultra vires and natural justice.

### NATURAL JUSTICE

The concept of natural justice is composed of two principles of English administrative law. The first is that a person should not be judge in his own case. The second is that a decision affecting the rights or interests of an individual should not be made until he has been given an opportunity to be heard.[97]

### JUDGE IN HIS OWN CASE

In the very nature of things the first of these two principles can have only a very limited meaning in the contemporary English context, for the typical situation is one in which a ministry proposes a certain program or policy, hears complaints directed to that policy, and then proceeds to carry it out with such modifications as it sees fit to make on the basis of the complaints. Everywhere in the world, including England, a central feature of administrative rule is precisely that administrators do serve as at least the initial resolvers of conflicts that are engendered with the citizenry by their programs. Indeed the typical English statutory scheme provides that the minister is the ultimate appellate authority for complaints against his administrative subordinates and his ministry's programs. English courts have never attempted "judge in his own case" challenges to such arrangements. At most they have created a rather shaky and unsure requirement that when the minister is acting to determine individual rights rather than in his political capacity, he must obey the second principle of natural justice, that of granting a fair hearing.[98]

The English have sought to alleviate the problem of administrative bias by the creation of a very large number of administrative tribunals.

These tribunals are imbedded within the agencies and largely staffed with agency personnel. Just as in the United States, where hearing officers have become administrative law judges, so in England there has been pressure to isolate these tribunals more completely from their agencies. But, as has been true here as well, these pressures have been resisted, for there is good reason to insist that the agencies must not be crippled by excessive judicialization of their decision-making processes. They are, after all, the repositories of both technical knowledge and ultimate operating responsibility. The English compromise has been to leave the tribunals well within the ministries but to create a Council on Administrative Tribunals to monitor their operation.[99] While the courts exercise some supervision over the tribunals, they do not hold that this massive structure of administrative judging violates natural justice. In practice, the first principle of natural justice is reduced to the insistence that the ministries and local government authorities follow the procedures for hearing and appeal established by statute and by their own regulations when they act as judges in their own cases.

FAIR HEARING

The second principle, that of fair hearing, has a bit more teeth. With a fairly high degree of consistency, English courts have held that a person has a right to a hearing before the taking of an administrative decision potentially adverse to his interests. Normally that hearing will be oral. The parties will be entitled to legal representation and may present witnesses and cross-examine. The principle of fair hearing requires that the party know the case he is required to meet and so implies that parties must be informed of all evidence the government proposes to consider in making its decision. The government must consider all evidence submitted by each party including his or her comments on potentially adverse evidence and on the case as a whole.

English courts, however, never succeeded in establishing (1) that the requirement of fair hearing applies to "legislative" as opposed to "judicial" decisions, (2) that administrative authorities must give reasons for the decisions they ultimately reach, (3) that they must give any particular weight to the evidence presented to them at hearings, or even (4) that the reports of hearing officers or tribunals must be made public. The minister is the ultimate arbiter of policy and is answerable to the Parliament, not to the courts, for his policy judgments. And what weight he gives to various evidence and arguments will almost invariably be held to be a matter of policy. Only after long struggle was it finally required that the reports to the minister of hearing officers or tribunals be made public. This development came by statute, not court decision. Similarly many statutes, including the Tribunals and Inquiries Act, now require that the minister give reasons for his decision although the courts have never made that demand independent of a statutory duty to do so. Thus the principle of natural justice may require the minister to go through the motions, but courts will not quash his decision even when it appears to the judges that he has decided against the weight of the evidence.

The tendency to extend natural justice requirements to various preliminary administrative decisions that precede final administrative determinations seems to have been reversed.[100]

ULTRA VIRES

While the doctrine of natural justice has been presented separately for clarity, it is typically treated by the English as a facet of *ultra vires*, [10] the very cornerstone of English administrative law. Indeed, with one exception, *ultra vires* is the only basis for court intervention in administration. That the *ultra vires* doctrine is central is the clearest of all signs of the ambiguity of the notion of judicial independence in England. The doctrine holds that, as long as an administrator is acting within the authority granted him by Parliament, his acts are totally beyond the reach of judges. We have already noted the enormous amount of parliamentary delegation to administrators of lawmaking power without fixed guidelines or standards. The *ultra vires* doctrine not only announces the total subordination of both judges and administrators to Parliament, but the freedom of administrators from most judicial supervision. If Parliament authorizes administrators to do what they please, and judges are not allowed to interfere with such parliamentary authorizations, then administrators are free to do what they please without fear of judicial correction.

As a practical matter the extent of judicial supervision of administration under the doctrine of *ultra vires* will depend on the judges' techniques of statutory interpretation. The ability of the American courts to interpret statutes so as to confirm their own policy preferences and block the ill-advised schemes of administrators is well known. It is typical of the English authorities on administrative law that they make much of those few instances of judicial statutory interpretation running against administrators that they can find. It is also typical that they can find very few, and many of those they do find are very old and probably would not be followed today.

PROCEDURE

As in the United States there are two central areas of statutory interpretation, the first whether the agency has followed the procedures specified in the statute, the second whether their actions are in accord with the purposes of the statute. Except for the proceedings of administrative tribunals, there is no general procedures statute in England comparable to the Administrative Procedures Act in the United States.[102] Most statutes, however, contain their own often quite rigorous procedures requirements. Particularly when local authorities, such as county governments, act as agents for the central government, and/or when private property must be taken for public use, procedures requirements are typically quite demanding in terms of notice, hearing, record, appeal, and so on. The courts, however, have settled down into an extremely low-keyed procedural review that only occasionally catches some local authority in a minor error. There is no suggestion, as there frequently is in the United States, that courts are using procedural review to interject an independent voice into bureaucratic policymaking. Indeed few procedural cases reach the highest courts, and almost none against the central government ministries. Given their sweeping administrative discretion, English administrators can always get their way in the end if they are patient: following procedures to the letter will in the final analysis almost always yield the decision they want.

LEGISLATIVE PURPOSE

When we turn to legislative purpose the same low judicial profile is evident. In theory the exercise of powers granted by a statute for purposes other than those mandated by the statute is *ultra vires*.[103] There are a few classic cases in which the administrator flatly contravened the clear wording of the statute and got caught by the judges. And there are a few remnants of clashes between conservative judges and socialist local governments in the twenties.[104] There is no real sign, however, that English courts will use the doctrine of legislative purpose beyond the narrowest scope of preventing open breaches of the clearest statutory commands.

ABUSE OF DISCRETION

Potentially the most promising avenue for establishing an independent judicial voice, beyond the more vigorous use of legislative purpose, would be along the "abuse of discretion" route. An administrative action so unreasonable or arbitrary as to constitute an abuse of discretion is *ultra vires*.[105] A number of factors inhibit the judicial employment of this doctrine. First, English courts have long held that, where a statute vests discretion, it is discretion to decide wrongly as well as rightly. That in retrospect a decision was wrong does not render it *ultra vires*. Moreover, should the issue be one involving an element of "policy," and most important ones do, the minister is answerable for the reasonableness of policy decisions only to Parliament.[106] Second, English courts generally will review administrative findings of law but not of fact.[107] As in the United States, there are of course gray areas, but on the whole English courts are extremely reluctant to dispute administrative findings of fact. As a practical matter it is extremely difficult to show that a decision was arbitrary when it is supported by an unchallengeable set of fact-findings. Third, except where a statute provides for appeal, in contradistinction to review, the standard of reasonableness is the most permissive standard employed in American administrative law, that is, whether reasons can be offered for the decision. English authorities constantly reiterate that the administrative law standard of reasonableness is not the common law standard or any kind of standard that will allow the courts to strike a balance between the reasons for and against the decision. In order to be held *ultra vires* an administrative decision "must be proved to be a decision that no reasonable body could have come to."[108] Fourth, many key statutes use such subjective language as "if the minister was satisfied that." Thus a mere showing that the facts on which the minister relied were not as the minister thought them to be is not a showing of arbitrariness constituting *ultra vires*.

While English courts have recently flirted with a "no-evidence" rule similar to those in the United States, even such a rule is considered a bit daring in the English context.[109] Such a rule would, of course, only hold unreasonable those administrative decisions for which there was no supportive fact-finding at all. On the whole English courts have not used the abuse of discretion doctrine expansively to extend judicial control over the vast discretionary powers of British government. It is indicative that most of the few recent cases involve local not central authorities and/or policy issues on which the central government has not yet stated a firm position[110] approved by Parliament.

In summary, then, the *ultra vires* doctrine begins with a declaration of absolute judicial subordination to Parliament—the only measure of illegal administrative conduct being its failure to live within the parliamentary law. And the doctrine ends in practice with a judiciary that will occasionally intervene against the most openly illegal conduct of local authorities but exercises very little supervision over the massive discretionary powers of the central government.

FOUR LEADING CASES

In the 1940s and 1950s judicial review of administrative decisions had become increasingly moribund. Since then there has been some revival of judicial authority that has been much touted by British and Commonwealth commentators as a "rebirth of administrative law" and an era of "judicial activism."[111] First of all it must be noted that even this revival was basically inspired and led by the parliamentary master rather than the judicial servant. For it was Parliament in the Tribunals and Inquiries Act of 1958 that clearly signaled that it wanted more judicial review of administrative proceedings. Among other things, the act abolished the finality clauses in most earlier statutes that had forbidden appeal to the courts from various administrative tribunals.

In the final analysis, the vision of renewed judicial independence from administrative domination rests on four cases which various English judges and some academic authorities have labeled as "landmark" decisions.

The first of these was *Ridge* v. *Baldwin*.[112] There the local police authorities in Brighton had dismissed a local police official without a hearing. The House of Lords found this to be a breach of natural justice. In the course of its opinions it unsaid some of what it had said in the 1950s about judicial withdrawal from review of administrative decisions. Indeed *Ridge* was part of a flurry of judicial activism in the period 1963–65. There are various explanation for this flurry, including changes in judicial personnel and a particularly bitter clash between the government and the law lords about compensation for some undersea oil claims. Whatever the reasons, the flurry was short-lived.[113]

The extent to which faith in *Ridge* may be misplaced is suggested not only by the subsequent decline in judicial activity but by a number of other factors as well. In *Ridge* the court is bold against a very minor local government authority which was deciding what was clearly a personnel rather than a policy matter. Moreover, it was a local authority whose discretion was very clearly limited by both statutes and central government regulations. Even *Ridge* says "that natural justice has no part to play where ministers have to attach importance to their policy."[114]

The second of these "landmark" cases is *Padfield* v. *Minister of Agriculture*.[115] It interpreted a statutory clause requiring that complaints be investigated "if the Minister in any case so directs" as not creating in the minister an unfettered power to refuse to investigate even for inadequate reasons. The case is particularly important because the law lords actually examined the reasons given and found them inadequate. This was the boldest adventure the courts had taken against a central ministry in many years. The law lords, however, did not even come close actually to challenging a substantive ministry decision.

The third of these cases, *Anisminic* v. *Foreign Compensation Commission*,[116] caused a great flurry at the time because it appeared to be a direct confrontation between Parliament and the courts. In fact it has been of only very minor importance subsequently in Great Britian, having been cited as significant in only three reported English cases, two of which did not apply it.[117] In it the law lords managed to interpret away one of the few finality or ouster clauses that had been left standing by the act of 1958.

Subsequently, however, the Court of Appeal has managed to uphold one of the surviving really important privative clauses.[118]

Some eight years after *Padfield*, the law lords again challenged the decision of a minister and again actually examined whether his actions were reasonable. The case was *Secretary of State for Education and Science* v. *Tameside Metropolitan Borough Council.*[119] In terms of what light it might shed on the supposed great revival since the 1950s, perhaps the most important thing that must be said about this case is that it caused a tremendous flurry of attention.[120] This flurry arose precisely because it was so unheard of for a British court actually to contradict a ministerial decision. Indeed the law lords in their decision had to rely heavily on *Padfield* because so little else was available.

There is no question that *Tameside*, when combined with *Padfield*, announces a judicial capacity to review the exercise of ministerial discretion that could have important consequences for administrative law. Nevertheless, a number of factors make *Tameside* a peculiar case. First of all, the governing legislation, the Education Act of 1944, specifically gave great educational policymaking autonomy to local, democratically elected bodies such as the Tameside Borough Council. The law lords stressed that they were protecting Parliament's intention to maximize the authority of democratic local bodies rather than asserting judicial prerogatives.

Second, in this particular instance the central government ministry could not enforce its policy directly against local authorities. Because of the way the act of 1944 was written, the minister of education had to go to the courts themselves and ask the judges for a writ of mandamus ordering the local education authority to obey him. In other words *Tameside* is not a case in which an individual citizen asks the courts to intervene against the administrative power of the central government that has made and carried out its own policy. Instead it is a case in which the central government acknowledges that it is too weak to carry out its own policies and asks the judges for help. Naturally judges feel more capable of refusing to assist administrators than they do in directly attacking policies that the ministries are implementing on their own.

Third, *Tameside* must be placed in its political context. The Labour Party controlled the government. At the time it was pushing through Parliament, in which it had a majority, a new education bill. That bill, however, had not yet become law. The Tameside Council was in the hands of the Conservative Party. It was pursuing education policies that were permitted by the act of 1944 but would be forbidden by the new bill once it became law. The Labour minister of education was attempting to manipulate some rather vague wording of the act of 1944 in order to force the new Labour policies on the Conservative Council *before* he had really gotten the statutory authority to do so. Moreover, the new statute would provide the minister with direct enforcement powers over the local authorities without the need for judicial assistance. In the *Tameside* decision the Court of Appeal and the House of Lords were not so much challenging ministerial authority as telling him to wait until he had it.

Finally a peculiar twist of the act of 1944 makes *Tameside* a two-edged sword insofar as judicial power is concerned. The act allowed the minister to intervene against a local authority when he found that *it* was acting unreasonably. The Lords hold in *Tameside* that the *minister* was not entitled to find that the local authority was acting unreasonably simply because he disagree with its policies or thought them not to be the best possible policies. Instead he could be "satisfied" that they had acted "unreasonably," as the statute put it, only if they were engaged in conduct "which no sensible authority" could have adopted. In short the act of 1944 puts the minister in the position that judges are usually in, that of deciding whether an action taken by an independent administrator is reasonable. In asserting that in such a situation the minister must use the most permissive standard of reasonableness, the judges are reasserting the doctrine that judges must use the most permissive standard of reasonableness in dealing with the policy judgments of the government.

Much of the proclaimed revival of judicial review in England is really wishful thinking by academic commentators and judges speaking off the bench rather than real judicial behavior. Or rather it is the typical lawyers' strategy of telling judges they have been doing something in the hope that this will embolden them actually to do it. While there are signs that British courts are now somewhat more open to challenges directed against administrative conduct than they were twenty-five years ago, the change in judicial attitudes is far greater in relative than in absolute terms.

The four recent, major cases do not so much declare a revival as announce the judges' refusal finally to be pushed entirely out of the field of judicial review of administrative decisions. *Ridge* undermines a doctrine created by the courts themselves. That doctrine declared that judges might review decisions made by administrators "acting judicially" but might not review those in which the administrator was acting administratively, that is, exercising policy discretion. *Padfield* and *Tameside* assert that judicial review is not entirely debarred by "subjective" clauses, that is, statutory language that allows a minister to act when he or she is "satisfied" or when it "appears" to him or her that something has occurred. *Anisminic* strikes at privative clauses that purport entirely to bar judicial review of some administrative decisions.

Declaring on an average of once every three years that one is still in the game is not the same thing as winning it or even making a modest score. Whatever the symbolic value of these four cases, neither they nor the handful of less important decisions that have followed them constitute a major check on British administrative authority, let alone a declaration of judicial independence from the sovereign powers of the British executive.[121]

ERROR ON THE FACE OF THE RECORD

It remains to examine one other area where the English courts do seem to have been active. We have noted that the very foundation of English administrative law is the notion of *ultra vires*. The courts act against administrative agencies not on their own independent authority but only to keep them within the bounds set by Parliament. Within those bounds the courts may not interfere with the agencies even when they act wrongly. To this general rule, the English courts have created one exception. They will quash even *intra vires* administrative judgments where an error of law appears "on the face of the record." This doctrine appears to be an activist judicial response to the enormous growth of statutory tribunals. Until 1958 most such tribunals enjoyed statutory immunity from appeal. Yet it appeared absurd in terms of any notion of the rule of law to allow such tribunals to announce openly egregious errors of law without correction. Subsequently it appeared equally absurd that a tribunal may make all of the "secret" errors of law it wants so long as none of them appear on the face of the record. Since 1951, when the doctrine was first announced, the courts have gradually expanded the meaning of record until it includes not only the opinion or statement of reasons given by the tribunal but the documents that are the basis for the decision and even oral statements of reasons for the decision made by the tribunal.[122]

Yet even this seeming assertion of independent judicial authority is far less independent than it seems and far more an exercise of parliamentary authority. The rule that tribunals are subject to judicial review for error on the face of the record means little if tribunals need not give any reasons of law on the record for the decisions they reach. And until 1958 tribunals generally were not required to make "speaking orders," that is orders giving reasons. The Tribunals and Inquiries Act of that year required that most tribunals and ministers exercising a duty to hold statutory inquiries give reasons and that those reason be incorporated in the record. The act was framed with the knowledge that the courts had already asserted the power to review speaking orders for errors of law. Thus it constituted direct parliamentary authorization for such review. Indeed the court decision that oral reasons were reviewable flowed directly from the act's provision on oral reasons. What has occurred here is a relatively minor judicial initiative into which Parliament has chosen to put teeth and vastly expand. It has done so as part of an overall scheme to bring the proliferating tribunals under some sort of control. As a result of the act many persons may pursue direct appeal by asserting that a tribunal has made an error of law and without showing that it has acted *ultra vires*.[123] The general effect is to bring these "lower courts" back into some degree of subordination to the regular judicial hierarchy. Thus the Parliament has partially counteracted one of the most serious erosions of judicial institutions that has occurred in twentieth-century England.

It should also be noted that jurisprudence based on error on the face of the record depends ultimately, as does *ultra vires*, on judicial styles of statuory interpretation. If judges are unwilling to substitute their interpretation of statutes for those of administrators, they are as unlikely to find *intra vires* errors of law as they are to find that administrators have acted *ultra vires*. So what was said in our examination of *ultra vires* must be said again here. English judges have shown remarkably little inclination to engage in independent statutory interpretation except in their occasional attacks on ouster and subjective clauses.

### ADMINISTRATIVE LAW IN AN ADMINISTRATIVE STATE

The overall pattern of English administrative law gives little comfort to the proponents of judicial independence. In the twentieth century England has become an executive state, an administrative state, a welfare state, and a socialist state. In such a state the very center of law and politics is the apparatus of central government. Yet the very foundation doctrine that the courts have proclaimed for dealing with that apparatus is that it is essentially immune from judicial scrutiny so long as it stays within the jurisdictional bounds set by Parliament.

This judicial surrender is all the more complete when it is acknowledged, as it must be, that the parliamentary power to which the courts pretend to be subordinating themselves has long since disappeared. In the last analysis *ultra vires* is a circular doctrine of surrender to administrative government. It proclaims that the courts will insure that the executive obeys Parliament. Parliament, however, has long since transferred all of its authority over day-to-day policymaking, and most of its ultimate authority as well, to the cabinet and the ministries. Ultimately *ultra vires* means only that the executive must obey itself. As to natural justice, it means no more than that the ministries must grant hearings before deciding whatever they please. The process of both parliamentary and judicial abdication has gone so far that there are serious doubts about whether the rule of law survives in

England at all.[124] And if it does, it must do so in the ideological commitments of the executive elite itself rather than in the constraining powers of the courts.

Nothing could be more touching than the way in which, in the face of this overwhelming political reality, English authorities on administrative law continue to cite and re-cite a handful of cases that preserve the doctrines of judicial review. For those cases are not only very few but almost invariably result in the chastisement of some local authority for firing a policeman or harassing the owner of a mobile home site. To the extent that judicial review remains an active force at all, it serves largely as a handmaiden of central administration in its attempts to rationalize and control the mass of local authorities and subordinate tribunals ultimately responsible to the central ministries.

### Conclusion

The insistence on judicial independence as an essential element in the conventional prototype of courts is largely derived from English experience. But it is largely derived from rather casual impressions of what the English courts appeared to be like in the eighteenth and nineteenth centuries. When the entire history of English judicial experience is reviewed, a far less clear picture of judicial independence emerges.

The common law courts began and flourished as faithful servants of a monarchical regime of conquest bent upon centralizing political authority. In the seventeenth century they transferred their allegiance from king to parliament without ever abandoning the theory of unified sovereignty of which the Parliament had become the principal beneficiary. In the seventeenth and eighteenth centuries the courts did succeed in building a substantial autonomy based on the institutional incapacities of Parliament and the marvelously impenetrable lump of lore-ridden common law, common lawyers, and common law courts. By the nineteenth century that lump was being broken up by a more effective Parliament. Only laissez-faire concepts of the proper scope of legislation obscured the reality that, once Parliament became the dominant lawmaker, the judges would return to a faithful subordination. The twentieth-century English courts have created a body of administrative law that almost totally subordinates the judges to the discipline of an administrative state.

All of this is not to deny that English courts have a considerable degree of judicial independence in the sense of freedom from day-to-day interference by the government in particular cases, although even here the government has not hesitated to reverse particular court decisions by legislation, sometimes retroactive legislation. Still less is it to deny that English courts are courts. Quite the contrary, it is to assert that the notion of judicial independence is so ambiguous and misleading that it cannot serve as a touchstone of "courtness."

As a general principle it would appear wrong to seize upon the judicial institutions of any one nation, write them large, and then insist that the institutions of other nations are truly judicial only to the extent that they correspond to the model thus derived. As a matter of particular historical analysis it is even more foolish to erect judicial independence as the *sine qua non* of courtness on the basis of a national experience which is actually a curiously subtle blend of judicial dependence and independence, and a blend in which dependence is ultimately the dominant motif.

# 3 THE CIVIL LAW SYSTEM AND PREEXISTING LEGAL RULES

The experience of English courts is usually offered to illustrate the element of judicial independence in the conventional prototype of courts. We have now seen that the English experience is ambiguous even on the question of judicial independence. It would be even more difficult to argue that English legal history supports the conventional element of judicial decision according to preexisting legal rule. For a legal system that openly proclaims that its law is made case by case by the judges themselves can hardly typify decision by preexisting rule. It has usually appeared that the Continental legal system, although not so clear-cut in terms of judicial independence, better satisfied the standard of preexisting rules. As opposed to the case law of England, the Continent enjoyed code law. The code is a complete system of legal rules. The task of the European judge is simply to select the appropriate rule from among those preexisting in the code and apply it to the case at bar.

Such a characterization of civil or Roman law systems, as the legal systems of such countries as France, Italy, and Germany are called,[1] is fundamentally incorrect. Indeed, contemporary authorities clearly proclaim the misleading nature of the contrast between Anglo-American law as case law and civil law as code law.[2] But what has not been so widely noticed is that, if even Continental judges do not consistently decide according to preexisting legal rules, then that element of the prototype of courts is not clearly applicable to either of the two major courts systems from which it was derived. For this reason I shall focus on the extent to which judges in civil law systems do decide according to preexisting rules given to them by their legal code.

A code law judge would be most completely bound by preexisting rules if his code were complete, consistent, specific, produced by a single authoritative legislator, and capable of rapid amendment by that legislator to meet changing circumstances accurately. No code can fully meet these conditions.

## The Roman Experience

The modern civil law systems of Western Europe are derived from Roman legal experience, as are those of Latin America, the former French colonies of sub-Saharan Africa, Japan, and Eastern Europe. Thus it is customary to begin any analysis of civil law systems with a description of Roman law.[3]

For our purposes relatively little need be said about the law of republican or early imperial Rome. In chapter 1 we looked at the formulary procedure of early Rome as a device for maintaining legitimacy through consent. From another perspective that procedure can be seen as producing a highly particularized law that is the very opposite of the general rules of broad applicability usually ascribed to Roman law systems. In fact until the Imperial period Roman law was highly particularized. It will be recalled that when two Romans sought triadic resolution of a dispute, they went to a third person who formulated a legal rule that both could agree was applicable to their dispute and should guide the iudex. The formulas of early Roman law were thus highly particular rules shaped to specific disputes that had occurred before the rule was invented. In a sense this was an ideal situation. For the iudex, the rule was not only preexisting but prefitted to the case before him. He could bind himself entirely by the preexisting legal rule without being confronted by the need to apply a general rule to a specific case. It is this need that leads most judges into case-by-case judicial lawmaking. In this sense the iudex may be the only judge we run across who really meets the conventional prototype.

In chapter 2 we have seen that the writs, which began as individualized royal responses to particular legal problems, evolved into more or less standard or generalized legal rules and procedures. Similarly in Rome, as the government officials called praetors were approached more and more often for formulas, they standardized their offerings. In both republican and imperial Rome statutes were occasionally enacted, but they certainly did not constitute a systematic and comprehensive body of law. The closest that the early Romans came to such a body of law was the Praetorian Edict. The edict, however, was only a long list of now standardized formulas that the praetor announced in advance he would make available to those coming to him for a legal rule. Eventually, on succeeding to office, each new praetor announced that he would continue the edict of his predecessor. So the edict became, in a sense, a permanent body of law. The Emperor Hadrian decreed that thenceforth each praetor must accept the edict of his predecessor and so it became known as the Perpetual Edict. Yet this law clearly retained its origins as a series of piecemeal responses to particular situations. Like the writ system, it was a long catalogue of narrowly drawn devices, each good for one specific type of conflict, rather than a systematically organized set of general legal rules.

Besides the praetors, *jurisconsults* were the other major source of the formulas used to guide the iudex. The jurisconsults were legal scholars who were consulted either directly by the litigants or by the praetors when they needed assistance in meeting a request for a formula. As we shall see in the course of this chapter and chapter 4, scholarly writing has played a far more decisive role in Roman and Islamic than in common law. The early Roman scholarship, however, took the form of *responsa,* that is, specific legal advice on the specific legal problem brought to the jurisconsult by the prospective parties. The jurisconsult did not write general legal treatises. The "books" of great early jurisconsults grew out of their *responsa.* Even the most ambitious of them are systematically grouped collections of rules, maxims, and formulas rather than general theoretical works. Thus, like the edict, each Roman work of legal scholarship consisted of very long series of relatively brief legal statements, each of which only specified what particular legal rule or procedure seemed best suited to a particular problem. For instance, the jurisconsults did not offer a general discussion of the nature of contract, but dozens of different rules each designed to be used to deal with with one kind of mutual agreement. Even a single jurisconsult might offer one rule for settling a case in which one man had agreed to sell horses to another and a different rule for a situation in which two men had agreed to become partners in a business.

In its origins then, Roman law is highly practical and particular rather than general, systematic, or theoretical. As the empire grew, law accumulated, particularly in the form of a mass of scholarly commentary by the now official jurisconsults and an ever growing list of imperial legal pronouncements which had the force of law.

### THE CODE OF JUSTINIAN

Eventually the Roman Empire split into two parts, with the eastern half governed from Constantinople. It was this empire, far removed in time, place, and culture from its Roman origins, that codified the Roman law. The Emperor Justinian gave a team of scholars five years to systematize the received legal materials. They produced the Code of Justinian or *corpus juris civilis.* It consisted of three parts. The Codex was what we would normally call a code, that is, a collection of the imperial statutes in force created by pruning, harmonizing, and rearranging the accumulated mass of old imperial decrees. The Digest was an anthology of excerpts from the writings of the jurisconsults. The Institutes was a brief textbook designed to introduce students to the law. Later a new part, the Novella, was added. It consisted of new statutes enacted by Justinian, some of them clarifying matters left unclear in the main body of the code.

One major purpose of the code was to reduce to manageable proportions what had become an overwhelming mass of legal materials. All the old statutory provisions not incorporated in the new Codex were declared no longer in force. The Digest established a pecking order among the hundreds of works of legal commentary, declaring a handful of jurisconsults to be most authoritative and the rest less so. Citation of any commentary materials except those appearing in the Digest itself is forbidden. In the eyes of its compilers, the Digest represented a purging of the whole body of scholarly legal writing, leaving only that which was correct and consistent and consigning the rest to oblivion. In a famous provision, the code commands that no further texts or commentaries on law are to be produced. The Institute and the Digest are not only the law but the only teaching about the law that are to be permitted.

The basic arrangement of the code was heavily influenced by that of the Praetorian Edict. The Digest materials were largely devoted to commentary on the edict. The Institutes reflected the traditional categories of Roman law: of persons, of things, and of obligations. Particularly in the Codex and Novella, the code goes far beyond matters of private law and incorporates many late imperial developments in government and public affairs. On the whole, however, it reflects the conservative biases of its compilers who sought to reestablish the legal virtues of classical times. The *corpus juris civilis* of Justinian is not a new or revolutionary code designed to sweep away the old law. Rather, it is an attempt to render a long and complex legal tradition simpler and more concrete so that it may be preserved and made to flourish in a somewhat alien environment.

Particularly important were the incorporation of the Institutes and the Digest directly into the code itself. For now a legal textbook and the scholarly commentary on law were an official part of the law itself. Indeed, both in bulk and in relevance to the mass of ordinary legal transactions, they were the main body of the law. Thus the academic or scholarly side of law has always played a central part in Roman law in contrast to its peripheral role in common law countries. (In England, as we have seen, common law was not taught in the universities. Until the twentieth century English lawyers were forbidden to cite the works of living authors and only four works of legal commentary were held to have authority comparable to case law.)

At the time Justinian's code was compiled, it was still part of a living legal tradition and was still understood as essentially an approved catalogue of specific solutions to specific problems. Lawyers probably still took it for granted that even generally worded rules or maxims in the Digest were in fact *responsa* and referred only to the particular type of case which had first elicited that *responsa*. By the time of Justinian, however, the formulary procedure itself had long since disappeared. New formulas, tailored to the needs of particular litigants, had not been produced for centuries. Thus, no matter what their ancient origins, the materials from which the code was made had long since become relatively fixed and were imposed on litigants rather than chosen by them. While the code consisted of many highly particular rules and maxims rather than a few very general ones, it represented a stage of legal development in which law had long since been substituted for consent.

The Western Empire had disappeared in the fifth century. The Eastern portion lingered until 1453. While remnants of Roman law remained in many places, the Code of Justinian was largely forgotten. In Western Europe, local and regional customary law was the basic law known to the medieval laity, although the Catholic Church had preserved much of Roman law in its own canon law.

### The Revival of Roman Law

The Renaissance was a rediscovery of ancient works to serve as models for new creative efforts. Like literature and art, law enjoyed such a rebirth in the city-states of medieval Italy. Late in the eleventh century, a complete manuscript of the Digest was found in Pisa. From that period on, Roman law was one of the principal subjects taught in the new Italian universities, particularly at Bologna, where at times as many as ten thousand law students from all over Europe were gathered.

No very satisfactory explanation for the enormous immediate appeal and rapid spread of the revived Roman law has been offered. It is clear, however, that the vehicle for the revival was the growing body of law teachers and practitioners, not the formal enactment of portions of Justinian's code into law. Medieval and Renaissance monarchs, princes, and emperors did a lot more legislating than they are usually given credit for, but they did not often simply pick up provisions of the *corpus juris* and make them into new statutes for their own jurisdictions. Instead the lawyers and judges of the regular courts introduced what they had learned in law school, at first in the guise of helping to interpret local statutory and customary law. While substantial elements of local law remained in Western Europe at least up to the time of the French Revolution, the revived Roman law became the dominant law of the forum, that is, it provided the vocabulary and conceptual apparatus used in their daily work by lawyers and judges.

The clearest illustration of the way in which Roman law returned to Europe is provided by its "reception" in Germany.[4] The bulk of Germany lying east of the Rhine had never been incorporated into the Roman Empire and had always lived under Germanic customary law. Italian, French, and even Spanish lawyers might purport to be rediscovering their "own" old imperial law and returning it to its rightful place, but German lawyers could not.

Even German lawyers, however, were aided by the belief that much of the old Roman law was *ius gentium,* a body of universal legal principles applicable to all people. The early Romans, like most primitive people, viewed law as essentially tribal. The *ius civili,* administered by the *praetor urbanus,* was the law for members of the Roman tribe. A separate official, the *praetor peregrinis,* was assigned to supervise foreigners living in Rome. Faced with foreigners from many different tribes, and so unable to use any single tribe's law, the *praetor peregrinis* supposedly built up a special law of his own. It was to be equally applicable to all foreigners because it purported to be based on legal principles common to all the tribes rather than the particular rules of any one. In reality the *ius gentium* was very much an extension of Roman law to meet new circumstances rather than a registration of legal practices common to a large number of tribes. Nevertheless, the claim to universality inherent in the *ius gentium* tradition, together with the more general claims to universality of Roman civilization, the Latin language and the Roman Catholic Church, enabled German lawyers to see themselves as acting quite naturally in injecting Roman law into German courts. Indeed, the cultural dominance of Roman, Catholic, and imperial ideas was so great that the Roman law was considered the *ratio scripta,* that is, true reason embodied in writing.

The German reception of Roman law is particularly striking for two reasons. First of all, it was native German legal ideas, not Roman, that dominated all of medieval Europe from Scandinavia to Spain. If any body of law had a claim to actual universality at the practical level, it was the German law that swept over Europe as the Germanic tribes themselves swept over the former territories of the Western Roman Empire. Second, during the period of the reception, Germany was not a single nation. It was broken into several hundred independent, quasi-independent, and partially independent political units with an incredibly complex pattern of political interrelations. Only the use of a common language allows us to identify a Germany in the welter of city-states, principalities, fiefdoms, imperial domains, bishoprics, and monarchies. In England we have seen that a common law arose because a central political authority existed. In Germany, Roman law became, and indeed was called, the common law even in the absence of political unity.

The vehicle for the German reception of Roman law was not the government but law teachers and practitioners. German princes did not enact Justinian's code into law in place of the existing German law. Instead Roman law was taught in the schools as a form of high culture. The study of the revived Roman law in the Italian universities had produced several centuries of scholarly writers whom we now refer to as the Glossators and Post Glossators. Their writings took the form of glosses or comments on provisions of the code, mostly on sections of the Digest which, it will be remembered, was itself an anthology of commentary. The Glossators used the scholastic method of careful and detailed commentary on a text, pointing out contradictions in its wording, logically working out the implications of its words, and clarifying and explaining its meaning. From a few words of text they produced an elaborately articulated set of general principles and logically derived solutions to hypothetical problems. The Post Glossators generally produced further commentaries on the commentaries of the Glossators. While the Post Glossators directed more of their attention than had the Glossators to the actual application of Roman law to real contemporary situations, the overall product of the Roman law renaissance was not a code or body of laws but a body of highly complex academic literature. The German reception was not the reception of a set of legal rules but the academic study of a number of authoritative textbooks about law and the addition of new scholarly writings by the German teachers of those texts.

As men who had been students of these teachers came to staff the courts, administrative agencies, and legal profession, Roman procedures and concepts infiltrated, reinterpreted, supplemented, and transformed the older German law rather than openly and abruptly replacing it. In Germany, as in Northern France and Spain, Germanic statutes and customary law in theory remained the fundamental law and in practice often resulted in important local deviations from the substance of Roman law rules. For instance, in many parts of Germany a widow would inherit a great deal more of her husband's estate than she would have under strict Roman law, which greatly favored male over female heirs. Because the lawyers and judges were thinking about law in Roman ways, however, very often what began as a German rule somehow or other turned out to have a Roman result. The Germans even revived the *responsa*. The judges would refer difficult legal questions to noted law professors. Particularly in the growing realm of commercial relationships, where local customs, which were largely agricultural, had little to say, Roman rules, procedures, and instruments were widely introduced.

The reception of the Roman law in Germany was essentially a cultural and academic rather than a legislative movement. Its vehicle was the training of lawyers rather than the passage of statutes or codes. The Holy Roman emperors and the various German territorial princes did foster the growth of legally trained bureaucracies and acted as patrons of the cultural movement. Both the specific doctrines of the Roman law and the supplanting of multiple local customs by a uniform jurisprudence favored the political centralization that all these rulers were attempting. Occasionally one or another of these rulers would enact a particular Roman rule into statutory law or decree that Roman rules were to be used where local custom was silent. Neither the emperor nor the princes, however, had sufficient political power to enact and enforce a code such as Justinian's.

On the eve of the French Revolution the Roman law in Europe was not a code enacted by a sovereign legislator and applied by a judge. Instead, the Roman law consisted of a body of academic commentary, largely on the Digest, which was itself an anthology of academic writing, and on the Institutes, which was itself a textbook. That body of academic writing was imposed on the judges not by statute but by education. A judicial decision was not the result of applying a statutory rule but of finding a solution to a particular case compatible with the views of a learned legal community of which the judge was a member.

## The Modern European Codes

Modern European Roman law is usually traced to the Napoleonic Code.[5] It is because of Justinian's and Napoleon's codes that we normally think of Roman law as code law, that is, a systematic, set of statutory rules that is the sole and complete law of the nation or other territorial unit. We have now seen that Justinian's code, particularly as it was applied to early modern Europe, was essentially a body of academic text and commentary rather than a set of statutory rules claiming to be the complete and exclusive law. It is also somewhat misleading to think of the Code Napoléon as a complete and exclusive body of statutory law.

In many ways it is the negative aspects of the Code Napoléon that are the most important. The French Revolution did, at least temporarily, sweep away the French monarchy. It was less significant for this reason, however, than because it swept away the legal status and privileges of the French aristocracy. Those privileges were entrenched in and protected by the customary, not the Roman, law, and the code displaced much of the customary law. As the revolution was spread over Europe by Napoleon's troops, aristocratic legal privileges were also reduced or destroyed in other nations. The initial reputation of the code rested far more heavily on its displacement of customary law than on its positive virtues.

The French Civil Code was enacted in 1804 and followed by four more codes between 1804 and 1811 which dealt with procedure, criminal law, and commercial law. The Commercial Code was largely a reproduction of royal commercial and maritime ordinances passed in the 1670s and 1680s and was generally felt to be inadequate. Subsequently it was supplemented by many commercial and maritime statutes. Thus what is normally referred to as the Code Napoléon was never a complete body of law. The Great Civil Code omitted a major segment of private law, that dealing with commerce. New statutes soon supplemented the code, not only in commercial law but other areas as well, so that it ceased to be the sole body of law.

Most important, the language of many provisions of the code was brief, often almost epigrammatic. Much of it consists of verbal symbols that did not contain the law but instead triggered certain lines of thought in the minds of those trained in the Roman law. In other words the code frequently presupposes rather than states the law and depends on the academic training of the lawyer to fill in the detailed substance behind the key word or phrase that it proclaims. Even leaving aside for the moment the growth of case law, the French code is not a complete, systematic statement of all of the law. It could not have been administered except in the context of a preexisting Roman law legal culture.

Indeed, the French code illustrates the ambiguity of the term "rule" that was discussed briefly in chapter 1. English and American lawyers tend to distinguish between "principles" and "rules." They use "principle" to refer to a very broad, fundamental legal statement like "no contract without consideration" (that is, a contract does not exist in a legal sense unless each person has agreed to give something of value in exchange for what he receives from the other.) They use "rule" to refer to a much more precise statement, such as the old rule that "a contract under seal implies consideration" (That is, courts will assume that something of value was really exchanged if there is a written contract that has been formally signed by both parties.) Such rules fill in the specific meaning of the principle. Thus, there are many rules that specify just what kinds of offers of what kinds of things do or do not constitute "consideration."

Most American and English lawyers would say that the French code offers many principles and few rules. French lawyers see the code as providing rules, but very general ones that must be explicated by legal learning. Thus, the French lawyer may insist that French judges do apply preexisting legal rules enacted by the code while the English or American lawyer might say that French judges created legal rules in accordance with the principles stated in the code. Both would agree, however, that the code was not and could not be the whole body of legal rules.

Belgium, the Netherlands, Switzerland, and, after some ups and downs, many of the Italian and German states introduced versions of the French code during the nineteenth century. After German unification in 1870, a great controversy arose about the creation of a single, unified Civil Code. The upshot was the great German Civil Code of 1900, which incorporated some specifically German legal traditions but was essentially Roman. The status of the received Roman law as the common law of Germany was of course crucial to the enactment of this code.

The German Civil Code is far more detailed, technical, and complete than the French code, but such a statement is somewhat misleading.[6] We have seen that much of the Code of Justinian consisted of a textbook and an anthology of academic writing. We have also seen that the Roman law was received into Germany essentially in the form of academic writing by the Pandectists, that is, German law teachers, who were themselves commenting on the academic writing of the Glossators and Post Glossators. The struggle over codification was largely waged between distinguished academics, and the final version of the code was largely the work of academics.

The German Civil Code is not so much a complete and detailed set of laws as an incredibly elaborate textbook about law. And subsequently it has been surrounded by a number of other leading textbooks. Thus the German lawyer or judge seeking to resolve a legal problem does not usually expect to find a specific, concrete, legal rule directly applying to the situation at hand. Instead, he consults the texts from which he learned law, confident that he will find the general concepts, principles, and methodologies that will allow him to work out the correct solution to any legal problem that might arise. It is in this sense that the code is complete. In many areas of human affairs, however, it offers even fewer specific rules than does the French code, and very often the specific rules it offers are shaped to nineteenth-century, not twentieth-century, life. Like the French code, the German code has been supplemented by legislation that usually takes the form of special statutes that stand alongside the code rather than being directly incorporated into it.

### Code Law and Case Law

Because a rough contrast is often drawn between common law as case law and civil law as code law, the similarity of common and civil law jurisdictions is often overlooked. It is true that the style of legal argumentation is somewhat different on the Continent than in Great Britain and the United States. Anglo-American judges often construct their opinions as mosaics of excerpts from, citations of, and comments about earlier judicial decisions. Even when the case is one of statutory interpretation, the wording of the statute may be buried in a footnote. In many instances, of course, the judge will openly proclaim that the source of the basic legal rule being applied is a previous decision rather than a statutory provision.

A Continental judge, however, will invariably cast the bulk of his opinion in the form of a direct commentary and interpretation of the relevant code provisions, but this style is somewhat misleading.[7] Almost invariably when a Continental judge purports to be drawing a series of definitions, doctrines, and conclusions from the code by logical exegesis, in reality he is acknowledging the body of legal doctrines built up around the bare words of the code by previous cases. While he does not necessarily cite the cases, other judges and lawyers know that he is not inventing new doctrines from scratch with just the bare words of the code to aid him. From the way he announces and applies the doctrines, they will be able to tell just which leading cases from the past he is following.

Moreover, although the main discussion will take the form of direct commentary on a code provision, some Continental decisions will contain explicit discussions of the previous cases usually designed to show that the present decision is in line with past ones. These discussions read very much like those by common law judges. To be sure, Continental judges are careful to phrase their commentary as if previous decisions are simply more or less persuasive discussions of what the code provisions really mean rather than independent acts of lawmaking. English judges, however, are usually careful to do something very similar. Typically they treat a precedent as evidence or example of an underlying common law rule not as a single piece of judicial legislation. Only American judges rather routinely treat a particular precedent as having actually created the law. Since World War II, however, there has been a growing tendency among German judges to adopt a quasi-American style, and so today, in many areas of German law, leading precedents are openly acknowledged to provide the working legal rules.

The extent to which Continental jurists rely upon case law is evidenced by the publication of the opinions of the leading appellate tribunals. Almost invariably these are annotated reports. With that deference to academic authority which, as we have seen, so often characterizes civil law, these annotations, prepared by well-known legal scholars, are often as influential as the opinions themselves in building up legal doctrine. Few European law students would be so foolish as to believe that they could understand the law exclusively by direct reference to the code without reading passages of authoritative texts, the leading decisions, and the annotations of decisions that surround nearly every clause of the code.

Indeed there are many areas of French and German law where the governing legal rules and doctrines take hundreds of words to express while the basic code provision consists of only a dozen words or so. All the rest has been created by judicial and academic commentary. In some of these areas, notably French administrative law, the body of judicially announced doctrine is so large and the wording of the code so meager that counsel and judges quite openly argue in a case law style fully comparable with that employed in the United States.[8]

### An Example of French Case Law

A brief examination of the French treatment of injury will illustrate the central role and particular style of French case law.[9] In Anglo-American legal systems this area of law is called tort. In Roman law countries, it is called noncontractual obligation because when one person injures another, he comes under an obligation to compensate the injured party. This obligation is not created by an agreement between the two parties, as a contractual obligation is, but by the act of injury which is called a delict.

ARTICLES 1382 AND 1383: LIABILITY FOR FAULT

The Civil Code has five brief articles on delict. They illustrate the point made earlier that the French code often announces general legal principles rather than stating specific legal rules. Articles 1382 and 1383 say that a person is responsible for the damage done by his acts when he was at fault, negligent, or imprudent. Together they total forty-five words and constitute the entire basic code law on delict. For several hundred years both Anglo-American courts and French courts operated their tort-delict law on this same basic principle of liability for fault or negligence. Yet the principle alone is too broad and general actually to be the entire law. English and American judges developed dozens of more specific tort rules in the course of hundreds of thousands of words of case decisions. For example, they created the contributory negligence rule. If acts of the injured party contributed in any degree to the injury, he could not collect damages even though the other party was at fault. They created the fellow servant rule. If the negligence of one employee injured another employee, the injured person could only sue his fellow employee and not their employer unless he could show that the employer too had been negligent. With a few notable exceptions, all these rules functioned under the overarching principle that without fault there was no responsibility. Most of the actual decisions about who had to compensate whom, however, were determined by these more specific rules rather than the principle standing alone.

No such rules were given in the French code. How did the French judges do without them? They didn't. They too invented them. Potential rules were proposed, elaborated, and tested and then were accepted, rejected, and/or modified, in a mixture of academic writing, arguments before courts, and court decisions. As we shall see in a moment, the relative weight of various contributors, and the form and the style of case law creation and analysis, are somewhat different in France than in the English-speaking world. Nevertheless, the rules of French delictual law, like those of Anglo-American tort law, are to be found in the old cases and are changed by the new cases. The French lawyer who memorizes the forty-five words of 1382 and 1383 has just begun his training in the law of delict.

FRENCH TEXTS AND TREATISES

This becomes clear from a glance at the actual textbooks used in training French lawyers. Law students use elementary texts in noncontractual obligation in preparing for their equivalent of American bar examinations. Such texts contain several hundred pages of discussion of articles 1382 and 1383 and of articles 1384, 1385, and 1386, which we shall discuss shortly. Although there are occasional references to cases, the textual discussion is largely presented as if it were a logical elaboration of the code provisions themselves. When rules that actually had their origins in case law are introduced and discussed, the author will typically present them as logical derivations form code language, and will write in very general terms about them. Often what is in reality a conclusion drawn from the interaction of the detailed holdings in a dozen leading cases will be presented by the author as an abstract proposition. He may offer no description of or even reference to the specific cases or only an airy general reference to the "jurisprudence," a term which the French use for the whole body of case law.

When the student has passed his examinations, however, he will practice delictual law with the assistance not of his elementary textbook but of a treatise on noncontractual obligation, often one written by the same distinguished professor who wrote his text. The treatise presents the materials at the level of specificity needed for the actual practice of law. Such treatises are cast in the form of general explications of the code provisions. They too often disguise as general statements of principle what are in fact summaries of the outcomes of many cases. But they also contain hundreds of paragraphs of description and analysis of specific cases. The French law student begins with the impression that the law is the code and various logical extrapolations from its words. The French lawyer ends up seeking to master extensive and complex bodies of case law both directly from the case reports and from the case analysis of the treatises.[10]

### ARTICLE 1384 AND LIABILITY WITHOUT FAULT

So far we have dealt only with 1382 and 1383, which present the basic principle of liability for wrongful or negligent acts. Articles 1384, 1385, and 1386 create exceptions to this principle. It is in the tension between 1382–83, on the one hand, and 1384, on the other, that French courts have made their most innovative bodies of case law.

While there is much flag waving about the revolutionary break of the Code Napoléon from the law of prerevolutionary France, in fact the code relied heavily on French legal traditions. Thus, 1382 and 1383 are revolutionary, at least in the sense of introducing a single, simple, sweeping rule. But 1384–86 introduce a series, of exceptions to the principle which are in reality a compendium of minor prerevolutionary legal rules that followed no particular principle. Thus, 1386 provides that the owner of a building is responsible for injuries caused by its collapse, and 1385 provides for the liability of the owners of animals for the damage they do. Both of these articles obviously derive from older rules of special liability for the owners of buildings and animals. Both deviate from 1382–83 because owners of these particular things are liable even if they have not acted wrongfully or negligently.

The crucial deviation, however, is 1384. It sets up a number of categories of persons who are liable, not only for their own wrongful or negligent acts, but for the acts of others. Parents are declared responsible for the acts of their children, employers for those of their employees, and teachers and artisans for their students and apprentices. Article 1384 also declares that persons are responsible not only for the acts of persons for whom they are responsible but for damages caused by "things under their guard."

The phrase "things under guard" is hardly self-explanatory. One traditional theory was that it referred only to the animals and buildings that are the subject of 1385 and 1386. To this day French courts casually tend to equate the phrase with "inherently dangerous objects," although the highest French courts have carefully avoided specifically limiting the phrase in this way. The phrase obviously has enormous potential for judicial choice, for it would allow the judges to throw nearly any accident caused by both a person and a thing under either 1382 or 1384.

FACT-FINDING FRENCH STYLE

What difference does it make, however, whether a tort case comes under 1382 or 1384? In fact, it makes an enormous difference, but to understand why, we must look briefly at the way French courts handle questions of fact. Their approach to fact-finding is quite different from that of Anglo-American courts. Probably because fact-finding traditionally was put in the hands of a secular jury, Anglo-American courts habitually decide questions of fact one way to the other on the basis of the weight of the evidence. French fact-finding traditions arose in the context of professional judges and religious courts. There was great emphasis on the moral obligation of the judge to be absolutely certain he had discovered the true facts. For instance, medieval English criminal courts did not hesitate to convict a person who continued to profess his innocence if the jury believed him to be guilty. At the same period in France, criminal courts required a confession before they would convict and in theory at least required that even a confession be corroborated by other evidence.[11] Modern French courts will very, very frequently simply conclude that there is not enough evidence to reach a factual conclusion. Often they refuse to make an authoritative finding of facts in situations in which an English or American court would hold that, for purposes of deciding the case, whatever version of the facts is most probably true will be taken as true. For instance, a well-known French case involved an unoccupied truck parked by the side of the road that was struck by a passing car, causing damage to the car.[12] Under French law, the operator of the truck was negligent if its parking lights were not on. There was firm evidence that the truck's lights were on forty minutes before the accident. There was no evidence that the driver had subsequently returned to the truck or that its lights had ever gone off. The French court held that, in the absence of any direct evidence of whether the lights were on or off at the moment of the accident, it could not reach any conclusion about whether the operator was or was not in fact negligent. An English or American court would almost certainly have concluded that the weight of the evidence required a factual conclusion that the driver was not negligent.

Faced with the proclivity of French courts to avoid conclusive findings of fact, plaintiffs who bring suit under 1382 are at a serious disadvantage. Unless they can get the court to make a finding of willful fault or negligence, they cannot win, and the court will frequently say simply that it cannot tell whether there was or was not fault or negligence. Even apart from these proclivities of French courts, the requirement that a plaintiff prove not only that the defendant's act caused the injury but also that he acted willfully or negligently is an onerous one that even Anglo-American plaintiffs often fail to meet.

### ARTICLE 1384 AND THE PRESUMPTION OF RESPONSIBILITY

Unlike 1382, article 1384 does not require that the plaintiff prove that the defendant was at fault, because it imposes liability without fault. French courts very early established the rule that 1384 entailed a presumption of responsibility, a presumption that could not be overcome even if the defendant could prove that he had not been at fault.[13] Thus, if a plaintiff could manage to bring the defendant under 1384 rather than 1382, he could win even if the court found itself unable to establish the facts conclusively. Indeed, the plaintiff could win under 1384 even if the defendant could prove that he had done nothing wrong. In a legal tradition that makes it very hard for plaintiff to establish the facts necessary to win, a legal presumption of those facts is of incredible value.

Nothing was clearer in the first fifty years after the code was written than that 1382 established the basic standard and 1384 some minor and narrowly limited exceptions to the great revolutionary principle of liability only for fault. In modern France as in the rest the industrialized world, however, two types of accidents have received central attention, industrial accidents and auto accidents. In the 1880s, the argument began to be heard in France, as elsewhere, that industrial injuries were an inevitable cost of manufacturing which, like all other costs, should be initially borne by the entrepreneur and then passed on to the consumer in the price of the product. When men are mixed with machinery for a profit, shouldn't the reaper of the profit pay for the damages caused by the inevitable collisions of steel with flesh? Why should the worker have to prove that his employer was negligent in order to get compensation for his injury? Some French judges tried to reinterpret the code to meet the industrial problem. Obviously, one solution would be to get industrial cases out of 1382. In one well-known case, a French court employing truly common law imagination, held that when a worker had been injured because a tree branch collapsed, the owner of the tree was liable under 1386. It argued that a rotting tree was like a ruined building so that its collapse was equivalent to the collapse of a building of the kind for which 1386 created liability.[14]

Clearly, however, it was not "buildings" but "things under guard" that opened the most promising avenue of escape from 1382. French courts began to hold that factory machinery constituted "things under guard" of the factory owner so that his responsiblity for injuries caused by the machines would be presumed under 1384. This approach was particularly important because, faced with the mysteries of new technology, French judges were often saying that no one could tell what in fact made boilers blow up and machines break down and then refusing to find the owners at fault.

This attempt to shift accident cases from 1382 to 1384 was muted by the passage of the Workman's Compensation Law of 1898, which replaced lawsuits under the Civil Code with a new procedure for workers seeking compensation for their on-the-job injuries.

VEHICLE ACCIDENTS

Auto accidents soon replaced industrial injuries as a major focus of the law of delict. The auto accident provides a perfect instance for judicial lawmaking. It falls precisely halfway between 1382 and 1384. When two cars collide, is the resultant damage caused by the drivers or the vehicles? A driver is clearly not "a thing under guard." If the driver causes the accident, then it is governed by 1382. Only if it can be said that the car caused the accident, can 1384 be brought into play with its almost unrebuttable presumption in favor of the plaintiff. And this presumption is particularly important in vehicle collisions, for in such accidents the facts are typically such that a French court is likely to say that it cannot find who was in fact at fault.

Initially the French courts could hardly find that the car, not the driver, was at fault in the typical collision situation. Such a finding too obviously offends common sense. The building up of precedent is as good a device for defeating common sense in France as it is in England or the United States. The French courts eased their way in to 1384 in cases that involved a mechanical defect in the vehicle and those which involved a parked vehicle from which the driver was absent. Having built a series of precedents in which the owners of vehicles were held liable under 1384, the Cour de Cassation was prepared to assert the absurd in the famous Jand'heur case of 1930.[15] It held that even in collisions of vehicles being driven, the driver and car fell under the "things under guard" provision of 1384. Indeed, it was argued to the court that to hold otherwise would contradict a clear and unbroken line of previous decisions holding that vehicular accidents fell under 1384.

Where courts build precedent to defeat common sense, there are usually good policy reasons. Obviously the French courts did not believe that car collisions were caused by the cars, not the drivers. They had come to believe, however, that trying to determine which driver was at fault as required by 1382 was unprofitable. They felt that the whole process of assigning compensation in auto accidents would benefit from concentrating on the extent of injury rather than the degree of fault of each driver. (American courts are coming to the same conclusion some fifty years later.) Thus, auto accidents had to be moved from 1382 to 1384, where responsibility was presumed and the issue of fault did not arise. "Things under guard" was the only statutory language available in 1384. A little absurdity about whether cars or drivers caused accidents was a small price to pay for the advantages of using that language in order to get the cases under 1384.

The Jand'heur case also involved a procedure peculiar to French law that highlights the role of judicial lawmaking. The organization of French courts is discussed more fully later in this chapter. Here it is enough to say that a decision of one of the French regional courts of appeal may go up to one of the civil chambers of the highest court, the Cour de Cassation. If that chamber reverses the court of appeal, the case is sent back down to a different court of appeal than the one from which it originally came. The second court of appeal may follow the chamber of the Cour de Cassation or again render the same judgment as did the first court of appeal. In the latter instance the case will usually go back up, this time not to the civil chamber but to a special chamber in which sit judges from all parts of the Cour de Cassation. The decision of that chamber is final.[16]

In the Jand'heur case, the court of appeal of Besançon held that accidents involving vehicles being driven fell under 1382. The civil chamber of the Cour de Cassation held that they fell under 1384 and sent the case back down to the court of appeal of Lyon. The court of appeal of Lyon repeated that they fell under 1382. The Chambres Réunies of the Cour de Cassation then decided with finality that they fell under 1384. This is clearly an instance in which the lower courts were saying, "Look, in the past we have always decided these cases under 1382. Do you really want to change the law." And the high court responding, "Yes, we really want to change the law."

In this way the French legal system moved from a negligence to a liability without fault standard for auto accidents solely by judicial pronouncement and without any formal amendment of the code. Just by way of contrast it might be noted that England, a common law country, and such civil law countries as Italy, Switzerland, and Belgium established new standards of responsibility for auto accidents by statute rather than judicial decision. Germany established a somewhat loose negligence standard by statute which the German courts then turned into something very close to a presumption of fault standard by judicial decision.

### The Style of French Case Law: Code and Company

In order to illustrate the importance of judge-made case law in France, I have deliberately chosen one of the areas of French law in which the code is least detailed. Much of the code gives more specific guidance and thus leaves less room for judicial innovation than 1382–86. Nevertheless, to a greater or lesser degree French judges do make case law under most of the articles of the code.

The importance of judicial precedent in French law is often hidden from outside observers by some peculiarities in French legal materials. While the citation of cases is beginning to creep into French opinions, French opinion writing style has always favored extreme brevity.[17] The opinion of the trial court typically contains the most complete statement of the facts and the legal reasoning behind its decision. As the case moves upward, the opinions become more and more cryptic. The opinions of the highest courts typically are little more than final orders with hardly any real explanation or justification. They are written as if the final holding flowed so directly and logically from the code provision involved that no explanation is required.

Yet precedents lurk in the background. Once a high court opinion is viewed against that background, it will usually become quite clear exactly which precedents the present decision is following. The precedents in a quite literal sense surround the opinion. In France not only the plaintiff's and defendant's lawyers but a lawyer for the government make arguments to the court where the case is considered an important one. Extracts from their arguments, and most particularly that of the government's representative, are sometimes even printed in French case reports preceding the opinion of the court. Moreover, in the highest French courts, one of the judges is assigned to "report" the case to his colleagues who are about to decide it. His report will not only summarize the arguments of opposing counsel, but provide analysis of his own. It will also appear occasionally in the reports just before the opinion of the court. All of these preliminary materials are replete with detailed case analysis in a style remarkably similar to that in an American brief. Lines of precedent are laid out. Individual cases are analyzed and distinguished academic authorities are cited.

Any skilled French lawyer could cross check the actual opinion with the preliminary materials and get a pretty good idea of what cases the court was following. For customarily the court's opinion will adopt a number of the general propositions advanced by counsel, government attorney, or reporter, while dropping the case law arguments that they made in support of those propositions. The court opinion thus provides a kind of guide to which parts of the case law arguments it found persuasive.

The reports of most cases of any general significance accompany the court's opinion with an annotation. These annotations are prepared by distinguished legal scholars, some of them professors of law and others judges of the high courts. They provide an extensive elaboration of the court's cryptic opinion, exposing its basic reasoning, fitting it to past precedent, and criticizing it both in terms of legal reasoning and public policy. Those who write these annotations are frequently the authors of the very treatises that contain extended analyses of the case law. Thus the case law (jurisprudence) and academic writing on law (doctrine) become inextricably mixed. English and American lawyers are accustomed to arguing from both cases and academic writing, but they tend to distinguish sharply between the two. French lawyers also argue from both, but are not so concerned to distinguish them. Often the notation on a case establishes its meaning for the future more clearly than do the few words of the opinion.

Often in the United States we speak of a decision as being rendered by "the judge and company" to emphasize the extent that the judge may rely on the work of opposing counsel in formulating his final opinion. A bare reading of French high court opinions might lead one to believe that French judges are in solitary communion with the civil code. Read in their context, and that is how they literally are read by French lawyers and judges, the French judicial opinion becomes a key to the large body of case law reasoning that surrounds it and on which often it ultimately relies.

Thus the French experience is one of "code and company," the company being a substantial body of case law and academic commentary.

### The Italian Experience

The Italian system shows the influence of French and German experience as well as Italy's own long civil law history.[18] The code is more in the French than in the German style. The Code of 1942 is essentially a reformed version of that of 1865. The 1865 code was basically French but was adopted at the very time that the German legal science of the Pandectists was sweeping over the Italian universities. Even more than in Germany, it is the law professor who dominates Italian law. The code was quickly surrounded by an enormous body of highly abstract academic writing, the doctrine, as it is called, which is not officially part of the law. Yet the doctrine so dominates Italian legal education and discussion, and without it so much of the code would be cryptic and incomplete, that it actually constitutes a central source of legal rules. The Italian legal system officially denies the existence of *stare decisis*. In reality, however, hundreds of volumes of case reports are published, decisions are routinely cited in arguments and opinions, and few lower courts would be so foolish as to ignore leading opinions by the higher courts. Because of the dominance of academic approaches to law, however, Italian opinions take a rather peculiar form. In a legal community where the professor is of far higher status than the judge, judges strive to make their opinions look as much like academic writing as possible. The specific fact situation of the case at bar tends to be underplayed, and accounts of it are frequently edited out of the case reports. The opinion generally will also underplay the particular in favor of the general aspects of the case so as to produce a *massima,* that is a general legal proposition, as similar as possible to the maxims produced in scholarly books and articles. Typically it is this maxim that will be cited by later courts. The Italian judge does not look for a previous case with facts as nearly similar to the present one as he can find. Instead he looks for one with a legal maxim that seems applicable to the facts in the present case even though that maxim may have been derived from a very different kind of fact situation.

Most Italian legal authorities admit that the code must be interpreted. They argue that its language cannot be absolutely precise and self-explanatory and that gaps must inevitably appear which must be filled with interstitial legal rules. Moreover, the orthodox position is that the principal guide to interpretation is not the specific intent of the actual legislators who enacted the statutory provision. Instead it is the intent of the statutory provision itself, its "real" purpose and rationale and the essential norm lying behind it, that are the keys to its interpretation. It is not what the legislature thought it meant, but what the judge discerns the law really means that counts. In short, statutory interpretation is an occasion for judicial lawmaking in Italy as in other places.

In summary then, the Italian situation is one in which the code and statutes do not create a complete, fixed, and certain body of legal rules. Academic writing introduce an important element of doctrinal controversy and change. Academically and judicially created changes are incorporated into the statutory law by judicial interpretation.

### LEEWAYS OF JUDICIAL INTERPRETATION

The Italian Civil Code contains specific provisions for judicial interpretation when the language of the code does not clearly determine the case at bar or when the case does not fall directly under a single code rule. A famous provision of the Swiss Civil Code of 1912 enjoins the judge who encounters a gap in the law to create whatever new rule he would have enacted were he the legislature. The Italian code is far more guarded. Nevertheless, the doctrinal position that the intent of the law, not the actual intent of the legislators who passed it, is to guide judicial interpretation gives the professors and judges substantial leeway. The German and French codes contain no such provisions. There has been a long-standing debate in both countries, however, between those favoring very free and those favoring more limited judicial interpretation. Often that debate comes down to a choice between two verbal formulas. One specifies that where a gap in the code exists, the judge should imagine what the legislature would do. The other specifies that the judge should imagine what he would do if he were the legislature.[19] While there clearly is a difference between the degree to which these two formulas encourage independent judicial lawmaking, in practice they reflect substantial agreement that incremental judicial lawmaking is necessary and proper.

In both France and Germany an extreme doctrine of judicial lawmaking, often called free decision theory, enjoyed a considerable vogue in the early twentieth century. It was a reaction to the older and patently false orthodoxy that the judges could and did mechanically apply the code to the cases before them without exercising any discretion. The free decision theorists argued that because judicial lawmaking was an inevitable facet of code interpretation, the judges ought to do their lawmaking openly and self-consciously. Since they were engaged in lawmaking, they ought not to do so solely by analytical means that sought a purely verbal extrapolation of new rules from old. Like a good legislature, the judges ought to look at the social facts and shape new legal rules that embodied good social policy.[20]

Free decision theory was always controversial and fell into bad repute during the 1930s. The Nazi regime in Germany and particularly the Fascist regime in Italy used it as an academically respectable cover for their attempts to force judges to subvert or ignore statutory provisions that protected the individual rights of citizens. After World War II, however, an increasing amount of academic commentary argued that, when fundamentally democratic regimes existed, judges might safely be given more lawmaking discretion without fear for popular liberties.[21]

### Code, Case, and Scholarship

We began then with the picture of a clear, complete body of preexisting legal rules embodied in a scientifically organized code. We conclude, however, with quite a different picture. First, even at the statutory level, the codes are not complete. In France, Germany, and Italy very large numbers of piecemeal statutes coexist with the code and the legislatures pass many new ones every year. Recodifications to incorporate these new laws are many decades apart. Second, the need for judicial interpretation of the code involving some level of case-by-case lawmaking is recognized in all code law countries. Third, while *stare decisis* is not officially recognized, hundreds of volumes of case reports are published, and French, German, and Italian lawyers routinely put their arguments to courts by citing precedents just as common lawyers do.

Fourth, and probably most important, the role of legal scholarship historically has been far more important in code than in common law countries. The Pandectists essentially wrote the German Civil Code, the first part of which is, like Justinian's Institutes, an academic textbook of the law written into the law itself. In Italy, "the doctrine" created by the professors is the basis of legal education, the principal source of statutory interpretation, and the model for judicial opinions. In France the status of professors is not as high, and that of judges correspondingly higher. The French code was a legislative rather than academic creation. Nevertheless, French legal scholars are viewed as at least the equals of judges, and the French style of scholarly commentary freely mixes description, critical analysis, and policy prescription. France retains the general Romanist notion that the real law is the received scholarly tradition, and the code and judicial decisions are merely attempts to specify and particularize that tradition. Interpretation of the French code is a lively mixing of scholarly and judicial initiatives.

The role of scholars in civil law countries has always been emphasized in the literature. What has not been sufficiently noted is the extent to which the existence of that role undercuts the clear and simple picture of civil law judges deciding their cases according to a set of preexisting legal rules neatly and unambiguously set forth in the national codes. Even leaving aside the ambiguities and gaps in the codes and the inevitability of statutory interpretation, Continental judges live in a world of academic legal commentary which is influential and often decisive. Far from being a fixed body of preexisting legal rules, Continental legal commentary is a mass of abstract discussions, general principles, specific criticisms, and policy recommendations. Like legal commentary everywhere it often confuses the *is* with the *ought*. Like academic commentary everywhere it is divided into schools of thought that sometimes converge and sometimes conflict with one another. Courts, which must operate within this matrix and are staffed by judges and attorneys proud of their academic training and qualifications, necessarily reflect this state of affairs. The European judge prepares his decisions as an integral part of a living, growing, and changing body of academically and judicially created legal principles, rules, interpretations, and proposals. Like the common law judge, he employs legal rules that partially preexist and partially are brought into existence as his decisions are made.

### European Court Systems

The extent of judicial discretion in civil law systems cannot be finally assessed without a brief look at the institutional setting. Each of the judicial systems of the Western European nations has features peculiar to itself.[22] Nevertheless, a certain common pattern emerges. In most there are basically four levels of courts. At the lowest level are hundreds of local courts, presided over by a single judge and using simplified procedures. They have jurisdiction over minor cases. At the next higher level will be courts of first instance that serve as trial courts in most serious cases and hear appeals from the lowest-level courts. These courts are usually presided over by a panel of three judges, use formal procedures, and are to be found in every major political subdivision. In France for instance, there are 172 such courts, at least one for each department with the larger departments having more than one. At the third level are regional courts of appeal that hear appeals from the courts of first instance and sometimes also conduct trials in certain special or especially serious matters. Typically such a court is presided over by three to five or even seven judges. Finally, at the highest level will be a single supreme court or court of cassation which hears appeals that raise particularly serious issues of law and sits in large panels, usually seven or more judges.

#### CRIMINAL COURTS

As with the American states, European nations have never quite decided whether to operate merged or separate civil and criminal justice systems. Roman law countries do not have a tradition of juries and never use juries in civil cases. Most have, however, introduced some sort of jury in serious criminal cases or provided for the appointment of several laymen to sit alongside the professional judges. Each European nation also has a criminal code quite distinct from the civil code. As a result, criminal proceedings are necessarily quite different from civil ones. Some European nations have two separate and parallel sets of courts so that there is both a criminal and a civil court at each of the levels we described in the preceding paragraphs. In others the criminal courts are special divisions of a unified court system. In many, some courts or judges handle both civil and criminal matters, but others specialize in serious criminal matters only.

While we have spoken of "a" court at each level, each of these courts may consist of many judges who divide up into panels (chambers, senates) to hear particular cases. For instance, the French Cour de Cassation has over eighty judges in all, but any single decision of the court will be rendered by one panel usually consisting of seven members.

### TRIALS

Romanist trial procedures are far different from those in common law countries, for the jury has been central to common law. Trials in Anglo-American countries must be shaped to present all the evidence and argument in a case at a single time and place and largely orally, so the jury can hear the whole case, reach a verdict, and then return to their private lives. Roman law courts have basically been staffed by professional, long-serving, judicial bureaucracies.[23] Typically they employ judges of lower rank to gather and prepare the evidence in written form and present it to judges of higher rank. A case proceeds by the filing, refiling, amendment, revision, and supplementing of a written case file over a considerable period of time. The parties have many opportunities to enter new evidence and argument and to respond to written pleadings filed by the other side. What appears to be the "trial" is only the final public proceeding in which the court finally decides the case that has been developed by the attorneys and subordinate judges in a series of preliminary proceedings.

### APPEAL

Appeal is also somewhat different. The first appeal from a trial court can usually be on questions of both fact and law. New evidence can be introduced, and often a whole new trial proceeding can be had. The appeals court will usually render a complete and final judgment of its own which substitutes entirely for that initially reached by the trial court. In other words, appeal is usually by trial *de novo,* as it often is in England as well, but almost never is in the United States.

We noted earlier that above the third-level courts of appeal there is typically a highest-level supreme court or court of cassation. Appeals to this court are usually only on questions of law. The court is sometimes called a court of cassation because in some countries it does not make a final judgment. If it finds that the lower court has made an error of law, it quashes or invalidates the decision and sends the case back for retrial, usually in a different lower court from the one where the case was first tried. The new trial is then conducted in the light of the court of cassation's statement of the law applicable to the case. In some countries, should the second decision also be quashed, the court of cassation may then render its own final verdict.

SPECIALIZED COURTS

In addition to the regular chain of courts, or the double chain of criminal and civil courts, most European nations have developed a number of specialized courts. In Italy commercial and civil law have been merged, but in France and Germany they have not. In the latter two a separate series of commercial courts exists and the jurisdictional boundaries between commercial and civil courts are complex. Most European nations have special labor courts that are often more like boards of arbitration than regular courts and may be staffed by a mixture of business and labor representatives and professional judges. Social security, agricultural, rents, tax, juvenile, and other special courts may also exist.

JUDICIAL PERSONNEL

There is a relatively common pattern of judicial recruitment and personnel management although there are substantial variations in judicial independence and status from country to country.[24] In most European nations, after attending the university as a student of law, a young person makes an initial choice of a legal career in private practice, as a government lawyer, as a civil service executive, or as a judge. (Many students with law degrees do not choose any of these alternatives but enter business or politics. In Europe law is a general degree roughly equivalent to a program philosophy, history, political science, economics, and sociology in an American university.) Unlike judges in England and the United States, judges on the Continent are not recruited from among experienced practitioners. Instead, a young person enters directly into the judicial service at the lowest judicial rank and works his way up to higher and higher judgeships until his retirement. Given the Romanist procedures described earlier, most of the youngest judges are employed at gathering evidence and preparing case files for ultimate decision by their judicial superiors. They then typically move from appointments as judges in the least important local courts up a career ladder that takes them to higher-level courts located in increasingly larger cities.

Judges are perceived by others and perceive themselves to be government officials. Therefore they share in the prestige that accrues to the government official in most European countries, but that prestige is relative. In Italy law professors are accorded more respect. In France service in the judicial corps is not nearly so prestigious as service in one of the elite corps of bureaucrats that perform the highest levels of government administration.

JUDICIAL INDEPENDENCE

These facets of the judiciary as government bureaucracy are crucial and interacting. First, the tie between the judiciary and a politically powerful legal profession that exists in the United States and Great Britain, where judges are chosen from among and remain in the circle of successful practitioners, does not exist on the Continent. We have seen that this tie is an important element in what we have usually called English judicial independence.

Second, unlike American and English judges who do not usually seek promotion from court to court, almost every European judge is seeking to rise higher in his service. They are particularly anxious to get a judicial place in the capital or in one of the other large cities that provide the social and cultural life desired by most university graduates. While European judges cannot be dismissed without exceptionally good cause, they are subjected to a great deal of discipline by their superiors, who control both their promotions in rank and their transfers to better courts in better places.

Third, because judges are a bureaucratic corps of government servants, who are in a sense employees of the ministry of justice just as other civil servants are employees of the ministry of agriculture or the foreign ministry, European judges have a great many ties of outlook and sympathy with other government executives. These ties are strengthened by their shared university experience, often in the same law faculties, and by their frequent working contacts. These ties are particularly close between judges and their fellow ministry of justice employees, the state prosecutors and attorneys. The social contacts of judges, too, are far more likely to be with other civil servants than with practicing attorneys—the reverse of the situation in the United States. The result is that European judicial services are likely to be closely attuned to the viewpoints of the civil servants who run the country.

In short, behind the facade of judicial independence may lie an assimilation and subordination of judges to the higher civil service. The reality varies greatly from country to country, often on the basis of particular historical experience. Post–World War II Italy felt that judges had yielded too much to the Fascist regime. As a result, while organized in the standard bureaucratic way, the Italian judiciary is an almost completely self-contained and self-controlled career service. Tenure and promotion are determined by a system of examinations and evaluations controlled by the judges themselves. The service is governed by the Superior Council of Magistrature, sixteen of whose twenty-four members are judges. The president of the republic, who in Italy is not a partisan politician, and seven practitioners or professors appointed by Parliament, complete the membership.[25]

At the opposite extreme is France, in which an antijudicial spirit still survives from the prerevolutionary period when local judicial bodies were bastions of medieval privilege. In spite of considerable rhetoric about separation of powers, the judicial service remains essentially a branch of the civil service. Promotion and transfer are really controlled by the Ministry of Justice. The High Council of the Magistrature is under the control of the political executive.[26] Clearly the fortunes of French judges depend on their conformity to dominant political opinion and the legal views of their judicial superiors. Like other French civil servants, judges typically are very desirous of reaching prestige posts in Paris or at least in one of the great regional centers of France. The political control of transfers and promotion is thus of tremendous importance.

The German situation lies between the French and the Italian. Traditionally there have been extremely close ties between the judges and the higher civil service, of which the judiciary in practice forms a part. Close parallels in education, day-to-day experience, life-style, status in the community, organizational setting, and career concerns have usually led to a strikingly similar world view among judges and career officials in the government ministries. This is not to say that the judges necessarily reflect the sentiments of the particular political party that holds office at the moment. The German civil service, like that in France, has a continuity of outlook and values quite apart from the politics of the day. It does mean that the German judiciary is unlikely to be a vigorously independent watchdog of government administration. Traditionally promotions, transfers, and discipline were heavily influenced by both the political and career civil service executives in the capital. The post–World War II constitution provides some safeguards against political meddling. The influence of partisan politics on judicial careers has largely been eliminated, but the traditional affinity of the judiciary to their fellow officials in the government ministries remains.

Thus the independence of European judiciaries presents varying and subtle problems. It is easy to contrast the political insulation of the Italian judiciary with the political subordination of the French. But neither is likely to affect the day-to-day work of French and Italian judges much. Far more important throughout Europe is that the judges are seen, and see themselves, as government officials who form one branch of a national higher civil service, the organization, incentives, and life-style of which are very similar to those of the other branches. Anglo-American judges are generally attuned to the norms and styles of the legal profession. Indeed, they often have to be reminded that they are government officials too. European judges tend to be attuned to the norms and styles of the higher civil services that do most of the day-to-day governing of European nations. They never have to be reminded that they are government officials, and hardly the highest prestige government officials at that. They do sometimes have to be reminded that they share professional values with the lawyers who practice before them. Judicial independence and judicial assimilation into the great fellowship of the executive level of government bureaucracy are always contending forces on the Continent.

### ADMINISTRATIVE COURTS

This tension is no doubt clearest in that peculiarly Continental institution, largely unknown in the English-speaking world, the administrative court. Roman law systems draw a sharp distinction between administrative and civil law. Administrative law governs the relations between government agencies, the relations between government superiors and subordinates within government agencies, and the relations between private citizens and such agencies. While some administrative law matters are heard in the regular courts, most are heard by special administrative courts. These courts are the major place where claims that a government officer or agency has acted illegally are heard. The situation is quite different from that in the English-speaking world, where such claims are typically heard by regular courts at least after administrative remedies have been exhausted.

The administrative courts of most European countries form a separate hierarchy with local or regional courts and a central court in the capital. Unlike the so-called administrative law judge or hearing officer in the United States, these courts are not embedded within particular agencies or ministries. The same court will hear cases one day that deal with alleged misconduct by the agriculture department and the next by the labor ministry. But neither are the administrative courts an integral part of the judicial system.[27]

The model for most European countries is the Conseil d'état.[28] The council is not only an administrative court but a general expert on administrative law, procedure, organization, and practice which performs a wide range of functions designed to insure the correctness and efficiency of French administration. Its litigation section handles its case business and is staffed by more than a hundred "auditors" and councillors. Junior or "second class" auditors are recruited directly from the graduating classes of the Ecole nationale d'administration, which is the elite school for training French government executives. Councillors are drawn by the promotion of auditors and by the lateral entry of high civil servants from the ministries, and occasionally of distinguished lawyers. Thus the council is not a court staffed by judges but an extremely elite segment of the high civil service designated to supervise the legal behavior of the rest of the civil service.

The litigation section uses an adversary procedure roughly like that of Continental courts. But after a private petitioner has initiated a complaint or appeal from a lower tribunal,[29] members of the staff of the council itself prepare and argue the case in his behalf and do so with the greatest vigor and professional skill. The French codes contain only a few short provisions on administration. The law of the council is the most open and explicit case law of any litigational body in Europe.

The French Conseil d'état has an excellent reputation as a guardian of the people against administrative illegality. In its invention of the doctrine of *detournement de pouvoir,* many legal observers profess to see a much stronger restraint on administrative misconduct than its nearest equivalent in the common law world, "abuse of discretion." Its work product is at the very highest professional levels and its staff resources excellent. About the only complaint against it is that its pursuit of absolute perfection leads to delays of two or three years or more in final decision.

Nonetheless, the Conseil d'état and most of the administrative courts of Europe consist of one set of elite administrators watching the rest of the administration. The principal result will be a tighter, more efficient, more disciplined, and more unified civil service and bureaucratic administration. While the form and often the substance are protection of individual legal rights against the state, the ultimate purpose is the improvement and autonomy of the administrative machinery of the state.

Institutions very similar to the Council d'état exist in most European countries. In Germany, which is a federal state, the Supreme Administrative Court rules on certain disputes between the state governments and between a state government and the central government as well as on purely administrative law questions. In Scandinavia, the ombudsman, an official who acts as a special protector of individuals mistreated by government, takes on some of the functions that would normally be performed by administrative courts. Throughout Europe the administrative courts live in a sort of halfway house between judicial control of public administration and bureaucratic self-discipline designed to insure the autonomy of the higher civil service.

### CONSTITUTIONAL COURTS

One final development, largely of the post–World War II period, must be added to this picture of Continental courts. Although France has had written constitutions since the revolution, judicial review of the constitutionality of legislation has always been rejected in France. The power of the Conseil d'état to resolve certain statutory conflicts and impose authoritative interpretations of statutes on government agencies is the closest thing to judicial review that the French have had.[30] Under the Constitution of 1958, the Constitution Council has certain limited powers to declare statutes or administrative regulations unconstitutional. The council is not, however, a court but a body consisting of all the former presidents of France plus three persons selected by the current president, three by the president of the Senate and three by the president of the National Assembly. Because

Switzerland has long been a federal state, its highest court exercises certain powers of review. Like England, however, the Continent has basically been dominated by notions of parliamentary sovereignty that preclude review. In the wake of World War II, Germany and Italy adopted new constitutions under American influence. Both provided for special constitutional courts with the power of judicial review. In both countries these courts have been active and popular and have added considerably to the general prestige of the judiciary. The German court has become a major political institution of very considerable power.[31] In both countries, however, the constitutional courts are rather explicitly recognized to be something other than regular courts. They are not expected to be "neutral" but instead to be active instruments for the promotion of the newly established democratic regimes and guardians against any backsliding into earlier antidemocratic political ways.[32]

In Germany the postwar constitution provides an important opening for judicial activism quite apart from judicial review. Provisions of the constitution specifically direct that judicial decisions not only apply the law but do substantial justice between the parties on the basis of desirable or established social norms. This rebuke to the extreme positivism that had marked much of earlier twentieth-century German legal thought has not gone unnoticed by German judges. They now feel themselves to have constitutional mandate to engage in a somewhat broader judicial discretion than came to them when their powers were defined solely in terms of applying the code.

### Conclusion

An attempt to apply the conventional prototype of "courtness" to the civil law courts of Western Europe yields a number of paradoxes and ambiguities. As we noted in chapter 1, even if those courts mechanically applied the codes without any interference from other arms of government, they would hardly appear independent to those classes of litigants systematically disfavored by the codes themselves. We have now seen that European courts do not mechanically apply a set of complete, self-explanatory, preexisting legal rules. Instead the codes are often incomplete or generally and ambiguously worded and necessitate a large measure of judicial creativity if appropriate legal treatment is to be found for litigants. Far from enjoying a complete set of preexisting legal rules, civil law nations, like common law nations, depend on their courts to legislate many of their legal rules as they conduct litigation. For Roman law is a curious mixture of highly specific solutions to specific problems and very sweeping academic generalizations. The central role played by scholarly legal writing in the evolution and day-to-day application of civil law, a role that we shall also encounter in Muslim law, further undermines the preexisting rule aspect of European courts. A surprisingly large share of the "rules" they apply consist of more or less abstract, academic doctrines either incorporated into the codes themselves or so central to legal education and legal reasoning that they are essential to the application of the codes. While many of these doctrines persist unchanged over considerable periods of time, all are embedded in the continuous dialectic of academic discourse in which nothing is finally fixed. Once the role of "the doctrine" (academic writing) and "the jurisprudence" (previous case decisions) is understood, the position that European courts decide on the basis of "preexisting legal rules" becomes as shaky as the position that English and American courts do so. As in England and the United States, when viewed statically, most cases do involve the more or less automatic invocation of a clearly applicable legal rule. Over time, however, it can be seen that the clearly applicable legal rule has changed, although the statutory provision has remained the same. In Europe, as in England and America, the change must be attributed to changing legal doctrines that are incorporated case by case in the body of the law.

A similar ambiguity exists in the area of judicial independence. If we limit the notion of independence very, very narrowly to the absence of direct outside interference in the outcome of a particular case, Western European courts are essentially independent. In a number of countries, however, and most particularly in France, the political regime actively controls the career opportunities of judges. In such countries judges who wish to succeed professionally are likely to give the regime the kinds of decisions it wants even though the politicians apply no direct pressure. Finally, in all Western European nations, the judiciary is a hierarchically organized civil service, more or less cut off from private practitioners, and with relatively close affinities and connections with the rest of the higher levels of the career government bureaucracy. Even when a European judicial service is free of direct control by elected political executives, it is likely to be closely allied with the career civil service executives who actually do most of the day-to-day governing. From the point of view of the private citizen this alliance may be far more significant than sporadic political interference in cases with peculiar political significance. For it may systematically bias the judiciary in very broad ranges of cases that involve social and economic issues on which the "administration" has a firm national policy.

Things that we all unhesitatingly call courts have been operating continuously in the civil law world since at least the fourteenth century—many would say all the way back to the time of republican Rome. Yet they have managed to operate all that time without a clear, complete set of preexisting legal rules, and they have only achieved a relative judicial independence.

# 4   JUDGING AND MEDIATING
## IN IMPERIAL CHINA

When we sketched the continuum go-between, mediator, arbitrator, and judge in chapter 1, we argued that in reality most of the triadic conflict resolution institutions of any society mixed all four in various compounds of coercion and consent. One of the world's largest and longest enduring judicial systems, that of imperial China, seems to contradict this proposition. For it is often said that, governed by the pervasive Confucian ethic, almost all triadic dispute settlement in China was done by mediation.[1] In short it is argued that Chinese judges did not mix judging and mediation but instead acted essentially as mediators and did little or no judging of the sort specified in the conventional prototype of courts.

### The Confucian Tradition and Mediation

A relatively unified China ruled by an emperor emerges in about 200 B.C. Beginning with a small state in what is now north central China, the emperors gradually extended their domains to and beyond the boundaries of present-day China. While incorporating a wide range of racially and linguistically diverse people, the Chinese empire achieved a remarkable cultural homogeneity at least among the upper classes. A number of religions and political philosophies swept through China from time to time, but a central body of religious, political, and social beliefs emerged early and continued to dominate Chinese intellectual life well into the twentieth century. This body of beliefs is conventionally called Confucianism after the ancient sage Confucius. Confucius himself was a synthesizer of earlier intellectual traditions, and many of the ideas and institutions associated with Confucianism evolved long after his death. Thus by Confucianism we mean not the ideas of a single philosopher set down in a specific body of writing but a long and dynamic intellectual tradition with a number of conflicting cross currents.[2]

Central to the Confucian tradition is the idea of harmony. Nature is harmonious. The first obligation of every person is to achieve harmony both with other human beings and with nature. Personal and social discord will inevitably bring other discord in its train. A continued quarrel between two individuals will bring misfortune to both and disharmony to their social setting. Disharmony within families and clans will bring disharmony to villages, villages to districts, and so on. The natural result of maladjustments among humans will be maladjustments between humans and nature so that social strife will lead to such natural calamities as droughts, floods, famine, and pestilence.

When conflict arises, the most compelling moral and pragmatic duty of the conflictors, and of any third party, is not to decide who was right or wrong but to restore harmony between the two parties. The person of greatest moral virtue is not the one with the more legitimate interests, but the one who is willing to yield more of his legitimate interests in order to restore harmony with his opponent. The best triadic resolution is not the one that correctly assigns right and wrong but the one that leaves both parties sufficiently happy to bring about a restoration of their previous social relationships.

The Confucian notion of law is thus a difficult one to express in Western terminology. Whether or not the Chinese had a concept of natural law similar to that in the West[3] is unclear, given the fundamentally different ways of conceptualizing nature in the two cultures. It is clear, however, that the Confucian tradition basically conceives of law as akin to or a portion of a mass of ceremonials and rituals. The regular performance of these rites will assist man to achieve harmony with nature and other men living and dead. The Confucian legal tradition is largely unconcerned with legal rights; it is concerned with the consistency of performance of fixed social roles and rituals that insure social harmony. In this sense law is largely a matter of prescribed social roles—father and son, teacher and student, ruler and ruled—and the traditional modes of behavior that define those roles. Law is etiquette, and the rendering of the accepted courtesies and deferences that are appropriate to each particular social interaction. If a son should speak rudely to his father or a man claim that his grandfather was an educated man when he was not, the law has been broken. In short law is essentially social harmony conceived of as stability of social role.

Because the Confucian sees law as essentially the regular perfor-mance of social roles and rituals, he does not think so much in terms of law enforcement as of law inculcation. Men must be educated to perceive the true harmony of things and how to achieve that harmony in their daily lives. Men of education will then by example and moral suasion teach the un-educated to live in harmony. The entire imperial educational, political, and social hierarchy was designed to create a chain of moral example and per-suasion running from the emperor to the most distant and lowly peasant. If rulers conducted themselves wisely and harmoniously and with the welfare of the subjects as their sole concern, then the subjects would respond posi-tively to their concern and example and would themselves lead exemplary lives.

The emphasis on harmony and stability on the one hand and the conception of social control through moral leadership and tutelage on the other are highly consonant with a mediatory style of triadic conflict resolution. For as we saw in chapter 1 the mediator's job is essentially to make both parties happy enough with the outcome and with one another to maintain or reestablish their previous working relationship. And a key factor in the success of mediation may be the mediator's ability to lead the parties to a mutually acceptable solution rather than to impose one upon them.

The Confucian support for mediation is far more direct and specific than this, however. Confucian moralists teach that when a conflict does arise, it is the person who is less assertive in pressing his claims or sacrifices his interests with an eye to achieving harmony who acquires the greater moral status. In a system that assigns one party the legal right and says the other party is legally wrong, the winner gets both whatever the dispute was about and moral credit for getting it. According to Confucian ways, the loser in a mediation, to the extent one can be identified, is likely to be assigned the greater moral credit because he sacrificed more in order to reestablish harmonious relationships with the winner.

This element in Confucian thought is extremely important to the success of mediation. For as we saw earlier, the great weakness of mediation is the risk of overclaiming. In a system where it is known in advance that the conflict will usually be resolved by "splitting the difference," there is a high incentive for party X, who has not been injured at all, to claim that he has been injured, say a hundred dollars worth, by Y. Party Y will respond that he has not injured X at all. But in a split-the-difference mediation, X will get $50.00, which is $50.00 more than he would have gotten if he had not created the conflict. Even when a legitimate conflict exists, often there is reciprocal bidding up of alleged damages. If mediation is a compromise, whoever claims to have been hurt the most is likely to get the most favorable settlement. Built into Confucian teachings is a major deterrent to this kind of overclaiming. It is the person who is least assertive in his claims who is seen as the more morally worthy and is thus likely to benefit from whatever control the mediator exercises over the outcome of the dispute.

### Legalism

In addition to this emphasis on harmony, stability, moral tutelage, and self-abnegation, there is a second strain of Chinese thought about law and conflict resolution. This strain can be viewed as a pragmatic element of Confucianism itself or as a second tradition of Chinese thought separate from and somewhat in conflict with Confucianism. As early as the third century B.C. the Confucians were challenged by a school of thinkers who are conventionally labeled the Legalists. Because the Confucian-Legalist debate was centered among policymaking elites and went on for a long period of time, it contains a multitude of dimensions. For instance the Legalists wanted a strong imperical navy and the Confucians did not. Moreover, as in such later struggles as that between Trotskyites and Stalinists, the winners sometimes took over positions from the losers and great debates raged about whether a specific idea or policy position truly belonged to one school or the other. For our purposes here it is enough to say that the Legalists tended to emphasize social control by imperial command sanctioned by severe punishment rather than social control by example and tutelage. The Legalists argued that a highly trained, disciplined civil service would be required to communicate the imperial commands and carry out the punishments. The greatest virtue of this civil service was to be its bureaucratic skills and loyalties rather than its ability to act as a moral exemplar. In Western terms the Legalists are treated as saying that rulers should depend on laws and impartial law enforcement rather than education and moral leadership.[4]

The Legalists as a distinct political group vying for control of imperial policymaking were resoundingly defeated by their Confucian rivals. It was this defeat and Confucianism's subsequent total dominance of Chinese ideology which some authorities have argued set China on its uniquely mediatory tack. For the Confucian judge, it is said, is not a legalistic applier of preexisting law but a moral guide seeking to restore harmony between those who have temporarily strayed into conflict.

### Mediation

Jerome Cohen has most persuasively written of the mediatory style of traditional Chinese justice.[5] Unofficial "peace-talkers" apparently were constantly at work in traditional China.[6] Only where these peace-talkers failed was there resort to more formal mediation. Not only did disputants frequently seek out a third-party mediator, but would-be mediators bustled into conflict situations uninvited. A good deal of social credit and power came to those who gained a reputation as successful mediators. Within the family, disputes would normally be settled by the father or grandfather as paterfamilias. But here, too, other esteemed members of a family or even outsiders might be called or thrust themselves into family disputes in which it was impossible to consult a paterfamilias or in which he would appear to be obviously biased. Two recurring situations of family life that called for such mediation were the dissolution of the family into smaller units upon the death of a paterfamilias leaving a number of sons vying for the family property and mother-in-law–daughter-in-law disputes.

In extrafamilial conflicts village authorities, village elders, clan and guild officials, government officials, members of the gentry, or simply persons who sought the role of mediator or had reputations as good mediators might be sought out or initiate mediation themselves. The first step was for the mediator or mediators to see each of the parties separately, gather the facts, and frame the issues. The mediators then usually consulted other prominent persons in the village or other relevant social setting. Then they proposed a solution, shuttling between the two parties in a mixture of go-between and mediation styles until the two parties reached agreement. Typically they met privately with each party, often in a teahouse. There was a great deal of eating and tea drinking and elliptical conversation and varying degrees of social pressure, with the pressure mounting gradually if the parties showed inflexibility in their demands.

In theory mediation was not compulsory. The parties were insured access to the regular courts by imperial statute. Again in theory, once a complaint was filed in an imperial court, mediation had to cease and the complaint be settled by a regular judge according to law. In reality, however, clans and guilds usually had formal rules and villages and families informal ones against going to court unless the possibilities of mediation had been exhausted. These rules were backed by strong social and economic sanctions including the threat of ostracism, which was the ultimate sanction in a society in which every individual gained his livelihood and social status through his web of affiliations with relatives and neighbors. Moreover, magistrates were in practice likely to put pressure on prospective litigants to mediate. Once an esteemed set of mediators had proposed a solution, the magistrate was likely to impose that solution if the parties went to court. So there was little incentive for the party dissatisfied with the mediators' proposals to go "over their heads" to the magistrate. Finally the magistrates themselves frequently employed more or less mediatory styles and arrived at compromise verdicts. In practice mediation sometimes continued to a successful conclusion during litigation and compromises were sometimes reached as a substitute for levying execution on a previous judgment.

The successful completion of a mediation was usually marked by a feast, theatrical performance or other social gathering to mark the restoration of harmony between the contending parties.

### The Chinese Code

This picture of Chinese judging as Confucian mediation, which so neatly contrasts traditional Chinese law ways with the Roman law tradition of the West, is dramatically shattered, however, by two dominant facts of Chinese political and legal development. In fact the Chinese had a very long, very detailed code of laws created by imperial decree. And in fact the

Chinese had a very hierarchical, very disciplined judicial bureaucracy to enforce that code.

As with nearly all traditional Chinese practices, the origins of the Chinese code can be traced back to mythic beginnings in the earliest Chinese states of the nineteenth century B.C. But from at least the Han Dynasty (206 B.C.–A.D. 220) there are definite literary remains of such codes. The earliest surviving code is that of A.D. 653, which contained over five hundred articles.

A fundamental reorganization of the code was accomplished during the Ming Dynasty. The Ming Code became the basis for the Ch'ing codes of the seventeenth and nineteenth centuries, which continued in force until the destruction of imperial rule by the Revolution of 1912.

The Ch'ing Code contained 436 articles grouped under seven main sections including administrative, civil, religious, military, penal, and public works sections. If we confine ourselves to the basic statutes, there is enormous continuity in the code, with more than 40 percent of the provisions of the Ch'ing Code substantially the same as those of the Tang Code written eleven centuries earlier. However, if we include what Professors Bodde and Morris call "substatutes," the code is both considerably longer and subject to considerably more changes. The Ch'ing Code of 1863 contained 1,892 substatutes in contrast with the 297 substatutes of the Code of 1500.[7]

The Chinese substatute lies somewhere between what in the West might be a statute revising an earlier statute and an administrative regulation or decree. It is also a kind of judicial precedent. Typically it was a ruling of the Board of Punishments in a particular case, confirmed by the emperor and worded in such a way as to announce that it was intended as guidance for the decision of future cases as well as the one at hand. From time to time the emperor authorized compilations of approved substatutes which would then exist side by side with the code. Then at subsequent recodifications, the approved substatutes would be integrated into the appropriate sections of the code itself although they would continue to be designated as substatutes.[8]

### SPECIFICITY OF THE CODE

It is in part because of the predominance of the substatute that the code has a degree of specificity remarkable to Western eyes. But a number of other factors also contribute to this specificity. First of all, many of the statutes themselves had their origin in particular imperial decrees designed to deal with particular problems of the moment. The Chinese code is essentially a collection of individual imperial decrees accumulated over long periods of time rather than a conscious attempt to construct a complete system of laws. Its arrangement of materials is often arbitrary, or the result of historical accident or coincidental administrative arrangements. Even trained officials frequently encountered difficulties in finding the code provision most appropriate to the factual situation confronting them.

Second, the code is highly particular because of the distrust of local discretion that is a hallmark of at least the later empire. The emperors spoke as specifically as possible because they wanted to leave local authorities with as little discretion as possible in interpreting the code.

Third, the code is highly specific because it was designed to regulate a society in which there were many degrees of social status and many social roles. Each of these statuses and roles owed highly detailed and specific obligations to every other. Unlike codes in the West, this one deals not with an abstract legal person but with highly specific social beings—fathers, sons-in-law, officers of the imperial bodyguard, salt merchants, and so on. There is a conscious attempt to multiply and refine provisions of the code so that exactly the correct level of governmental intervention will occur which will restore social harmony in the light of the precise social status of each of the parties.

### SEVERITY OF THE CODE

Lest the impression be left, however, that the Chinese code is a deft and benevolent instrument for reforming the wayward, it must also be said that much of its detailed specificity comes in provisions stipulating exactly which form of death penalty is appropriate to which social offense. The bulk of the code was administered at the capital by the Board of Punishments. In general the Chinese were more likely to speak in terms of punishments than laws when referring to the code. There were five main categories of punishment: (1) beating with a light bamboo stick, (2) beating with a heavy bamboo stick, (3) penal servitude, (4) exile, and (5) death. Within each bambooing category there were five degrees of punishment ranging from 4 to 40 blows. Penal servitude involving a combination of bambooing and servitude ranging from 20 blows and 5 years on upward. Exile was internal, as it was in czarist Russia, and involved a combination of blows and transportation to a place 2,000 li, 2,500 li, or 3,000 li from the place of conviction. Given the social and economic importance of family ties to the Chinese, such a punishment was extremely severe and would doom most of those exiled to a life of poverty and ostracism. A second form of exile was military exile to serve in the frontier garrisons. There were three forms of death penalty: strangulation, decapitation, and death by slicing. The first, although it was probably more painful than the second, was considered less demeaning. The third was a slow death by torture.

For each of these penalties there were various mitigations. Fines were frequently substituted for blows and shorter terms of servitude or exile for longer ones. Sentences of strangulation and decapitation were decreed either as immediate or after the assizes. If the latter, there was a considerable but indeterminate chance that the sentence would subsequently be reduced, typically to exile. Most of the work that we would normally call judicial involved determining exactly the appropriate punishment for the offense under consideration.[9]

A few examples will provide a sense of both the detail and the severity of the code.[10]

> Boulais 1080a. Strangulation after assizes for theft eventuating in attempted but unsuccessful rape.
>
> Boulais 940. Military exile for the production of gunpowder and its sale to salt smugglers.
>
> Boulais 997. Deliberately releasing a horse that subsequently gores or kicks a person to death.
>
> Boulais 1167. A junior relative extorting property by intimidation of a senior relative.
>
> Boulais. 1482. Extortionate demands made by servants of an official resulting in the suicide of the victim.
>
> Boulais 1226. Mother-in-law who having been detected in adultry by daughter-in-law murders daughters-in-law in order to conceal adultery.
>
> Boulais 1506. Parents who direct their son to commit an immoral act and then fearful of discovery attempt suicide.

FLEXIBILITY OF THE CODE

When most provisions of a code are so highly specific, it is likely to miss a great many things that the law ought to cover even when it is very long. The imperial legal system had two methods of extending the code to cover situations not explicitly treated in existing provisions. The first was a highly formal method of lawmaking by analogy. Most legal systems employ analogy to meet new situations. We have seen that the judge-made portions of English common law are either analogical or at least pretend to be so. In Islam analogy was one of the lesser and less approved modes of expanding the body of law in a system in which legislation is theoretically forbidden. Even in Roman law systems, where in theory all new lawmaking is supposed to come by statute, analogy is sometimes used in the guise of judicial discovery of what scope the legislature intended for an existing statute.

The Chinese technique of analogy is often substantively similar to that used in common law countries. For instance, Bodde and Morris report a case in which a woman is punished for falsely confessing the murder of her son in order to shield the real killer. Since no statute specifically deals with this situation, the offense is handled by analogy to the statutory offense of "hushing up" the killing of a son. In other instances a theft from a Buddhist monk by his disciple and theft from a temple are treated as analogical to theft by a junior member of a family from a senior member and theft of objects used for imperial worship.

In other instances analogy is used in a more Romanist way to pursue the intent of a statute beyond its literal words. For instance, Bodde and Morris report a case in which a man who drove his mule recklessly was punished by analogy to a statute punishing one who "deliberately releases an animal."

In form, however, the analogical technique varies considerably from that typically found in the West. A statute of the code specifically authorizes and indeed requires the use of analogy when no statute is precisely applicable and provides for review of analogical decisions by "the superior magistrates" and by the emperor. Thus analogy was in the first instance a matter of judicial lawmaking but ultimately a matter of imperial legislation in the form of approval of a "lower court" decision. Indeed, many of the substatutes seem to have their origin in such imperially approved analogies.

A second technique for filling gaps in the code was the catch-all statute. The code contained statutes punishing doing "what ought not to be done," and "vicious scoundrels who repeatedly create disturbances and without reason molest decent people." A statute punishing the violators of imperial decrees was interpreted to apply to acts which the emperor would have forbidden if he had thought of them. Such catch-all statutes gave the code considerable flexibility.[11]

We have now discovered that a legal system in which judging has conventionally been thought to consist essentially of mediation in fact contained a very large, very detailed code whose principal concern seems to have been to meet out exactly the right degree of punishment for each and every wrongful act. And the punishments are extremely severe. How could a judge who is supposed to be a mediator finding a solution that will make both parties happy also be the applier of a body of law that clearly assigns wrong to one of the parties and then severely punishes him? Surely one party is going to go away very unhappy in a law case that necessarily results in one party being executed, exiled, and/or beaten. The prevalence of mediation as a judicial technique and the existence of a Draconian code are both widely recognized facts among China scholars, but it is not easy to see how the two facts can be reconciled.

A PENAL, NOT A CRIMINAL, CODE

The reconciliation usually is to treat the code as essentially a criminal code. It might be that all private disputes between man and man were handled by mediation while only criminal or public law matters were handled by the imposition of preexisting legal rules in the judicial manner. We have seen that the Chinese thought of the code as essentially a schedule of punishments. The bulk of its provisions were administered by the Board of Punishments. Almost every article of the code takes the form of defining a wrongdoing in highly specific terms and assigning a punishment to it. Clearly then the code is a penal code. In the West we have generally used the terms penal and criminal synonymously, but they are not necessarily the same.

The Chinese code is a penal code but it is not exclusively a criminal code. Articles 75 to 156 of the code, covering the family, land and property, marriage, moneylending, and public markets, were supervised by the Board of Revenue rather than the Board of Punishments. Other groups of articles dealing with administrative, religious, and military matters and public works were assigned to other appropriate boards. Thus the Chinese themselves seem to have formally recognized divisions between criminal, civil, public, and ecclesiastical law parallel to those in the West.[12] Even though punishments are attached to many (but by no means all) provisions of the civil and administrative law segments, it would be misleading to label them criminal law. They are typically aimed at providing rules for the same citizen-to-citizen and bureaucrat-to-bureaucrat conflicts that are covered by Western private and administrative law.[13]

CIVIL ELEMENTS IN "CRIMINAL LAW"

Moreover, the almost two hundred articles of the code administered by the Board of Punishments contain many civil law elements cast in the form of penal laws. Bodde and Morris for instance report statutes handled by the Board of Punishments involving:

— destruction of the house, walls or other property of another person—the cost of restoration will be calculated and offender sentenced as he would be for unlawfully taking property of the same value but *offender must also pay for the work of restoration*
— falsely claiming to have lost property entrusted to one by another
— imposing restraints of trade to achieve monopolistic profit
— embezzling the property of another
— theft
— homicide through malpractice
— taking excessive interest
— negligent homicide
— "deliberate" release of an animal so as to cause death and driving horses or carts quickly resulting in death (the board explicitly

applies an "unforeseeable or unavoidable" standard and treats the statutes as covering negligent homicide but not pure accident)
— killing or injuring by mischance, that is seeking to kill one person but actually killing another
— homicide during an affray
— accidental homicide (without malicious intent, where death was neither foreseeable or avoidable).

At first glance these provisions may appear to be essentially criminal in nature rather than designed to resolve disputes between private persons. However, the customary Chinese practice was to attach both civil "damages" and state punishment to the same statute—a practice which we have also seen in the intermixing of tort and crime in early English law. The destruction of property statute has been listed first because it states this mixture so explicitly. The extensive scope of this mixed criminal-civil solution to problems which in English law would be called trespass, tort, bailments, restraint of trade, conversion, contract, malpractice, debt, and wrongful death is to be fully appreciated, however, only when the Chinese practices of redemption and return of property are noted.

The substitution of fines for the five punishments was widely practiced particularly to mitigate the harshness of the statutory punishment in the light of circumstances peculiar to the particular offense or offender. Indeed, when it was granted, such redemption, as Bodde and Morris call it, typically reduced the punishment to a nominal one. For instance the redemption to be paid by women or aged persons convicted of a capital offense came to about half an ounce of silver. What is significant for our purposes here is that redemption was routinely substituted for punishment in cases of accidental or negligent injury or death. In such instances the amount involved was substantial rather than nominal. It was paid to the victim or his family rather than the government. In other words when what in Anglo-American law would be called a tort was involved, redemption became civil damages. Moreover, quite apart from redemption, in cases involving illegally held property, the property was routinely seized and returned to its rightful owner.

Certain other provisions involving homicide also underline the civil side of Board of Punishments jurisdiction. Any criminal guilty of a capital crime amnestied by the emperor was required to pay 20 ounces of silver to the family of his victim. A number of statutes require the culprit to pay funeral money to the family of the victim. In addition the Board of Punishments ordered such payments in many other cases in which it reduced the death penalty to life exile. The overall policy seems to have been to compel money payments to the families of homicide victims except in those instances in which the perpetrator was actually executed. Because execution rarely took place except for what in Anglo-American countries would be labeled felony-murder, the Chinese actually had a system of civil liability through money damages for wrongful death. This was a system of strict liability or liability without fault in the sense that damages were paid for both negligent and purely accidental homicide.[14]

Quite apart from the redemption aspects of the law of homicide, there is an important aspect of private or civil law hidden even in the death penalty for homicide. In the West such a penalty is today preeminently criminal rather than civil, a severe punishment imposed by the state in the hope of deterring future criminal conduct. Traditional Chinese law incorporated a different notion of such a penalty. The Chinese believed in *ti ming*, the notion that social harmony would be restored after a killing by the death of the offender—quite literally a life for a life. Thus the death penalty for homicide was not only a state punishment but a means of resolving the private conflict between the family of the deceased and that of the killer.[15]

Finally the criminal law aspects of the Chinese code are usually exaggerated because the principal source for the substance of traditional Chinese law, aside from the code itself, has been the reported cases of the highest courts of appeal sitting in the capital. Under the Chinese system of appeal, few cases other than those involving third, fourth, or fifth punishments were reported to the capital.[16] In China most cases which in the West would be labeled civil would involve remedies such as restoration of property, redemption or payment of rents, or at most bambooing and so would never move on to the higher courts. Thus the traditional Chinese legal materials generally available to scholars tend to give a highly misleading picture of the proportion of criminal to civil matters handled by the Chinese judicial system as a whole.

Even the thirteenth-century manual of cases translated by Van Gulik, which was designed to highlight the detection capacities of an ideal magistrate, reports a number of inheritance cases.[17] Examination of a nineteenth-century local court archive on Taipei indicated that civil cases accounted for between 15 and 20 percent of the docket and criminal cases about 30, with the rest of the court's time devoted to what we would normally label administrative or public law matters.[18] There were cases involving marriage, divorce, land boundary, rent, sale of goods, monetary loans, trespass, water rights, mortgages, pledges, security transactions, bailments, contracts, and bankruptcy. Among them were several in which only civil remedies were employed without the application of any punishment. For instance in a debt litigation, the magistrate authorized a lender to collect rent pledged on a loan until the borrower had repaid a debt which he denied owing. Hsiao reports that farmers in a hilly region of Szechwan routinely borrowed each year from Shensi merchants and when they failed to repay promptly were routinely sued in the local Szechwan *yamen,* where their indebtedness was often scaled down by a sympathetic magistrate.[19]

### Mediation and Law

In summary then the supposed domination of mediation in traditional Chinese judicial practice cannot be reconciled with the existence of a long, highly detailed, and severe code by a facile distinction between criminal law and civil mediation. In reality the code provided preexisting legal rules for a wide range of civil relationships and wrongs. Even the appellate records available show that Chinese judges did resolve many essentially civil disputes through the application of these rules and arrived at dichotomous judgments of legal right and wrong under them. The Chinese were not devoted exclusively to mediation as the tool for resolving private conflicts.

Yet it would be incorrect to reject the traditional view running from Escerra to Cohen that the Chinese preferred the restoration of harmony between the parties to the assignment of legal right and wrong. The Chinese arrived at a rather subtle mixture of mediatory and legalistic elements. The Confucian canon itself incorporated diverse and potentially contradictory concepts of governance. Nine Confucian classics served as the basis of the examination system through which government administrators were selected. These nine works were the central core of orthodox political and legal theory. Of them the *Analects of Confucius,* particularly as interpreted by Mencius, most forcefully depicts rule as the fostering of harmony through moderation and moral example, and is thus most favorable to mediation as a judicial technique. The classic work most specifically concerned with government, however, is the *Record of Rituals.* This work emphasizes rule by command and authoritative enforcement of the edicts of the ruler. The *Rites of Chou,* which particularly emphasizes lawmaking and enforcement as central to politics, was admitted to canonical status almost a thousand years before Mencius. It was the most legalistic of the classics and clearly played an important role in imperial rule, particularly in the Ch'ing era.

Perhaps part of the difficulty of sorting out the strands of Chinese legal thought is the confusion created by the Legalist movement. While the Legalists as a distinct political faction vying for imperial favor were defeated, Legalist ideas were incorporated into Confucian ideology and governmental practice. First, and most important, the Chinese did adopt a legal code. No one confronted with the sheer size of that code, the immense effort expended at its periodic revision, and the bureaucratic resources devoted to its enforcement, could say that the emperor sought to rule entirely by moral example rather than legal command. Second, the Chinese created a highly trained, highly disciplined bureaucratic hierarchy charged with carrying out the law. Thus, in line with Legalist teachings, a reliable chain of authority was created to bring the commands of the emperor from the capital down to every portion of the empire and to enforce them there. Third, the code itself is not only extremely detailed in its prescriptions and prohibitions but assigns extremely severe punishments.

These Legalist devices, however, have been confucianized. The code exists but was viewed as a supplement to the more central mode of Confucian rule. That mode remained moral example and the adoption of policies that would contribute to the welfare of the people. The bureaucracy was highly trained and disciplined, but what it was trained in was the Confucian classics rather than administrative and law enforcement skills. And even the lowest government officers knew that their primary responsibility was the Confucian fostering of harmony and welfare through paternal guidance, not the rigorous enforcement of the law. Finally those administering the punishments of the code seem less concerned with the deterrent effect of punishment than with choosing that degree of punishment which would restore a harmony or balance in the particular human situation confronting them.

In other words the Chinese do have a large body of carefully administered law designed to shape human conduct. That body of law, however, is designed to provide punishments and civil remedies as a supplement to the more central Confucian modes of insuring social harmony: example, education, mediation, and sound public policy.

THE PARABLE OF THE ANGRY MAGISTRATE

A good illustration of the Chinese mixture of mediation and the application of preexisting rules carrying harsh punishments is to be found in a passage from a manual of instruction for local magistrates paraphrased by a Western resident. The manual is in the form of brief exemplary histories or cases. In one of them a local judge is confronted by a notorious criminal. The judge appears to lose his temper, a most un-Confucian mode of judicial conduct, rather strange for a manual of judicial practice to hold up by way of example. The judge storms from the room screaming at the defendant that his crimes are so hideous that no penalty in the code is sufficiently severe and a special punishment will have to be invented. A few moments later the judge reenters the courtroom, seeming visibly to master his temper, and tells the criminal that in spite of the terribleness of his crimes he will only be subjected to the punishment mandated by the statute, (usually a quick and relatively painless beheading). Having demonstrated his fidelity to law, the judge completes the formalities of the case.[20]

Clearly the problem for the judge is how to gain the consent of the loser, how to achieve at least some degree of mediation or mutual consent of the two parties to the outcome. For the outcome is that one party, the government, wins, and the other, the convicted criminal, loses his very life. The judge seeks to introduce an element of Confucian mediation or yielding, even in the context of a totally unyielding penal law, by appearing to lose his temper and then moderating his conduct by "only" imposing beheading. The criminal, suddenly faced with the agonizing prospect of torture, is then supposed to accept gratefully "only" losing his head.[21]

As this little parable shows, the Chinese were aware of the potential conflict between Confucian mediation and Legalist administration of statutes and sought to find working compromises between the two.

## The Imperial Administrative-Judicial Structure

In order to understand the actual mixture of mediation and litigation traditionally employed in China, it is necessary to look at the basic administrative-judicial structure of the empire. While the prevalence of mediation may in part be explained by its compatibility with Confucian ideology, the widespread use of mediation is also part and parcel of a general administrative strategy designed to control a vast territory with minimum cost and minimum risk of political upheaval.

The basic administrative structure of the empire is extremely simple although in practice certain overlaps and hiatuses of authority existed and indeed seem to have been consciously cultivated as a means of checking the power of one local official with that of another. At the capital, the emperor sat surrounded by a half a dozen or so major boards or committees, each responsible for some aspect of imperial administration. These boards governed by the preparation of memorials presented to the emperor. Only his signature and/or marginal comments on a memorial turned what was essentially a piece of advice into an official state policy.

The empire as a whole was divided into roughly twenty-two provinces, each headed by a governor. Two or three provinces were frequently grouped under a governor general. Each province was divided into a number of major subdivisions headed by a prefect, and each prefecture was in turn divided into a number of districts headed by a local magistrate.

### THE DISTRICT MAGISTRATE AND HIS YAMEN

All together there were about thirteen hundred local districts. The governors and governors general each had a number of subordinate high officials. Each prefect had a number of subprefects. About half the district magistrates had assistant magistrates. There were also military, educational, and salt officials scattered about. Nevertheless, only about three thousand administrative officers bore direct responsibility for an empire of vast size and population. Each district magistrate bore the entire local governmental responsibility for a district that rarely ran under two hundred thousand people and was often substantially larger.[22] The magistrate ruled the district from a city whose population alone was in the tens of thousands and was surrounded by dozens of villages. And village is a misleading designation in China. For a Chinese village may vary from a few dozen houses to a commercial and industrial center of thousands which might be a city in everything but official designation.

The district magistrate's office or court (*yamen*) was staffed with an assortment of gatekeepers, runners, and jailers who performed the manual and menial tasks of the office. The runners were a cross between messenger, bailiff, and policeman. The menial servants of the *yamen* were, of course, essential to the tasks of the magistrate, but they themselves constituted one of his more serious problems. Illiterate, and so poorly paid that they were on the verge of poverty, they took bribes, stirred up trouble in order to get more work, and practiced theft and extortion. Government runners were one of the classes of persons specifically denied admission to higher government service. The typical bandit or swindler in Chinese fiction is a former *yamen* runner. Each magistrate had a coroner who was a semiskilled person but of low social status.

The bulk of the routine work of the *yamen* in collecting taxes, administering justice, and doing public works was done by the clerks. The magistrate was subjected to extremely detailed and rigorous supervision by the administrative hierarchy above him. Most of the supervision took the form of an endless exchange of documents governed by highly complex regulations. The clerks prepared these documents and kept the records supporting them. The clerks, unlike the magistrates, came from the local area administered by their particular *yamen*. Typically they served for many years as one magistrate after another circulated through the *yamen*. From continued experience they came to know the details of government regulations far better than their superiors. While each *yamen* had an official quota of regular clerks, magistrates invariably greatly exceeded their quotas so that the actual number of clerks in a district *yamen* seemed to have run from a few hundred in the smallest to perhaps as many as several thousand in the largest.

The clerks were government employees on government salaries. Clearly they constituted too large and too entrenched a bureaucracy for the magistrate to control single-handed. This was particularly true because the magistrate was, as we shall see shortly, a generalist without much specific training in governmental affairs. The magistrate's principal weapon in this unequal struggle with the clerks were his "private secretaries."[23] As the term implies these men were chosen and paid by the magistrate himself. Typically there were somewhere between two or three and a dozen such secretaries in a *yamen*. They lived in the *yamen* in close contact with the magistrate and were relatively isolated from the clerks. They supervised the legal system, taxes, accounting, and document preparation and the flow of work of the *yamen*.

The private secretaries were administrative experts particularly in law and taxation.[24] They were scholars, that is, persons who had the education required for admission to the ranks of the magistrates. Many actually held fairly high degrees. Some eventually became magistrates themselves. Unlike most magistrates, they had usually received special training in law or taxation as well as a general scholarly education. They were persons of high social status treated as "guests" of the "host" magistrate. If they encountered serious disagreement with their magistrate, the honorable course for them was to resign.

First among the private secretaries in status, salary, and power was the legal secretary. Besides a general literary education, he had usually undergone a period of private tutorial instruction in law and legal processes conducted by a former legal secretary. The magistrate's legal work was the most sensitive and closely supervised of his relations with his superiors. The legal secretary was the special guardian of this area of work. His job was to keep his employer out of trouble. This was not easy to do in a system with a highly elaborate body of law, a very strict set of administrative procedures and regulations, and very severe punishments for even minor errors committed by government officials.[25]

District magistrates were particularly dependent on their legal secretaries because in the Ming and Ch'ing periods prospective magistrates no longer studied law but concentrated almost exclusively on literary and philosophical discourse.[26]

The magistrate was confronted with a highly detailed and complex law code, an even more detailed and complex body of administrative regulations,[27] several massive official and semiofficial compilations of precedents and a general body of legal literature that as early as the third century A.D. ran to over 7 million words.[28] While an academic doctor of laws title did sometimes exist in China, the legal secretary was the closest thing to a professional lawyer that existed in imperial China. Even the legal secretaries were essentially an eighteenth- and nineteenth-century development.[29] The secretary for taxation was almost the equal of the legal secretary. In addition to the tax business of the *yamen*, civil litigation involving property and financial transactions were usually handled by him rather than the legal secretary.

The legal, tax, and other secretaries prepared the endless flow of reports and replies to inquiries from above that were required by the hierarchical system of imperial administration. Since the reputation, rewards, and punishments of the district magistrate depended almost entirely on how correct and convincing these documents were, the secretaries literally held his career in their hands.

Aside from the legal and revenue secretaries, the first real specialists were to be found at the provincial level. Only summary, periodic reports of cases involving no more than bambooing were made to the prefecture. More serious cases were automatically reported through the prefecture to the provincial capital. Each province had a provincial judge who was a subordinate of the governor but was the representative of the Board of Punishments in Peking. He received the recommendation of the district magistrate in each appellate case. The defendants and witnesses traveled to his court and he reheard the entire case. His findings became the record on appeal if the case went higher. Moreover, the district magistrate was not allowed to make use of analogy while the provincial judge was. So for major trouble cases the Provincial Court became effectively the real trial court. Cases involving punishment heavier than penal servitude, all cases involving homicide, and cases in which analogy was used automatically were sent on to the Board of Punishment at Peking after receiving approval by the governor. Other cases were reported collectively to the board at intervals. Appealed civil cases passed from the district magistrate to the provincial financial commissioner rather than the provincial judge. They rarely involved sufficiently high levels of punishment to pass onward to the Board of Revenue at Peking.

The Board of Punishments at Peking was the final appeals court except for cases in which the death penalty was invoked. They went on to a body known as the Three High Courts and eventually to the emperor for final ratification. There was an extremely elaborate system for commuting death penalties that involved the various Peking decision makers. When a higher authority reversed the provincial court, the case was sent back to it for redecision. The redecided case then again traveled upward for final approval.[30]

In a sense the Board of Punishment's decisions were essentially sentence reviews. Its decisions are generally involved with whether a given fact situation best fits under one or another of the myriad highly specific code provisions. In other words the board is concerned about exactly which crime it should hold the defendant has committed rather than about whether he is guilty or innocent. Actual findings of guilt and innocence seem to have been almost solely in the hands of the district and provincial courts. The board's major concern seems to have been to insure that the appropriate punishment had been awarded. Often its extremely elaborate arguments about whether a given fact situation falls under one statute or another seem to be little more than an attempt to choose that statute carrying the punishment it deems most appropriate. Yet the board does seem to have been concerned with substantive statutory interpretation as well. Bodde and Morris report a number of cases in which great pains are taken to show that an offense falls under one statute rather than another even though the penalties provided by both are identical.[31]

Besides the system of automatic appeals, the losing party might appeal. Upon final approval of a judgment at any level of appeal, the case was retransmitted down the appellate ladder and final execution undertaken by the district court.

We have now set the local magistrate in the matrix of those above and below him. Above him was a very demanding hierarchy. Below him was an area of large size and population, an unruly army of runners, and a large, technically knowledgeable, locally entrenched bureaucracy. At his side were a handful of his personal administrative experts, and perhaps an assistant magistrate. But he personally bore the legal responsibility for every governmental act and many nongovernmental ones in his district.

THE NATURE OF THE DISTRICT MAGISTRATE

There were a number of different routes to the magistry and consequently a number of different kinds of local magistrates.[32] For instance some of the most celebrated local magistrates had served as legal secretaries for many years before entering the civil service. They came to the magistry with a quite exceptional level of experience and technical competence. At the other extreme there were periods in which half or more of the magistrates had purchased their appointments without having demonstrated any particular competence, although even most purchasers had had a good deal of scholarly training.

Nevertheless, it is possible to depict a more or less typical local magistrate. Entrance into the civil service was by a series of examinations. Successful passage of the local examination led to the title licentiate, the esteemed social status of scholar and the possibility of official employment. Success at the next higher level, the provincial examinations, was the normal mark of eligibility for the district magistrate and higher civil service positions. Those passing the provincial exams might compete for the metropolitan degree in exams given periodically at the capital. Only about two or three hundred of these degrees were awarded every three or four years. Holders of this degree therefore constituted the intellectual elite of the empire. Students might take any of these examinations a number of times. So the empire always contained large numbers of aspirants in their twenties and thirties and well up into middle age. More important, there were more provincial and even metropolitan degree holders than there were available appointments in the civil service. Men who completed their education in their twenties would normally expect to wait ten to twenty years for an official appointment and then might hold one such appointment lasting three to five years without ever receiving another.

The examination system itself was a triumph of Confucian learning over Legalist institutions. The civil service was elaborately hierarchical with many ranks, and many forms of supervision by superiors over subordinates. But the major qualification for entry into the hierarchy was passage of examinations, which tested not administrative skill or legal knowledge but mastery of the classical literary and philosophical texts of Confucianism. In the early dynasties one or more of the essays assigned concerned governmental processes and public policy. These topics were later dropped. During the Ming and Ch'ing dynasties ever increasing emphasis was placed on literary accomplishments.

Local magistrate was formally the lowest-ranking appointment in the administrative hierarchy. In reality it was a far more difficult and demanding post than that of assistant prefect or junior member of one of the boards or academies in the capital. Thus the career patterns of local magistrates were somewhat anomalous. Almost invariably the local magistrate came to his job as a first appointment having held no other civil service position. He usually came in his thirties or forties because of the long delay in obtaining appointments. He could expect to hold office from three to five years. But he would not expect subsequently to work his way up to the higher ranks of subprefect, prefect, and so on. Typically after his term as local magistrate he would either receive no further appointment or, if he had done very well in this difficult post, he might move on directly to a governorship or a high office in the capital.

In short it would be a mistake to visualize the local magistrate as a very young, very junior officer, a kind of second lieutenant just out of officers' training school. Typically he was a person of mature years. He had usually acquired considerable experience as a member of the gentry engaged in local affairs or in his family's economic and social enterprises during the years he waited for appointment.[33] He expected the local magistry to be either the most important official job he would ever hold or at least one of the major attainments of his career.

Yet by law he could not serve in the province from which his family came and so he was always initially ignorant of the area he had to govern. He knew how to write poetry rather than deal with the maze of laws, regulations, and government forms that determined his official life. Thus the local magistrate exhibited a curious mixture of experience and inexperience, knowledge and ignorance, beginner and mid-career executive. It should be added that an imperial statute required that local magistracies in areas that were known to have an unusually large press of business and/or a particularly unruly population be filled by persons who had already held a local magistrate's appointment elsewhere.

### DUTIES OF THE DISTRICT MAGISTRATE

We have spent so much time on the local magistrate because he is the basic trial judge in imperial China. In chapter 1 we argued that, considering all of the legal systems of the world, the typical judge was not an independant, specialized judge, but the general, all-purpose local administrator whom, for short, we called the district officer. The Chinese local magistrate is a preeminent example. He was the government, the whole government, for the district in which his *yamen* was located. Among his multitude of responsibilities was that of holding the local court.

First and foremost, like district officers everywhere, the local magistrate was responsible for maintaining the peace of his district, often with the assistance of a small military garrison, but often with nothing but his runners and the prestige of his office. He was also in a sense the high priest of the official cult and spent many hours attending various rites and ceremonials. He was required to lodge and entertain all visiting government officials, an extremely onerous responsibility in districts along main travel routes. Again like most district officers, he was the source of most of the central government's information on his district and prepared an endless series of tax censuses, returns, reports, and responses to special inquiries as well as an enormous number of documents pertaining to the operations of his own office. He was involved in local public works, particularly water conservation and control projects. He was the disaster relief officer in a nation to which fire, flood, drought, famine, earthquake, and war were endemic. He shared local political and social status with the local gentry, without whose cooperation he would almost certainly fail to govern successfully. So a great deal of his time was devoted to highly delicate maneuver among powerful local interests. He supervised a considerable government establishment, including his own *yamen*, a jail, and a government granary. He had at least a peripheral connection with the maintenance of the military garrison, the educational system, the imperial courier service, and the government salt monopoly. Because of his status as a scholar, and because the Chinese believed that the display of virtue by officials was the best mode of governing the potentially unruly masses, the magistrate necessarily spent a good deal of time displaying his patronage of the religious, cultural, and martial arts of the community.

Among all these activities two tended to become preeminent because of the demands of the hierarchy above the district magistrate. The first was the suppression of crime.[34] Special reports had to be made of the number of crimes in the district and the elapse of time between the reporting of a crime and the prosecution of the criminal. Magistrates who apprehended large numbers of criminals quickly were specially regarded; those who left crimes unsolved were punished. Not that the local mandarin ran anything like a modern police establishment. In a jurisdiction of several hundred thousand people, there must have been thousands of violations of the criminal law each year. A magistrate whose records showed the discovery and solution of a few dozen a year was considered exemplary.

The regime was concerned essentially with murder, banditry, the large affrays to which the Chinese were very prone, arson, and very large thefts. The stream of routine petty theft, assault, and the like was, as in most societies, largely unreported and when reported handled rather summarily by the magistrate. In the event of serious crime, however, the magistrate, aided by his coroner if a body was involved, was expected to investigate personally and bring the culprit to justice. Then he was expected to arrive at precisely the proper recommendation for punishment under exactly the correct statute. His judgment would be reviewed at the prefectural and provincial levels and finally by the Board of Punishments and the emperor. Thus on the basis of his education in the classics, the local magistrate was to combine the skills of a great detective, a wise trial judge, and a subtle drafter of legal documents that would stand the scrutiny of the greatest legal minds of the realm.

The district magistrate's second major task was the collection of taxes. The imperial tax system was a demanding one, involving payment in silver from landowners, many of whom were subsistence farmers perenially short of cash. The magistrate himself rarely traveled outside his city into the dozens or hundreds of villages in his district where the bulk of the taxpayers lived. He did not have a staff of tax collectors beyond the tax secretary and tax clerks who also remained in the *yamen* and to whom the taxpayers or their representatives traveled to make their payments.

Indeed the difficulty of collection was so great that total payment was hardly even an ideal, let alone the working goal of administration. Targets were set in terms of proportions of the totals recorded by the Board of Revenue in the capital. Local magistrates collecting a high proportion of the total due were rewarded. Those collecting too low a proportion were punished and often dismissed. Just as for crime control, a constant stream of documents, each of which had to be exactly correct, flowed in and out of the local *yamen*. Silver had to be stored, guarded, accounted for, and transmitted. Silver in China was not in the form of a uniform coinage but of bits and pieces of various shapes and sizes and degrees of purity. As a measure of insurance against famine, in some areas some taxes were collected in kind. The tax grain then had to be stored in a local government warehouse, accounted for, and guarded from pilferage.

Thus the magistrate was faced with the almost constant emergency of falling behind in tax collections and the sporadic emergencies of serious crime in his district and visits from touring dignitaries. Because in these three areas he was under the most direct and demanding eyes of his superiors, he could not hope to survive unless he could handle them expeditiously, correctly, and with a fair measure of success. Because he was most under the eyes of the locals in religious and cultural rites and ceremonies, his performance at those also had to enjoy a high priority.

### THE MAGISTRATE AS TRIAL JUDGE

It is against this background that the local magistrate's performance as the sole local judge must be assessed.

Because of various recesses and holidays, criminal cases were heard only six or seven months a year and civil complaints in something less than six. The magistrate was, however, required to give immediate attention to grave crimes and to reserve six to nine days a month for civil complaints during those months when civil court was in session.[35] All cases were initiated by individual complaint. Upon receipt of a criminal complaint, the magistrate initiated an investigation either personally or through runners, or both, and if a death was involved through his coroner. In civil complaints typically he interrogated the parties to determine whether a valid cause of action existed. Following preliminary investigation a formal rescript was prepared stating the reasons why a complaint was either accepted or rejected for trial and, if appropriate, setting a trial date. The parties then filed the necessary legal documents although few magistrates actually reviewed these before trial. They usually relied instead on a summary prepared by their legal secretaries. Since most cases were criminal in form, even in what were actually civil cases the defendant might be jailed before trial and plaintiffs seek delays to put further pressure on defendants to settle. There were statutory time limits on the interval between complaint and trial, but they were often ignored. In the period before trial the magistrate might dispatch runners to investigate and to summon the parties and witnesses.

Except in treason cases, trials were public, and magistrates were urged to heed public opinion.[36] In criminal matters the accused was dragged in chains before the bench. Torture was used freely in the courtroom to extract testimony and confessions. Even in more or less civil matters, complainant and defendant appeared personally and in an obsequious manner and were often treated harshly by the magistrate who sat on an elevated bench above the kneeling parties and witnesses. Present in the courtroom were various clerks, attendants, and runners, but the legal secretary was forbidden to attend. The aim of the court was to secure confessions. Those confessing signed a written deposition.[37]

The magistrate retired after the hearing to prepare a formal order which included a summary of the evidence and a proposed disposition or verdict. In actuality the secretaries usually prepared these orders. In case where appeal was automatic these orders took the form of recommendations to the magistrate's superiors. They became final judicial orders if and when they were approved by the appropriate level of the hierarchy. In other cases they took the form of a final verdict or in civil matters of an interim order that the two parties wrote bonds of willingness to accept. Should the parties be unwilling to enter into such a bond, they could appeal.[38]

Only the elderly, those with degrees, youths, women, and members of prominent families were sometimes allowed to send representatives instead of appearing in person.[39] There was no place in either procedure or official contemplation for attorneys as such, although some persons did prepare legal papers for others. In the countryside there were sometimes "litigation sticks," half-literate former government clerks or runners, or failed students, who stirred up litigation and, for a price, helped file the necessary papers. From a number of imperial decrees forbiding the practice, it appears that examination candidates and students, who after all might well have been in their thirties or forties and have studied for years, sometimes hung about the *yamen* picking up legal business.

The prospective litigant had to run a guantlet of runners, clerks, and gatekeepers, each demanding a bribe, before he managed to file the requisite papers. The legal secretary was generally the final bastion to be overcome. The magistrate also typically expected a substantial gift. In addition to these unofficial bribes or fees, there were also official litigation fees that went to the government treasury.[40] Magistrates were traditionally paid a very low salary, far below the cost of administering their office, and so they took gifts from many sources as a matter of course. In the Ch'ing Dynasty a substantial salary supplement was introduced "to nourish honesty" but even then the magistrate's official income usually ran below his expenses. The magistrate who lived solely on his own income and personal resources seems to have been a rare exception.

Litigating involved not only substantial monetary costs, but substantial literary skills in drafting the requisite documents and considerable sophistication in the ways of government in order to steer the documents through many channels, each of which was prone to delay or confuse matters in order to gain additional gifts. For those who resided in the countryside, there was also the burden of traveling to the city and lodging there while awaiting proceedings.[41] The costs of litigating were not only substantial but unpredictable. It was impossible to know in advance just how many or what size bribes would be required once the litigation process got underway. Moreover, it was not unknown for the magistrate to decide in favor of the litigant who had provided the largest gift or came from the family with the best connections.

### TRANSLATION OF CIVIL TO PENAL COMPLAINTS

An additional risk of litigation inhered in the Chinese legal process. The code was, after all, cast almost entirely in the form of severe punishments even though many sections covered essentially civil matters. Thus those seeking judicial relief in an essentially civil matter might suddenly find that the magistrate had converted it into a penal one in which one of the two parties might well be sentenced to a beating or exile. For instance a dispute over a land boundary might end with the magistrate finding that one of the parties had made a false land claim in violation of the statute against false claims. The punishment prescribed by the statute was bambooing. So not only would the rightful owner receive the land but the looser would receive a severe punishment as well. The more complex the factual and legal issues, and thus the more the need for third party resolution, the less predictable were the chances that one of the two parties, and which one, would suffer penal sanctions. Van Gulik reports two cases in which disputes over the ownership of chattels resulted in the property being assigned to one of the parties and the other being fined.[42] Land transfers were usually by written document so that land litigation often became a dispute over the authenticity of such documents offered as proof of ownership. A successful challenge to the authenticity of such a document might lead not only to an award of the land to the challenger but the punishment of the loosing party for forgery.[43] Refusing to pay rent was a violation of the code punishable by whipping. A tenant who lost a rent case with his landlord might not only be ordered to pay the rent due but be subjected to corporal punishment. Van Gulik reports an inheritance case in which the plaintiff, daughter of the deceased's first wife, claims that a child of his second wife was not legitimate, so that the plaintiff is entitled to inherit as sole legitimate heir. Upon a determination by the magistrate that the child of the second wife was legitimate, he not only ruled adversely on the plaintiff's inheritance claim but punished her "for having calumnated her stepmother."

So the conversion of an essentially civil suit to a penal one could lead to torture, corporal punishment, or exile for one of the litigants as well as civil remedies to the other. It could also lead to a sudden and disastrous escalation in legal expenses. For if the magistrate chose to take the suit as a serious criminal complaint, a horde of *yamen* runners might descend upon the locale of the dispute to conduct an "investigation," which typically turned into a campaign of extorting all the loose cash in the neighborhood.

This uncertainty about the limits of litigation arose precisely because the local magistrate was the complete district officer and wielded judicial power as only a subset of his total executive authority. He did not obviously and automatically limit his litigational judgments to the scope desired by the litigants. His dual role as moral mentor and local wielder of the total coercive powers of the empire led him to deal with any problem, including those that came to him in a litigational frame, as completely as the problem, not the litigants, seemed to demand. Thus a single judicial order might require restoration of property, payment of cash restitutions, seizure and disposal of property, public apology or humiliation, corporal punishment, penal servitude, or a combination of any or all of these remedies.

More important, the magistrate was not simply or even primarily a law enforcer, but the father of the people. If he wanted to, he could, on the one hand, settle nearly any litigation by a nonpunitive mediation involving compromise between the claims of the parties. Or he could find one party legally correct and the other in violation of the law but in such a way that he could confine himself to essentially civil remedies. On the other hand, given the complexity and severity of the code, he could nearly always deal out unlimited misery to one or both of the parties if he wanted to.

### Mediation, Litigation, Avoidance, and the Rationing of Judicial Services

There is probably no society in which there is not a set of wise saws about avoiding litigation like the plague. Such sayings were, however, particularly prevalent in China. There was a definite and very strong pattern of avoidance of litigation. The costs of litigation were arbitrary and could not be anticipated. Litigation required literary skills that most inhabitants did not have. Litigants submitted themselves completely to the powers of the magistrate. A suit that began over a few dollars worth of property might end in the economic ruin of a family and the exile of its head to a distant province.

Indeed, and this is the key point, if there had not been a strong pattern of litigation avoidance, and strong reasons for it, the imperial justice system could not have operated at all. In spite of the Confucian teachings on moderation and yielding, there is no particular reason to suppose that the Chinese were by nature a peculiarly nonlitigious people. Chinese history is full of riot, civil disorder, banditry, and affray. At least in South China, villages frequently armed themselves and fought fixed battles over disputed land, livestock, or water rights. This was not a peculiarly nonconflictual culture. As it was, much of the magistrate's time was spent on litigation. Remembering that he was the sole trial judge for hundreds of thousands of persons, litigation would surely have swamped him entirely if the Chinese had been prone to use him as one of their principal triadic figures.

This situation is not peculiar to the magistrate's judicial functions. The whole official business of the empire was conducted by amazingly few government officials at amazingly low cost to the imperial treasury at least so long as we exclude the extravagances sometimes practiced in the capital, which had little to do with administering the countryside. At every hand the Chinese found ways of supplementing the district mandarins with various devices and organizations that cost the government little or nothing. This was particularly true when the problem was one of extending government policies down into the villages where the magistrate almost never went.

### MAGISTRATES, GENTRY, AND VILLAGE OFFICIALS

The principal art of imperial governance was to create numerous cheap transmission belts of imperial policy into the countryside while so balancing one against another that none could become a rallying point of local resistance to centralized rule. First and foremost was the magistrate himself, who always came from another province and so was without local ties, came to office late and for a short time, was overworked and underpaid, and was subjected to severe disciplinary measures. Second was the gentry, who like the officials were generally scholars, who lived both in the cities and in the countryside, and who had a common interest with the government in preserving law and order. While the gentry did provide much of the pressure for stability in the countryside, almost every local rebellion in China was led by dissident members of the gentry.

Aside from the gentry the principal governmental intervention into the villages was a dual, and often in practice overlapping, system of collective responsibility. The villagers themselves selected from among their own members one official for police and one for tax purposes. The village police official was responsible for the general peace of the community and particularly for reporting the presence of strangers and troublemakers to the *yamen*. In theory he stood at the apex of a system in which every ten and then every hundred families were grouped together, each group under a head and each bearing collective responsibility for wrongdoing committed by any of its members. The village tax official was responsible for maintaining a tax census of families in his village. Typically both of these officials would be moderately prominent peasants but not gentry, and usually not among the family heads and "elders" accorded highest social status in the village. They often brought unpleasant responsibilities to the villagers and were subject to serve punishments for failure to meet their responsibilities to the government.[44]

### CLAN, GUILD, AND VILLAGE ELDERS

Besides the gentry and these peasant officials there existed a number of other authority structures. The prominence of clan organizations varied greatly in various places, being generally far stronger in the South than the North. Frequently the clan was the principal social organization of one village and relatively unimportant in the next. A clan was composed of persons of the same name tracing descent from a common ancestor. The clan might or might not hold extensive common property or engage in collective enterprises. Well-established clans had a clan head and a series of clan officials and underofficials or elders. In the cities guilds of persons engaged in the same trade or business, and often from the same place of origin, also appointed official leaders and governed their members under their own regulations. Most villages, whether or not clan organization was prominent, recognized a set of elders, that is, persons whose demonstrated skill at managing their own affairs, scholarship and/or service to the village entitled their opinions to special respect. By custom, religious teaching, statute, and government policy, the head of every primary family had unquestioned authority over it and responsibility for the conduct of its members.[45]

Just as imperial policy dictated the employment of these various authorities to minimize the burden of the district magistrate in keeping order and collecting taxes, it employed them to reduce the burden of litigation on the magistrate. In part because of Confucian teachings about moderation, in much greater part because of the prudent desire in most peasant societies to keep out from under the eyes of the government, in part because of the high costs and risks of litigation, and in part because of social pressure from fellow clan members or villagers, persons in conflict tended to resort to these various local authorities rather than going to the magistrate for resolution of their conflicts.

The village residents charged with policing and taxing responsibilities were used as triadic conflict resolvers in spite of their low social status.[46] Village elders sitting singly or as a body heard many village disputes and were probably more significant dispute settlers than the government's appointed village police and tax officials because they were of higher social status.[47] Where the disputants were of the same clan, clan seniors often heard disputes. The regulation of some clans provided that where fellow clansmen were involved in a dispute over land or debt, they must seek mediation by clan elders rather than going to the magistrate. Only

when clan mediation was unsuccessful might they engage in formal litigation. In those towns that had merchant or craft guilds, the guild leaders
heard disputes. Members of the gentry were apparently chosen by disputants to aid in the resolution of their conflicts.[48]

Courts of official jurisdiction for both civil and criminal disputes
existed throughout the empire. Gentry, elders, clan and guild leaders, and
village policemen and tax census takers had no such official authority. Given
these two facts of juridicial life, triadic conflict resolution done by persons
other than the district magistrate necessarily took the form of mediation;
that is, so long as official courts with official sanctions remain available even
in theory, unofficial triadic conflict resolvers must attract the consent of
both parties. If either party prefers to submit himself to the official third, or
is gravely unhappy with the outcome of the unofficial triad, he could simply
break the unofficial triad by resorting to the official court.

Thus the prevalence of mediation in China may be attributed in
part to Confucian ideology, but more fundamentally it is the inevitable
result of an imperial structure of government which in theory is absolute
and all pervasive and in reality shifts as much of the burden and cost of
government as possible onto authority figures not on the government
payroll. Superficially there appears to be a contridiction between a highly
legalistic code and a mediatory style of conflict resolution. This apparent
contradiction turns out to be a typically Chinese solution to the problem of
running an enormous empire as cheaply as possible and with an optimal mix
of hierarchical control and dispersion of local authority. The legalistic code
and the prevalence of mediation supplement rather than contradict one
another. Mediation conducted by nongovernment persons reduced the flow
of cases into imperial courts to proportions manageable by a very thinly
scattered judiciary. It resolved most conflicts at the lowest possible level and
without expense to the government.

There is much more involved, however, than a simple two-stage
system in which local authority figures mediate most cases while the most
serious go "up" to the district magistrate for legal decision. First of all, the
existence in the background of an expensive and risky legal process provides
both parties with a high incentive to go to mediation and accept its outcome
rather than face the expense and risk of going to court. Second, the district
magistrate himself may proceed in a mediatory style or, as frequently seems
to have happened, encourage the parties to settle their problem by private
mediation. That is, proceeding to court does not imply the total rejection of
mediations in favor of legal judgment, as it tends to do in the West, because
the Chinese judge as general administrator and father of the people can cast
himself as mediator until he chooses to do otherwise. And the fact that he

can, at will, don the mantle of terrible enforcer of a Draconian code no doubt gave him enormous advantages as a mediator, moving him in the direction of binding arbitrator.

OVERCLAIMING

Finally, and perhaps most important, the existence of office and law—of magistrate and code—sitting on top of a predominantly mediatory system tended to cure the major paradox or self-contradiction of mediation, overclaiming. In ascertaining the facts, the mediator may be able to discover that one or both claimants are engaged in false claiming or overclaiming. His announcement of the true facts, together with social pressure for a just settlement, may lead the false claimer to profess his own acceptance of a low award or none at all. Given the difficulty experienced by most triadic conflict resolvers in discovering the true facts, however, the overclaiming problem is likely to be endemic to a mediatory system.

A solution to the overclaiming problem employed by many societies is to superimpose a legal-judicial system over the mediation system, allowing resort to a judge for any party who believes himself to be a victim of a false claim or overclaiming strategy by his opponent. Mediation may work best when both parties know that an excessive claim aimed at maximizing a split-the-difference payoff will lead an opponent to reject mediation, where split-the difference is most likely to occur, and instead go to a law court, where it is less likely to occur.

Chinese mediation by nonmagistrates exists in the context of a court system to which a party unwilling to mediate may resort.[49] Mediation undertaken by a magistrate himself exists in the context of a body of procedural and substantive law that will allow a magistrate affronted by an excessive or false claim to shift the proceedings from a mediatory to a punitive mode and assign direct punishment to the false claimer or overclaimer.[50] Thus the magistrate as administrator of a highly specific, detailed, and severe code is not a contradiction to the proclaimed mediatory thrust of Chinese dispute settlement but an essential component of mediation aimed at curing its major ill, false claiming or overclaiming.

VILLAGE DISPUTE SETTLEMENT

Beyond the problems of overclaiming, the existence of a body of strict law and a magistrate to enforce it has other important consequences for the use of mediation at the village level. But before speaking of these it is useful to enter an important caveat about village mediation. There is a tendency among scholars of Chinese law to assume that informal legal settlements at the submagistrate level are necessarily mediated settlements. But we know from a great many other rural village societies that local settlements may be based on local customary law rather than pure mediation. No matter how informal a local proceeding may be or how much it depends on the consent of both parties to appear, its outcome may rest not on the discovery of a solution mutually satisfactory to the two litigants but on a decision about which has a claim that is strictly in accord with the detailed and specific local customary law. Our knowledge of customary law in China is almost nonexistent, but what we know about Chinese culture and village life in general certainly suggests that custom played a strong role. It may be that in such areas as family relationships, landlord-tenant relations, and landholding, conflict resolution by the application of preexisting customary rules may have been as important as pure mediation.

Hsiao cites an instance in late nineteenth-century Yunnan in which a youth caught stealing corn from a neighbor was summoned before a meeting of village elders and sentenced to death under the customary law of the village.[51] Village clans and guilds sometimes adopted formal bodies of regulations of their own which amounted to fairly complete codes. In some instances clans incorporated large segments of the imperial code into their own regulations.[52] Thus it would be incorrect to equate all "informal" or nongovernmental triadic conflict resolution with pure mediation. Much of this "private" dispute settlement may have been done by the application of preexisting bodies of "private" or local legal rules.

Perhaps the clearest indication that much Chinese mediation was in fact not mediation but lay or private adjudication by persons administering preexisting legal rules but holding no official judicial post is to be found in the tea drinking and feasting that all observers agree was an integral part of "mediation." For it was the "loser" who usually paid for the tea. Martin C. Yang notes that in his own village when a successful mediation had concluded in what Yang translates as a "negociated peace," both parties shared the expense of the feast. But if one of the parties conceded fault or was found to have been at fault by the elders, he paid for the feast.[53] Similarly in guild mediation, the losing party might be required to pay for a feast or a theatrical performance for the members of the guild.[54] Clearly then the Chinese themselves distinguished between two kinds of nongovernmental conflict resolution. One was a pure mediation in which some compromise was reached between competing interests. The other was an informal triadic dispute settlement in which one party was assigned the right and the other the wrong. The right and wrong were defined in some instances by general moral sentiment but in others by preexisting customary, local, or imperial legal rules. This is a far cry from the Confucian yielding and compromise which is supposed to make the Chinese so prone to mediation rather than adjudication.[55]

LAND DISPUTES

Customary law and the imperial legal system may have combined largely to displace mediation in one important area of potential conflict, landholding. China was overwhelmingly agricultural and much emphasis is conventionally placed on the continuity of the basic pattern of Chinese agricultural life over many centuries. Such continuity no doubt existed in the long term, but in the short term landholding was not particularly stable in China. During times of flood, famine, war, and rebellion, districts, even whole provinces, might be depopulated. Subsequently they would be repopulated by migrants from other districts and provinces and the return of some of the original inhabitants. The expansion of Chinese agriculture out of the fertile river valleys into marginal mountain and desert lands has been almost continuous over the course of Chinese history. Major new irrigation and water control projects occurred sporadically, often to be followed by the gradual deterioration of what had been accomplished. Much of the arable land was in flood plains in which shifts in the channels of watercourses and flooding might rearrange the basic geography. Large families led to frequent division and redivision of land among sons and grandsons. This tendency toward fragmentation of holdings was counterbalanced by concentrations that came about as particularly prosperous farmers sought to expand their holdings. In an economy marked by subsistence farming, the shortage of cash and the necessity for cash to pay taxes, crop failures, and other misfortunes would bring about a great many sales of land which would tend to concentrate in the hands of those who did have money.

Prosperous peasant families with substantial landholdings and cash reserves usually seem to have lasted only a few generations before their holdings were again dispersed. At least in the eighteenth and nineteenth centuries and probably much earlier, agriculture near major cities tended to become "capitalized." The prosperous gentry and merchants of the city would buy land with their spare capital. At the same time much of the land would be converted from subsistence to cash crop farming to feed the inhabitants of the city. Because individual cities waxed and waned as commercial, political, and artistic centers, this capitalization would be occuring in some places and breaking down in others at any particular moment. Finally marginal land was constantly being reclaimed from waste or returning to waste as short-term economic, demographic, and climatic cycles dictated.

All of these phenomena meant that there must inevitably have been many disputes over land ownership. Mediation in land disputes is peculiarly subject to false claims or overclaiming described earlier. For if the normal solution to a land dispute would be to award a portion of the land to each disputant, anyone could easily expand his landholdings at the expense of his neighbors simply by claiming part of their land. Moreover, in any society that has the institution of formal title to land, that is, of legitimate sole ownership of a specific piece of land, a dispute over ownership of a specific piece of land, is likely to inspire the question: "Who really owns the land." This is a question that naturally leads to a winner take all rather than a mediated answer. Either X has title or Y has title.

The Chinese did in fact have a land title system. Tax liability ran with land. The principal responsibility of the village tax assessor was to gather and maintain information about who held what land. The district magistrate's tax clerks were principally engaged in correlating such records. During the imperial government's tax reform drive of the eighteenth century, the "fish scale" registers were created. These registers were land ownership maps designed to facilitate tax collection. Most important, the Chinese practice was to transfer land by formal written document, or deed, at least when purchase rather than inheritance was involved. These deeds were then registered with the magistrate for a fee.[56] The magistrate's seal on the document was evidence of its authenticity. In the eighteenth century, there are imperial regulations directing magistrates to keep records of the fees collected for this registration and other regulations aimed at ending certain abuses of the registration system such as the collection of double fees. Village police and tax collection (*pao-chia* and *li-chia*) authorities were also charged with keeping track of land transfers.[57] All of these eighteenth-century measures are clearly reforms of practices that had existed for some time, not the initiation of brand new policies. Thus, while the Chinese did not have a comprehensive land registry, they did have a system of tax records and officially authenticated title deeds that made it natural for them to ask "who has legal title" when a property dispute arose.

Of course, there are some land disputes that do seem to call for mediation, particularly landlord-tenant disputes over rents and the conditions of tenancy and disputes over title to previously waste land recently brought under cultivation. But many boundary and ownership disputes must inevitably have resolved themselves into questions of who in fact had title to what. And surely the best evidence of such ownership must have been the official stamped deed. An alternative would be the tax records showing that the family of one of the parties had paid taxes on the disputed land continuously for a long period of time. There would have been no reason for parties involved in a land transfer to incur the trouble and expense of registering it with the magistrate unless they expected to use the stamped document as proof of legal ownership.[58] So, it would seem probable that many land disputes were not settled by split-the-difference mediation but by determining that one of the two disputants had legal title to the land and should receive all of it while the other party had no such title and would receive nothing.

At present such all or nothing solutions to land disputes must be inferred from our knowledge of the existence of title documents and records because we have almost no direct knowledge of how magistrates handled land cases. As we noted earlier our knowledge of substantive legal proceedings in China comes almost entirely from the collections of major cases handled by the Board of Punishments and other boards in Peking. Only cases involving serious physical punishment reached those boards. Land cases would not involve such punishments unless the magistrate threw them into the penal mode by treating them as instances of making false claims. Moreover, many land disputes were probably not treated as judicial cases at all but would be referred to the magistrate in his administrative capacity as supervisor of official records indicating ownership. Consequently, few land cases are to be found in the appellate records of the boards. But that does not mean that there were few such cases nor should it be assumed that such cases were mediated. Van Gulik reports a case in which, boundary markers having disappeared and the deed of sale having been lost, ownership of land was determined by consulting tax records.[59] It is probable that many land cases were settled as they would have been in Western courts by a determination of which party had legal title established either by customary possession, title deed, or government record.[60]

### OVEREMPHASIS ON LITIGATION AVOIDANCE

Finally, in assessing the sweep of mediation in imperial China, there has probably been an overemphasis of the tendency to avoid litigation among the Chinese.

Again the fact that our knowledge of Chinese substantive law comes from the codes and appellate cases probably leads us somewhat astray. The cases we see are either cases that were extremely serious from the start—involving a death for instance—or cases that got out of hand, beginning small but ending up involving very serious penalities requiring review by higher judicial bodies. After reading dozens of cases in which the Board of Punishments solemnly debates about whether the defendant shall be sliced into little pieces or merely beheaded, one readily comes to believe that any sane Chinese would avoid going to court whenever he could. This impression is reinforced by our knowledge of the various gifts, fees, and outright bribes often involved in the litigation process.

Nevertheless, given the general level of efficiency of the magistrate system over many centuries, it would seem probable that many Chinese in many places at many times would feel that resort to the magistrate rather than to local mediation would bring speedy and fair resolution to their dispute without involving excessive costs or risks of punishment.

The charms of local mediation by village elders or gentry are often exaggerated or romanticized. Elders and/or gentry often represent social, economic, and political interests that are at odds with the interests of one of the disputants. Almost inevitably such persons have a web of local affiliations that one of the disputants may view as suggesting partiality to his opponent. As we saw in chapter 2, many persons will prefer to escape from purely local justice to a more distant court less entangled in local interests and inequalities. It is precisely for this reason that judicial services offered by central regimes are an attractive device for winning local support for such regimes. Not only was the district *yamen* often a more hospitable place than it would appear to be from the horror stories in appellate records, but local mediators were often far more partial, corrupt, and selfish than a good mediator should be. Recent research on run-of-the-mill cases in a district *yamen*, as opposed to appellate decisions, indicates that the Chinese may not have been as reluctant to bring routine cases, including civil ones, to the magistrate as is usually supposed. This research also indicates that magistrates were capable of rendering routine decisions in such cases, some in mediatory style and others by winner-take-all application of the preexisting statute.[61]

## Conclusion

In chapter 1 it was argued that judicial systems almost invariably employ a mixture of mediation and winner-take-all decisions based on preexisting rules. In contradiction to this argument is the conventional wisdom that one of the largest and longest lasting of the world's judicial systems, that of imperial China, consistently avoided winner-take-all in favor of mediated resolutions of conflict. This view of imperial Chinese practice is based on the supposed dominance of Confucian ideology and its insistence on the virtues of harmony, moderation, and yielding rather than the proclamation of legal rights and wrongs. We have seen, however, that the existence of a very long, detailed, and severe imperial code brings the conventional wisdom into question. For the application of such a body of preexisting rules carefully defining legal wrongs would appear to be incompatible with an exclusive reliance on mediation.

Our examination of this apparent contradiction then suggested that Chinese ideology contained a strong strain of reliance on the administration of formal legal rules and punishments as a mode of governance running parallel to its teachings about government as moral leadership and tutelage. Chinese ideology was not as insistent on mediation and as condemnatory of the application of law as is sometimes believed.

Second, the prevalence of mediation in China was based less on the denigration of law per se than on the desire to carefully husband and ration the scarce judicial resources available. We have seen that all regimes must ration official conflict resolution services. Imperial China sought to administer a vast empire with a very small number of district officers, each of whom had complete administrative and judicial responsibilities for hundreds of thousands of people. Thus much of the insistence on "mediation" in China consists of a series of incentives and devices designed to channel most conflict resolution chores into nongovernmental hands. This tight-fisted policy toward judicial resources, combined with the equality tight-fisted monopoly of government over legitimate coercive authority, meant that most conflict resolution inevitably had to be mediatory. For most such resolution had to be done by private persons, and those persons had to rely on mutual consent of the parties because they were rigorously excluded from the governing authority necessary to enforce nonconsensual judgments. Thus it is not so much a matter of legal decision being denigrated in favor of mediation as it is a matter of legal decision being a scarce resource monopolized by government.

Third, we noted that it was the very existence of this official law applying as an alternative to mediation that made mediation itself workable. The existence of an official judicial alternative to mediation, and the capacity of the district administrator to shift at will from mediation to law application, provided an essential corrective for the tendency to overclaim that is endemic to mediation.

Fourth, while the evidence is scanty, it appears probable that there was more reliance on customary law and the assertion of legal rights based on legal documents and government records than has been supposed by conventional mediatory interpretations of imperial Chinese law. At the very minimum it is essential in dealing with Chinese materials not to lump all triadic conflict resolution by nonmagistrates under the heading mediation. To the extent that village elders and others who have customarily been called mediators imposed their services on conflicting parties, employed preexisting written or customary rules to arrive at decisions assigning right to one of the parties and wrong to the other, and enforced these decisions by threats of severe social and economic sanctions, they were more lay judges than mediators. An as yet undetermined but clearly substantial part of what is conventionally called Chinese mediation is in fact such lay judging. And here again the principal explanation of its prevalence lies not in some Confucian antipathy to judging but in the shifting of the burden of adjudication from those who are on the government payroll to those who are not.

Finally, the Chinese magistrate is neither solely a mediator nor even solely a mediator in civil cases and solely a judge in criminal ones. Rather the Chinese district magistrate more clearly incorporates in his own person the whole continuum from go-between to judge than any triadic figure we are likely to encounter in the modern West. While in theory he was required to act as judge once a complaint had been filed, in practice he often delayed litigation while he or others acted as a go-between or mediator.[62] When he himself acted as mediator, the constantly implied threat that he would transform himself into a Draconian judge should he be dissatisfied with the attitude of the parties or their refusal to consent to the outcome he proposed made the magistrate a mediator so powerful that he barely remained a mediator at all. In suggesting in advance that, should one of the parties persist in litigating, his own verdict was likely to reflect the settlement reached by clan, guild or village elders, or gentry, the magistrate came close to employing binding arbitration. Once litigation had begun, the magistrate might still in reality mediate the dispute.

Even if he reached an official verdict, it might be one that went part way toward meeting the claims of each of the parties. At the judging end of the continuum he might act as an official judge applying a preexisting code law and applying civil remedies in civil cases and criminal punishments in criminal ones. Moreover, the nature of his office and his code allowed him to transmute civil cases to penal ones at his pleasure. Thus in assigning legal right and wrong, he could not only provide the legal winner with the remedies to which he was entitled but impose sanction on the loser far beyond any contemplated by either party when they initiated litigation. Thus he combined capacities for the most consent-oriented mediation with capacities for coercion-oriented judging far greater than we encounter in most Western judges.

It must be concluded then that, while the legal system of imperial China stands as strong evidence that mediation can be as central to triadic conflict resolution as the conventional Western prototype of the judicial officer applying law, its existence does not contradict the proposition that legal systems inevitably mix mediation and what is commonly called judge-ing.

# 5   THE COURTS OF ISLAM AND THE PROBLEM OF APPEAL

In chapter 1 we saw that appeal is a nearly universal phenomenon because, in addition to contributing to the stability of the triadic structure, it yields great advantages to the regime in terms of increased legitimacy and hierarchical control. Nevertheless, one of the world's major legal systems, that of Islam, is generally seen as having little or no appellate dimension. The survey of Islamic materials presented here will focus on the problem of appeal.

## Kadi Justice

Such a focus is particularly appropriate because Western perceptions of Islamic courts have been seriously distorted by a kind of accident, an accident that occurred in part because of the general absence of appeal in Islam. The accident is a Weberian one. In his seminal work on legal systems, Max Weber made use of what has become a famous construct, "*kadi* justice."[1] The term evoked the image of a somewhat scruffy Muslim holy man sitting under a tree and deciding cases on a purely ad hoc basis as the morality or equities of the conflict struck him. *Kadi* justice was to be contrasted with justice dispensed by a Western judge deciding cases according to preestablished, general legal rules rather than his moral or religious impulses of the moment. Like so many of Weber's constructs, "*kadi* justice" was for him an "ideal type," whose value lay in its analytical usefulness rather than its correspondence to the actual behavior of any particular set of people in any particular society. Weber was not summarizing empirical findings about the actual behavior of real *kadi*s but seizing upon a colorful figure of speech in order to dramatize the contrast between rational-legal judicial decision making and highly particularized decision making based on religious inspiration.

The figure of speech was memorable, however, precisely because it appealed to a set of Western prejudices, and particularly central European ones. In Weber's day Europeans' general vision of the Islamic world had been shaped by their contact with the Ottoman Empire in its final stages of decay in the turn-of-the-century Balkans. While Germany was a major center of Arabist studies, to the average literate German, the word *kadi* suggested a half-literate, tattered, corrupt, fat man in a fez acting with complete arbitrariness amidst the ruins of a failing Oriental despotism.

Because Weber has been so powerful in shaping subsequent thinking about law, his figure of speech has more or less accidentally preserved the popular prejudices of his day as about the only thing most Western students of law and courts think they know about Islamic judicial institutions.

Weber's picture of the *kadi* has its roots in three aspects of Islamic law.[2] First, Islamic law is often highly particularized. It does not treat of contract in general, for instance, but has one provision for contracts of sale for dates and quite another for sale of houses. Second, Islamic law treats not only of what is legally right or wrong but also of what is morally good, better, and best. The *kadi* may punish any act that seems to him to merit punishment. Third, Islamic law does not generally know appeal, so that the judgment of the *kadi* is usually final. These three factors taken together, and seen through the eyes of an outsider, tend to create a picture of the *kadi* as deciding each case just as he pleases based on the particular moral claims of the litigants without the need to rationalize his decision on the basis of any general body of law. The reader must guard against applying this stereotype to the materials presented in the remainder of this chapter.

## The Legal Culture of Islam

With this warning that there is no necessary connection between what the Islamic judges called *kadi*s do and what Weber called *kadi* justice, let us move on to our central question: Why don't we encounter appeal in Islamic law as we do in nearly all other legal system? There are two basic explanations available, one cultural, the other institutional or, if you like, political.

### ABSENCE OF LEGISLATION

In order to understand the cultural explanation, we must briefly sketch the evolution of Islamic law (*sharia*). In Islam the words of the Prophet as recorded in the Koran and in the sayings ascribed to Muhammad by certain authenticated traditions are the sole body of legislation. While the interrelation between secular and religious authority has been complex and fluctuating over the course of Muslim history, in theory at least the caliphs, who were the highest authorities of Islam, were merely protectors of the faithful and not sovereigns. In the early years of the Abbasid caliphate (following A.D. 750), there were proposals for codification and legislation, but they were conclusively rejected. Thus aside from the Prophet and his words, Islam does not know legislators or legislation.

This rejection of legislation either causes, or at least is an integral part of, a number of distinct characteristics of Muslim law. Most bodies of law show a distinct disinclination to change. Deprived of the opportunity to make new law consciously and openly, Islamic law has been especially conservative. Perhaps more important, as a system of law it has never had to respond to the kind of single, central direction and unification that would flow from a sovereign wielding acknowledged lawmaking power.[3] Deeply embedded in Islamic legal and theological thought is the notion that what is true in law and religion is determined by the consensus of the faithful rather than the command of any living being. The Muslim treats such a consensus as a blessing but a rare one. The absence of a sovereign other than Muhammad himself is part of a deeper cultural acceptance of very great diversity of opinion within the overall consensus of the community of the faithful. For the Muslim it is neither particularly strange nor particularly offensive that two or three or six different versions of the law of the Prophet should exist side by side.

Finally, the absence of legislation subsequent to the words of the Prophet has resulted in a highly particularized body of law. While Muhammad did attempt some relatively systematic and general comments on some legal topics, most of his law consists of highly specific utterances on the day-to-day disputes brought to him for settlement by his immediate followers. Thus there are no general statutes on tort, contracts, and the like, but only a body of particular sayings of the Prophet. For instance, Muhammad denounces *ribā*, transactions in which amounts of gold, silver, wheat, barley, dates, or raisins exchanged are unequal or delivery delayed. But the Koran states no general rule for what kinds of commodities are subject to *ribā* prohibitions or even an explanation of what these particular six commodities have in common.

The absence of legislation does not mean, however, that Islamic law confines itself to the bare words of the Koran. Indeed, the legal pronouncements in the Koran are so sporadic, particularized, and incomplete that they could not serve as the body of law even for a relatively simple village society, let alone the empire that Islam became. The first great body of supplementary law consists of the authenticated "traditions" of the Prophet (*hadith*). After the death of the Prophet, his followers treasured memories of his sayings and actions and passed them on to their descendants. An enormous body of traditions thus arose, many no doubt invented to do service in the sectarian conflicts that constantly racked the Muslim world. The elaboration of traditions, and picking and choosing among them, were methods of filling out and clarifying the fragmentary legal materials of the Koran itself. For several hundred years this was the principal task of legal commentators. The building up of a more or less complete body of law through the "discovery" and "authentication" of traditions was enthusiastically pursued. It even was held that where conflict or uncertainty existed, the traditions were to be considered more authoritative than the words of the Koran itself.

THE SCHOOLS

From a time only very shortly after the death of Muhammad, Islamic legal commentary proliferated at an incredible rate. Hundreds of commentaries appeared on the words of the Prophet found in the Koran. The search for the true traditions of the Prophet resulted in an enormous amount of quasi- and pseudo-historical authentication and elaboration. This work usually took the form of seeking to trace the traditions back from their most recent prounouncers through an unbroken chain of earlier authorities and holy men to the very mouth of the Prophet. These commentaries on the Koran and the traditions were produced not by judges but by jurisconsults, independent scholars learned in the law.

As a result of early dynastic quarrels among the heirs and successors of the Prophet, Islam, the community of true believers has, almost from its first triumphs, been divided into two major (Sunni, Shi'ite) and numerous minor sects. The vast Muslim empire and sphere of influence once stretched from the Philippines in a broad belt through India, Persia, and the Arab lands and across North Africa, with offshoots into East Aftica and Spain. Different regions were dominated by different sects although in some areas members of various sects lived side by side. The Shi'ites and a number of the minor sects each had their own school of legal commentators. The main or orthodox body of believers (the Sunni Muslims) recognizes four major schools of legal commentary. There were in addition a number of others that did not quite achieve full status although at least one, the Zabirite, lasted for centuries.[4] By the second half of the eighth century, six or more schools had established firm control of the law. The four major Sunni schools were each identified with the name of a single great commentator (Abu Hanifa, Malik, Shafi'i, Ibn Hanbal). But it was the collective writings of all the commentators belonging to a given tradition, not a single synthetic work by a single author, that constituted the law of any given school. Just as the consensus of all the faithful, when it could be found, defined religious and legal truth, so the consensus of the commentators of a given school constituted the legal truth of that school. When one scholar is identified as the leading member of a school and his work cited as authoritative, it is because his writings are seen as representing the mean or consensual position within his school. The diversity of opinion within a given school was often great, and opinion was often graded as "dominant," preferable" in certain circumstances, or "weak." While in theory the *kadi* would follow the dominant opinion of his own school, in practice he might follow the preferable or weak opinion in order to do justice in a particular case.

Should the consensus of one school on a particular legal point differ from that of another, then that was part of the diversity of opinion among the faithful that was also a blessing from God. Each school might continue to assert its own differing legal holding. Indeed the continuing diversity of the schools is sometimes described as a tree whose beautiful network of branches and twigs all spring from the same trunk and roots. Every Muslim fell under the legal authority of one but no more than one of the schools.

In some areas adherents of various schools lived side by side, each under their own law. Where no consensus on a point of law existed among the commentators of a given school, then each might continue to assert his own position.

The four major schools differ on many specific points of law, but it is not easy to generalize about their differences. The school of Abu Hanifa arose in Kufa, one of the new barracks or garrison cites created by and for the warriors of Islam as they conducted the conquest that shaped a vast empire in the course of a hundred years. The school of Malik flourished in Medina, a holy city because of its associations with the Prophet, but also one that had been a settled commercial community with its own legal traditions long before Muhammad was born. Hanifi jurisprudence tended therefore to be more militant and in some sense more purely Muslim. Maliki jurisprudence rests more on the pre-Muslim customs and usages of Medina, particularly in being somewhat more receptive to commercial practices which might, under the most rigid interpretations of the words of the Prophet, smack of *ribā*.

Shafi'i is a later figure, one of the great synthesizers of Muslim law, who sought to settle the quarrels between literalists and those commentators with a bent toward more speculative and creative jurisprudence.[5] He is a skilled casuist who typically saves the letter of the Koran by demonstrating that somehow or other the letter can be interpreted to meet the exigencies that the real world has thrown up. Shafi'i stresses the agreement of the faithful as a test of legal correctness. The school of Shafi'i is the most complex, subtle, and synthetic of the schools. To a certain extent it is the dominant school in the sense that the others have tended to accept its general methodology of cross comparison and integration of the Koran, the traditions of the Prophet, and the agreement of the faithful. All of the major schools also seem to accept the method of analogy widely practiced by the Shafi'ites to work their very limited initial materials into a fuller body of law.

The Hanbali school may be seen as, to a degree, the opposite of the synthetic sophistication of Shafi'i. Ibn Hanbal was a fundamentalist theologian who taught that there should be no human commentary on the words of the Prophet. A martyr to his beliefs and a hero to the street mobs of Baghdad, his legal commentary consists simply of a massive collection of traditions of the Prophet.

## LAWMAKING AND THE SCHOOLS

The vast body of legal scholarship created by the schools became the working law of Islam. It elaborated and proliferated the scanty and scattered legal pronouncements of the Koran. Although a few of the traditions of the Prophet collected in the writings of the schools may actually be traceable to Muhammad himself, most of them must be new law made by the schools and legitimated by ascription to the Prophet. Also at the earliest stages a great deal of local custom (*urf*) was undoubtedly incorporated into the commentaries, particularly by the Hanafi school relying on the traditions of bedouin warriors and by the Maliki with their tendency to legitimate Medinan commercial practice. Although later the schools came to formally reject custom as a source of law, it clearly was important initially. We have already noted that Shafi'ite reliance on analogy (*giyas*) is common to most of the schools. Analogy is an extremely powerful lawmaking method where, as in Islam, the original corpus is a series of highly particular and incomplete legal pronouncements. *Ribā* again provides a good example. An endless series of analogies were drawn between other commodities and the original six. Those that were held to be like gold, silver, wheat, and so on fell under the prohibition against uneven or delayed exchange. Those that were held to be unlike them did not.

Beyond tradition and analogy most of the schools, with the notable exception of the Hanbali, of course, engaged in various lawmaking practices labeled opinion (*ra'y*), preference (*isthsan*), consensus (*ijma*), and public interest (*isthislah*). There are long debates and interschool differences about when, and to what extent, these devices are to be used and their degree of legal authority. In general, however, they are built on the acknowledgment that the koranic and traditional materials are incomplete and sometimes contradictory, as are the subsequent commentaries. The latest commentator must of necessity on occasion choose between various applicable, but incomplete or conflicting, preexisting rules. In doing so he may be guided by his own preference, but preference in the sense of what appears to him to fit best into the general teachings of Islam and his school. He may seek to discover the consensus of the faithful or of his own school and declare it to be the law. Or he may choose the one of two conflicting or potential rules that appears most to meet the needs of the community, particularly as expressed in their own customary practices.[6] Thus in Islam we find a mixture of rational, legalistic, democratic, and utilitarian bases for supplementary lawmaking by commentators.

Finally, Islamic law, like most other legal systems, employs a set of special technical usages to allow the legal profession to modify some legal rules in order to meet unforeseen circumstances or to ease the burdens of legal administration. In the West we frequently encounter legal fictions or presumptions designed for these purposes. In Islam we find devices (*hiyal*). The strict letter of the Sharia contains prohibitions on interest, and derivatively on any uncertain or speculative elements in contracts, as well as several other doctrines that would render commercial activity impossible. The devices are designed to circumvent these doctrines. For instance there is the loan by double scale. Party A purchases an object from B at a lower price at date 1, and B would at the same time agree to buy the same object back from A at date 2, at a higher price. Party A's purchase price is the loan, and B's purchase price is the repayment. The difference between the two prices is the interest.[7]

The schools obviously did engage in a great deal of lawmaking. They also did a certain amount of synthesizing, at least when great scholars like Malik or Shafi'i sought to integrate various sources and methods of law-finding and harmonize conflicting interpretations. But the schools did not systematize, generalize, or codify Islamic law. For the most part the scholars wrote commentaries upon commentaries upon the Koran and the early collections of traditions of the Prophet. The commentators proceed by detailed exegesis on a particular saying of the Prophet, usually by posing an imaginary fact situation that comes close to but is not quite the same as the one for which the Prophet first shaped his pronouncements. The books of commentaries show only rudimentary attempts at systematic arrangement by subject matter and little or no attempt to frame general rules or categories. The typical form is one in which the Prophet's text is announced, together with the particular situation in which it arose, say the exchange of dried figs by weight. The commentator indicates how other commentators of his school have interpreted this saying and extended it to other very similar fact situations. Then he provides his own applications. Each book of commentaries is a long series of such exegetical commentaries on discrete rules and their attendant fact situations. There is no assurance that all of these discrete discussions add up to a complete code of law, nor any assurance that the rules for various specific fact situations are in harmony with one another.

Moreover, the opportunities for lawmaking by the commentators of the schools was limited very early. Tha basic collections of traditions (*hadith*) were frozen by about the tenth century. At about the same time comes the "closing of the gate" of legal theorizing (*ijtihad*). From this point the orthodox consensus of the various schools is taken as fixed and very little scope is left for further innovation. This fixing appears to be largely the result of the work of Shafi'i. He emphasized that the traditions (*sunna*) of the Prophet must dominate the orthodox consensus (*sunna*) of each individual school. He also placed great emphasis on the consensus (*ijma*) of the whole community of the faithful. This dual emphasis may have been designed to unify Islamic law. In the actual event, what happened was that each school managed to identify its own particular teachings with the traditions of the Prophet and to preserve many interschool differences above and beyond the points of interschool agreement (*ijma*). The end result was that the law of Islam was frozen in the tenth century through its identification with the unchangeable *sunna* of the Prophet and unchallengeable *ijma* of the scholars. And the divided legal teachings of the schools was itself one of the central features that became fixed. After that point the schools continued to produce new manuals for the guidance of judges and students, but their compilers ceased to employ the lawmaking techniques used by earlier commentators. The medieval manuals remained the basic corpus of Islamic law until various reform movements of the twentieth century. Until very recently Islamic commentators bound themselves very firmly by the doctrine of *taqlid*, strict adherence to the teachings of their school as expressed in its medieval manuals. And the compilers of those manuals had already foresworn the conscious use of such methods as preference and opinion.

The jurisconsults (*mufti*) continued to offer opinions (*fatwas*) on disputed points of law both to private litigants, who went into court armed with as many *fatwas* as they cared to purchase, and to the *kadis* themselves. Indeed, official *muftis* were attached to many courts, but their opinions had no official sanctions, and the *kadi* was not required to accept them. Nevertheless, particularly in the nineteenth century, compilation of *fatwas* came to have some authority as legal texts complementary to the medieval manuals.[8] No doubt they contained a good deal of covert lawmaking.

### Islamic Legal Culture and Appeal

From these materials on legal culture it is possible to construct an explanation of why there is generally no appeal under Islamic law. First it must be recalled that one of the major purposes of appeals courts is to provide uniform legal rules so that the law will not be one thing in one trial court and quite a different thing in another. In Western legal systems this uniformity is typically achieved through the announcement of general legal definitions, concepts, and doctrines by the highest courts. These pronouncements then provide guidance for the future decisions of lower courts. The legal environment of the *kadi* was far different from that in the West, however. He worked in a world of highly particularized legal rules rather than general legal concepts. His job was to find which of hundreds of very, very specific and detailed rules most closely fitted the particular facts before him. In doing so he was cut off from the original wording of the Koran and traditions, and even from the great scholarly texts. Instead he referred only to the frozen medieval manuals of his school. He was himself forbidden to work by preference or public interest or any kind of independent legal theorizing (*ijtihad*). Instead he was limited to the most narrow kind of analogy in the interstices of already highly detailed and particularized rules. The work of Shafi'i and others had by the tenth century firmly frozen the legitimate sources (*usūl*) of law as the Koran, traditions, consensus of the schools, and analogy. Thus no legal authority beyond the immediate case could attach to the pronouncements of any legal tribunal.

    In such a system appeals courts would be robbed of many of their major functions. They could not announce uniform legal rules or doctrines. Only the words of the Prophet or the consensus of the community of the faithful can do that. In other words, in a legal culture that rejects all law-making, there can hardly be appellate lawmaking. Indeed, appellate courts could not do any of the kinds of doctrinal pronouncement in which Western appeals courts engage. For the legal culture rejects generalization, broad conceptualizing, and any sort of direct reinterpretation of the basic law. The Hanbali tradition is the extreme statement of rejection of broad reasoning upon the words of the Prophet, but that rejection runs deeply through all of Islam. In a legal culture that rejects generalized legal reasoning, even the most "hard cases" come down to a rather arbitrary choice among a number of highly concrete and particularized rules. There can be little or no attempt even to rationalize the choice. Thus there would appear to be no reason why a second choice by an appellate court would be any better than the initial one made by the trial *kadi*.

    Not only would Islam rob appellate courts of the power of legal generalization and rationalization, which is one of their principal legal tasks in the West, but it would rob them of their ultimate weapon in the struggle for institutional legitimacy. In the West it appears obviously intolerable that, given two trial courts applying the same statute, one should say it means one thing and the other that it means the opposite. Because appeal is the major insurance against this nonuniformity, it is almost impossible for Westerners to accept the abolition of appellate courts, no matter how much they are opposed to the policies being pursued by those courts at any given time.

    In Islam, however, no overwhelming compulsion toward uniformity of law exists. The multiple sects and schools are, of course, the most dramatic evidence of Islamic tolerance of diversity. (Of course sectarianism may exist in religious traditions that show little or no tolerance for diversity, as say in Western Christianity. But unlike Islam each Christian sect has historically tended to deny that the others are sharers in the true faith.) More fundamentally, however, the Islamic cultural stance is to be seen in its mutual acceptance of consensus and diversity among the faithful as equally gifts from God, and the recurring metaphor of diversity as the branches springing from the trunk of the great tree of Islam. Not only are there many differing schools of law but, as we have seen, differing opinions within a single school are tolerated. Even the Islamic notion of consensus is generally one of spontaneous and evolving agreement rather than one of imposition of uniformity. Thus appellate courts are not essential to counter the terrible vice of nonuniform law because legal nonuniformity is not considered a terrible vice.

In short, one explanation of the absence of appeal in Islam is that Islamic legal culture is not a fertile ground for the elaboration of uniform legal doctrines, which is a main task of appeals courts in Roman and Anglo-American legal systems.

### The Incompleteness of Cultural Explanations of the Absence of Appeal in Islam

Explanations of the absence of appeal in Muslim courts based on the legal culture of Islam are not entirely satisfactory for a number of reasons. First of all, as we have already seen, imperial China had a legal code as highly particularized as that of Islam and seemed just as adverse to the formation of general legal concepts or doctrines. It relied heavily, too, on working by small-step analogies from particularized legal provisions taken as fixed. Yet it had a highly elaborate system of appeal.

Second, while after the tenth century the body of law was taken as immutably fixed, why did appeal not arise before the tenth century? While the existence of the schools during even the earliest period might have precluded a single system of appeal, why was there not a highest appeals court for the *kadi*s of each school? The fact that law enunciation and development during the early period was in the hands of jurisconsults rather than the *kadi*s themselves would not have precluded the formation of appellate courts advised by leading jurisconsults in the same way that trial *kadi*s were advised by such jurisconsults. In short during the formative period of Islamic law, when independent legal theorizing (*ijtihad*) was very much in evidence, appellate court lawmaking would have been appropriate to the legal culture, and yet it did not arise.

Third, even after the closing of the gate of *ijtihad*, a number of factors might have combined to encourage judicial lawmaking. Legal rules were particular and incomplete. There was a continued use of reasoning by analogy as a judicial technique. There was a very large body of commentary literature. All of this might have left room for considerable appellate judicial lawmaking at least within each of the schools. Certainly many other legal cultures, most notably the Anglo-American, which in theory limit judicial lawmaking to reasoning by analogy, have witnessed the growth of considerable appellate lawmaking.

Fourth, even if the formal doctrines of each of the schools were theoretically fixed, each *kadi* still had to "apply" this large body of formal rules to the cases before him, many of which inevitably would not quite fit into the preexisting, highly particularized rules. This is a classic breeding ground for judicial lawmaking and thus for appellate work, if only to correct trial courts which have chosen the "wrong" rule or made the "wrong" analogy. Here again the imperial Chinese practice is revealing. Indeed, in the Maghrib, the Western island of Islam running across North Africa, we do encounter the practice of court decisions (*amal*) taking on an independent legal force.[9]

Fifth, the notion of the consensus of the community or the consensus of the jurisconsults is deeply embedded in many legal cultures. We have encountered it in connection with the German "reception" of Roman law. Yet large amounts of lawmaking at appellate court levels go on in many such cultures. The appellate judge or the jurisconsult simply announces himself as the spokesman for the consensus of the community. The requirement of popular consensus need not be a bar to the announcement of law by a single high source. Instead the very cultural need for consensus may become one of the values supporting an appellate court that announces uniform rules in the form of "discovering" the consensus latent in the community. And this need for consensus might have served as a strong weapon of appellate court discipline against the tolerance of diversity that characterizes Islamic culture.

In summary then, the three basic cultural peculiarities of Islamic law are (1) the particularization of legal rules, (2) the rejection of institutional lawmaking beyond the words of the Prophet, and (3) consensus as the mode of discovering what the true words of the Prophet were. But, as the Chinese example shows, particularization alone would not prevent the growth of appeal. And the formal rejection of judicial lawmaking and the formal confinement of judges to the method of analogy has not prevented growth of appellate lawmaking in other cultures. Finally, the notions of law as the consensus of the community exists in many legal cultures in which we do encounter appeal.

It is possible that the peculiar combination of these three dominant features of Islamic legal culture together with its peculiar tolerance of diversity of opinion are enough to explain the absence of appeal in Islam. But the presence of one or more of the same features in other societies that do have appeal makes such an explanation doubtful.

### Institutional Explanations of the Absence of Appeal in Islam

We turn, therefore, to institutional factors of the Islamic legal system that might better explain the absence of appeal. To understand these factors, we must embark on a brief sketch of the growth of Islamic legal, political, and religious institutions. This sketch will reveal two basic institutional factors that are highly relevant to the problem of appeal in Islam. The first is the existence of two judicial systems, one secular and one religious. The second is the weakness or absence of hierarchical structures in both the political and religious organization of Islam.

### RELIGIOUS AND SECULAR COURTS

The Sharia, that is, the law of Islam, cannot simply be called either a purely religious law or an all-encompassing law governing all affairs both secular and religious. The Sharia is the path to righteousness. It guides the faithful to an ideally pure existence rather than prescribing minimums of acceptable conduct. All of it is concerned with the believers' duties to God, and most of it is devoted to what Westerners would call religious obligations such as prayer, pilgrimage, and various kinds of abstinence. Substantial portions of it concern marriage, divorce, and inheritance, matters that initially were considered to be essentially within religious jurisdiction in the West. In this sense the Sharia is religious rather than secular law. But the Sharia also contains prohibitions against a number of major forms of crime, stipulations about the validity of various kinds of commercial transactions and agreements, and provisions about the holding and transfer of various kinds of personal and real property. In that sense it is a secular law or at least had the potential for becoming such a law, particularly given the dominant role of religious values in traditional Muslim society.

### THE UMAYYADS

In the actual event, however, Islam did not develop a single, unified body of law or court system but instead created two parallel legal systems, one of which, with the caveats noted above, can be labeled religious and the other secular. The first Islamic dynasty, the Umayyads (661–750), who controlled a rapidly expanding empire, show an institutional pattern that we have urged is typical of imperial rule. Both judicial and administrative power were vested in the caliph. His judicial powers were then delegated to the host of subordinates who exercised territorial or functional, administrative control, such as provincial governors, army commanders, treasury officials, market inspectors, and water supply officials. Provincial governors were the principal judicial officers, but they left actual dispute settlement to the *kadi*s. At this point, however, the *kadi* was simply the legal secretary to the governor, appointed by him and exercising his delegated authority. Decisions by the *kadi* were reviewable by the governor. The *kadi* replaced the *hakan,* the triadic figure whom disputing Arabs had selected by mutual consent to mediate their disputes. Thus at first the *kadi* handled only "private" disputes voluntarily brought to him by both parties. This is a typical pattern of a new central political regime supplanting purely private triadic dispute settlers with public officials. The police (*shurta*) were in complete control of investigation, arrest, trial, and punishment in criminal matters.

Before the end of the Umayyad caliphate, however, the *kadi* was ceasing to be simply an administrative officer providing dispute settlement services on behalf of the territorial governor. By 715 or 720 the custom had arisen of appointing *kadi*s only from among the scholarly specialists in the Koran.[10] Thus the *kadi* began to become a religious expert rather than simply an administrative subordinate.

### THE ABBASIDS

This tendency, begun under the Umayyads, is rapidly carried to its extreme under the next dynasty, the Abbasids. The Abbasids represented a militant religious reaction to the incipient secularism of the Umayyads. Abbasid policy emphasized the central role of the faith in the new Arab empire. One wing of that policy involved the formation of the *kadi*s as a separate profession of religious scholars. The *kadi*s ceased to be administrative subordinates of the governor and became specialized judges confining themselves entirely to the Sharia. In this sense the *kadi* becomes an independent religious judge rather than a secular subordinate administrator.

It must be remembered, however, that the caliph's regime itself is not a secular one in the Western sense. The Abbasid emphasis on Islam was at the same time an elevation of Islam and an elevation of the caliph, who as defender of the faithful wielded both religious and secular authority. While nominally supervised by a chief *kadi*, the *kadi*s in reality served at the pleasure of the political authorities. In practice that usually still meant the caliph's territorial governor.

### THE SECULAR COURTS

At the same time that the religious aspects of the *kadi*'s role were emphasized, and indeed partly because of this emphasis, a second body of law and courts arose. We have already noted the trial jurisdiction of the *shurta* which was far more extensive than the police court jurisdiction for minor offenses that we encounter in many legal systems. The caliphate took over from the Byzantines the institution of "inspector of the market" (*muhtasib*), a local official responsible not only for maintaining the orderly operation of the marketplace but for settling commercial disputes according to the local customs of the market. In Islam, as in medieval Europe, they could play a particularly important role because religious objections to profit and interest on loans were deeply embedded in the general law. This is not to say that the inspectors of the market were totally isolated from the Sharia and employed a totally distinct body of law. As with most older institutions taken over by the faithful, this one was Islamicized. The *muhtasib* was generally regarded as in inferior of, if not a subordinate to the *kadi*.[11] However, a great many of the "devices" of Islamic law are designed to reach a compromise between the Sharia and customary commercial practices. Thus the jurisdiction of the market inspector was not some sort of haven or island of antireligious law. Nevertheless, the inspector was not a *kadi* and his decisions were not pronouncements of the Sharia.

From the earliest times the administrative side of the caliphate contained an office known as the *sahib al-mazālim,* the official in charge of complaints.[12] *Mazālim* jurisdiction included complaints against government officials, land law, and whatever else the government chose to define as a complaint. *Mazālim* courts could and did announce doctrines of substantive law additional and supplemental to the Sharia in the form of administrative regulations or policies of the government. The relation between this *mazālim* court system and the *kadi*s is not clear-cut and varies greatly from time to time and place to place. It is clear that the Sahib al-Mazālim was totally independent of the court of the *kadi* and indeed could hear complaints against the *kadi* as against all other government officials. But in some instances *kadi*s held both Sharia and *mazālim* jurisdiction and many *mazālim* courts had a *sharia* jurisconsult in attendance. Moreover, particularly in active military zones, the *mazālim* courts might take on almost complete jurisdiction.

The authority of the *mazālim* courts was derived from that of the caliph. The caliphate expanded its own lawmaking powers, and thus the powers the *mazālim* and the police courts, in two ways. First, under the name *siyasa,* which means roughly administration or public policy, the caliphs did in fact legislate particularly in the areas of police, taxation, and criminal justice.[13] The Sharia condemned only a few offenses, and for those it specified particularly severe punishments (*hadd*). Prosecutions for other offenses, and even for Sharia offenses when the authorities wanted something less than *hadd* punishments, were brought in the secular courts. The caliph defined both the substantive and procedural aspects of the non-*hadd* criminal law. Moreover, the caliph might impose whatever punishments (*ta'zir*) he thought were necessary to serve as a deterrent to bad conduct even in noncriminal disputes.[14]

Land and tax litigation were normally brought before the master of the treasury. The Sharia said little or nothing about such matters. The seizure and reassignment to the faithful of great tracks of conquered land was a key feature of the Islamic political economy of conquest. Since the caliphs assigned this land, major land disputes ended up in the *mazālim* courts rather than before the *kadi* because they were essentially problems of military administration rather than ownership. Thus the totality of the caliph's administrative powers was very great.

Moreover, as defenders of the faithful, the caliphs attributed to themselves the status of religious scholars. They could announce their personal interpretations of the Sharia just as could any other legal scholar. Thus the vast administrative discretion of the caliphate could be given a gloss of Sharia legitimacy by the caliphs themselves.

It is always a great mistake in analyses of traditional Islam to make a sharp distinction between secular and religious authorities or jurisdictions. For until the fall of the Ottoman Empire after World War I, the Islamic world knew no purely secular governments, except where, as in India and Indonesia, Muslims were conquered and reduced to the status of a protected religious minority. Nevertheless, we can observe a large body of law and courts, basically involved in the secular-administrative sector of the Caliphate's vast authority, operating separately and in parallel to the courts of the *kadis*. These courts conceived of themselves as applying the rules and policies of the caliph and other territorial rulers rather than confining themselves to the Sharia. In this sense a secular legal system exists side by side with the religious law of the *kadis*.[15]

The growth of an alternative system of law and courts was encouraged, perhaps even necessitated, by two aspects of the Sharia. The first was its incompleteness, which we have already examined. The second was its strict and demanding rules of evidence. Under Sharia procedure it is almost always both necessary and sufficient that two male adult Muslims testify orally to the truth of the claimant's (*mudda'ī*) position. If two such witnesses cannot be produced, the defendant (*mudda'ā alayhi*) wins by taking an oath of denial. If two such witnesses do appear, about the only option open to the defendant is to attack their moral and religious character. There is no cross-examination, and *kadis* do not normally weigh opposing evidence.

These evidentiary problems were so severe that they spawned a special official, the *sahib al-rodd*. His function was to hear cases rejected by the *kadi* because the claimant could not meet Sharia standards of proof although he appeared to be justified in his claim. The police courts and the *wali al-jarā* (official in charge of crimes) heard evidence from dubious witnesses, cross-examined, extracted confessions, and heard and weighed circumstantial evidence. The *mazālim* courts used discretionary procedures outside the Sharia.

Thus with the appropriate qualifications that must always be made for Islam, the primary institutional fact of the legal system is that there were two basic structures of law, courts and judicial procedures. One was essentially secular and directly linked to the political and administrative authorities. The other was religious and directly linked to the Sharia tradition as embodied in the teachings of the schools of jurisconsults.

## Appeal and Sharia Courts: Appeal as Hierarchical Control

As a result, some of the uses of appeal are not relevant to the Sharia courts of the *kadis*. Appeal as a sample of administrative performance was irrelevant because the *kadis* were not in the main line of administration. Appeal as a means of hierarchical control and coordination was irrelevant for the same reason. To the extent that the caliphs and subsequently the Ottoman sultans did exercise control over their domains, it was through a chain of territorial administrators and tributary monarchs, a chain to which the *kadis* were only loosely connected. (It is true that in the declining days of Islamic empire the *kadis* took on more and more of the duties of local government, but that was precisely because the hierarchical chain of government administrators was disintegrating.) In short, to the extent that appeal is an instrument of hierarchical control, and we have seen that it is largely as such an instrument that appeal is attractive to government, it was far more relevant to the secular side of Islamic legal institutions than to its system of religious courts.

The relations between church and state are extremely complex in the history of Islam. Nevertheless, it always remained relatively clear that the law of Sharia pertained to the religious aspirations of the faithful while the police and administrative law and courts of the caliphs and sultans[16] were the principal governors of the more mundane aspects of public policy. Yet to label the Sharia religious is not in itself a satisfactory explanation of why appeal as hierarchical control is absent. In the ecclesiastical law and courts of the Roman Catholic Church of Europe, where far clearer lines are drawn between religious and secular law than in Islam, we do encounter an extremely elaborate system of appeals very heavily freighted with the function of maintaining papal control over widely dispersed subordinates. It is not that *kadi* courts are religious, but the nature of Islam as a religious community, that explains the absence of appeal.

The Islamic religious community, unlike the Roman Catholic one, has only the weakest hierarchical structure. The caliph is in theory both the successor of Muhammad and the chosen of the people, but he is only defender of the faithful, not proclaimer of the faith. There are no equivalents of Apostolic succession, dogma, or papal infallibility, or of cannon law made by the Church as subsidiary to Divine Law. The caliph or *imam* may make no law on the central questions of religion. At best he is one among the many jurisconsults. He may protect but has no superior claim to enunciate the consensus of the faithful. In some of the Islamic sects, their own religious leader achieved the status of Prophet or even a kind of God. This development leads to absolutist regimes, combining full religous and secular powers, such as the Fatimids in Egypt and the Persian monarchy. But in the Sunnite mainstream no such dominant religious authority emerges. Islam has no ultimate human religious lawgiver, nor any hierarchical organization of priests and bishops culminating in such a lawgiver.[17] For a religious community that lacks both the doctrine of a single, central, dominant human pronouncer of religious truth and a hierarchical structure of priests and religious institutions, one of the principal attractions of appeal, its hierarchical control dimension, is missing.

Thus the Sharia courts did not need to be mustered in a hierarchical fashion to achieve the secular tasks of territorial rulers since those rulers enjoyed a second legal and administrative system for such purposes. And they did not need to be hierarchically organized to support the hierarchical structure of the religious community because there was no such structure in the religious community.

The religious fragmentation of Islam is a part of its more general fragmentation. Although political institutions such as the caliphate and the Ottoman Empire often claimed centralized authority, in reality Islam was usually divided into a large number of independent territorial states. Even within areas that acknowledged the nominal rule of a single caliph, imam, sultan, or emperor, typically there were a series of city-states or praetorian provinces with very few lines of authority running from local to central authorities. Because *kadi*s were appointed by the government authorities, Sharia judicial organization reflected the general lapses in hierarchy of the political regime. Somewhere in the background a head *kadi* might exist, but in reality there was rarely a unified corps of *kadi*s or any single central appointing authority. *Kadi*s, like other government officials, usually lived in essentially local worlds.

The *kadi*'s law was a segment of a universal religion. The *kadi*s were officials appointed by city or state secular regimes. As purveyor of the universals of Islam, the *kadi* cannot be totally incorporated into whatever local political hierarchy exists. Yet he is also not incorporated into any universal religious hierarchy since there is none. Governing authorities did sometimes try to discipline *kadi*s. There are instances in which regimes attempted to apply test oaths and purge the ranks of the *kadi*s in order to achieve religious uniformity or compliance to the regime's policies.[18] But these attempts are relatively rare and usually unsuccessful. Thus the *kadi* lived in an essentially local nonhierarchical situation. He was usually appointed by local authority, and his duty was to one of the schools of a religious law in which neither the school nor the religion had a single central authority. In such a nonhierarchical world the absence of appeal is hardly surprising.

### Elements of Appeal in Islam

This close linkage between the vicissitudes of Islamic political and religious hierarchy and the absence of appeal can be further demonstrated through an examination of the elements of appeal actually to be found in Islam. Those elements are in fact substantial. Initially, no distinct appeals mechanism was necessary in Islam because of a constitutional theory of delegation apparently inherited by the Arabs from the Byzantines. All political, legal, and religious authority belonged to the caliph. He might delegate portions of that authority to subordinates, who in turn might redelegate it. But the delegator retained full and complete jurisdiction and authority over all matters delegated. Thus the caliph and his governors retained full judicial authority even when delegating judicial tasks to the *kadi*s. The notion of a higher level of appeals courts above the *kadi*s does not arise because a litigant dissatisfied with the *kadi*'s decision or reluctant to go to him in the first place could place his case directly before the highest political authority. While not actually spoken of in this way, a system of appeal by trial *de novo* conducted by the delegating authority existed. There are scattered recorded instances of caliphs reversing the decisions of a *kadi* or sending a case back to him with new instructions. Because initially the political authorities retained such complete judicial jurisdiction, they had no need of special appellate courts. Subsequently two interacting forces intervene to disrupt this appellate system. First, as the *kadi*s came to be seen as servants of the Sharia, experts in a religious law rather than simple legal subordinates of caliph and governor, they became increasingly independent of day-to-day control by the political authorities. Second, as the central political, military, and religious authority of caliphs and their governors decayed, they tended to give up personal exercise of their judicial authority.

Thus we have a paradox. Precisely because initially the caliphs concentrated such enormous religious and secular judicial authority, they needed no special appellate institutions or procedures. As a result, Islam ended up with no appellate institutions at all once the powers of the central authorities waned.

Closely connected to their personal judicial powers to try cases, the caliphs, sultans, and governors exercised another authority, that of *mazālim*, or complaints. We have already seen that *mazālim* jurisdiction was part of the second and "secular" line of Islamic courts. Three elements of *mazālim* jurisdiction intersect to make it an appeals jurisdiction imposed over the *kadi*. First, it is a court of complaints against government officials, and the *kadi* is a government official. Second, it is a kind of equity court designated to do substantial justice in cases in which for any reason the *kadi* has been incapable of doing justice. Typically this incapacity arose because the procedural or substantive rules of the Sharia were too rigid or narrow to remedy the injury. Sometimes the transgressor was a person so powerful that the *kadi* was unable to reach him. The failure of the *kadi* to reach a *correct* legal decision, however, was also viewed as an incapacity remedial by the *mazālim* court. Third, the *mazālim* jurisdiction is peculiarly connected to the head of the regime. It is a device for correcting the misconduct of his own lesser officials. It is also a device for bringing the full power of authority to bear against powerful individuals who resist the jurisdiction and judgments of the *kadis'* courts. *Mazālim* jurisdiction inheres in the caliph, sultan, or governor. So does the general power to hold court. So the two are often not distinguished or are seen as additive or supplementary to one another. The *mazālim* jurisdiction, therefore, empowers the head of the regime to hear and remedy complaints against a *kadi* brought by those who have lost cases in the *kadi's* court or otherwise suffered from his conduct.[19]

What is most striking about the development of *mazālim* jurisdiction over time is that whenever a caliph, sultan, territorial governor, or *wazir* (prime minister, major of the palace) was in the ascendancy, concentrating political power in himself, he tended to exercise *mazālim* jurisdiction actively and personally. Indeed in such instances *mazālim* jurisdiction tended to expand so far that it not only supervised but sometimes displaced the *kadis'* jurisdiction. Whenever central government was in disarray, however, we find that the governing authority ceases to exercise *mazālim* jurisdiction personally and instead delegates it to a special corps of subordinate judges. And when *mazālim* jurisdiction is exercised by such subordinates, it usually is specifically excluded from taking appeals from *kadis'* courts. Moreover, in the weakest periods of central authority, the *kadis* themselves often are granted *mazālim* jurisdiction.[20]

In short, if we trace the major appeals institutions of Islam over time, we find that appeal tended to flourish as political power become concentrated and wane as political authority was dispersed.

### The Ottoman Empire: A Case Study in Islam, Hierarchy, and Appeal

If the absence of appeal in Islamic law is indeed related to the absence of centralization rather than to the absence of concern for the loser at trial, we should expect to find the introduction of appeal where Islamic institutions did become centralized. The great intersection between Islam and centralizing tendencies occurred in the Ottoman Empire, which dominated much of the Muslim world from the fourteenth through the nineteenth century.[21] The Ottomans were originally nomadic Turkic tribesmen from Central Asia who settled in what is now the western portion of modern Turkey. From that base they gradually built their empire at a cost to both the European Christians to their west and north and the Muslims to their east and south. At its highpoint, the empire swept from the Balkans and Greece into the Caucasus, through Turkey, and thence along the eastern and southern shores of the Mediterranean all the way to Algeria and Tunisia. With the exceptions of Persia and the interior of Saudia Arabia, the Ottomans either directly or indirectly ruled the whole heartland of the Islamic faith. The sultan was both the emperor and caliph,[22] and the religious capital as well as the secular capital of most of Islam was Istanbul.

The Ottoman Empire only reached its ideal of complete centralization of authority in the sultan partially and for brief moments. In the seventeenth, eighteenth, and nineteenth centuries even the moments got briefer and briefer until they disappeared. Nevertheless, the ideal of centralization was there and so was the reality during the reigns of some of the great early sultans.

Certainly, the ideal of centralization was reflected in the judicial institutiosn of the empire. The *kadi*s held the sultan's commission. They enforced both the Sharia and the *kanun,* that is, the secular laws enacted by the sultan. The *kadi*s played a major role in territorial administration, not only in the levying of criminal penalties, but in the supervision of the tax system and in the management of the large religious trust funds that were an important feature of Muslim life. The *kadi*s and *bey*s shared authority as conveyors and enforcers of the commands of the sultan.[23]

The judicial personnel system was centralized and hierarchical. Under the ultimate authority of the sultan, the two *kadi*s of the army (*kaziasker*), one for the European and the other for the Near Eastern sectors of the empire, appointed all the *kadi*s for their respective territories. Later, some of the authority of the *kaziasker*s was partially lost to the new office of chief of Islam or grand mufti (*seyhulislam*). This mufti not only appointed and supervised lesser mufti and the general body of the learned men of the faith (*ulema*) but appointed the more important *kadi*s. There was a hierarchy of *kadi* positions with appropriate graded (and quite high) salaries, honors, and territorial jurisdictions numbering about five hundred in the eighteenth cenutry. In short, the corps of *kadi*s exhibited the standard pyramidal organization running from rank-and-file local *kadi*s up to the *kaziasker*s and the *seyhulislam* who were appointed by and responsible to the sultan. Moreover, the *kadi*s, like other imperial officers, were subject to the scrutiny of the roving inspectors that the sultans sent out from time to time. The sultan and his high officers could and did summarily remove local *kadi*s from office.

Given the general imperial thrust toward centralization and the hierarchical organization of judicial personnel, do we encounter the expected appellate institutions and procedures? The answer is a qualified yes.

There were appeals, but there were no appeals procedures or appeals courts as such. The absence of specialized appellate institutions and procedures was perhaps due in part to the fact that the absence of such institutions was already a central characteristic of Islamic law when it was taken over by the Ottomans. But just as in the development of English law that we have already traced, appeal was stunted essentially because another mode of judicial centralization was employed, that of centralized trial courts. Like many sovereigns close to their tribal origins, the sultans were personally the supreme font of justice, much as the early English kings had been. The sultan held court wherever he was. The grand vizier, highest officer of the sultan and the delegate of his authority, also held court. The *divan*, or council of the sultan, like the Privy Council or Star Chamber, was both an administrative cabinet coordinating the business of government, and an important court. And so was the *divan* of the grand vizier. Since all of these persons and groups reflected the personal justice of the sultan, which of course was a complete justice, each could hold whatever trials it pleased.

In the empire every court was a court of first instance for whatever cases were appropriate to its level of prestige. The two *divan*s were in a sense supreme courts, but they served as courts of first instance for cases important enough to attract their attention. The grand vizier personally decided those cases he wished to hear with the advice of the *kadi*s who attended the *divan* if the case involved the Sharia. Other Sharia cases he turned over to these *kadi*s for trial. The head of the Financial Office (*defterdar*) had a court of his own to deal with monetary disputes between the government and individuals. The Admiral heard all cases involving the fleet. Most important, the *kaziasker*s had trial jurisdiction over all cases of inheritance, marriage, and emancipation in which *askeri*s were involved and had direct personal jurisdiction over all members of the standing military forces. Given the basically military character of the empire, nearly everyone above the rank of peasant and artisan, and outside the *ulema*, was an *askeri*, that is, a soldier. Moreover, because most of the land of the empire was held as military fiefs (*timar*), almost all land disputes arose between persons who technically were members of the standing military forces. As a result the courts of the two *kaziasker*s heard nearly all the major real property cases that arose and a substanial share of all cases involving the political and social elite of the empire. Thus elaborate appeal mechanisms were not terribly necessary as a device for centralization because the most important cases were likely to be heard directly by the central government itself.

While technically forbidden by Islamic law, a party dissatisfied with the judgment of one *kadi* could try another. Traditionally the *kadi*s made their decisions rather summarily without lengthy opinions either written or oral. Given these two practices, an appeal was not necessarily differentiated in any way because it was an appeal. No special procedures or courts were necessary when a litigant, dissatisfied by the decision of a local *kadi,* went to a regional or provincial *kadi,* and then, dissatisfied there, went on to one of the highest courts of the realm sitting in the capital, or indeed to the sultan himself. For each of the courts involved, the trial was a trial de novo rather than a "review" of what had been done below.

In spite of the absence of special appeals mechanisms, an absence we have just explained, numerous authorities testify to the existence of appeal and to the fact that the sultan, the grand vizier and their respective *divan*s, stood at the apex of appeals.[24] The *kaziasker*s attended the sultan's *divan* and the *kaziasker*s and four of the most important *kadi*s that of the grand vizier. After sessions of the *divan* itself, the high officials who attended it customarily split up, each to hear further business of particular concern to him. Cases would also be heard at these sessions. The two *divan*s sat both as trial courts in regular lawsuits and as administrative superiors hearing complaints against their subordinates including the *kadi*s. Appeal took the form either of a trial de novo or a complaint against the corrupt or unjust acts of a lower *kadi*. This was yet another reason why appeal does not appear as distinctly in the empire as in other places. It was often merged, as we have noted elsewhere in this chapter, with the general complaints jurisdiction of various mixed judicial and administrative bodies. The *kaziasker,* for instance, heard appeals not only in the *divan* but independently from decisions of the military governors of towns and provinces concerning the affairs of their subordinate government officials.[25]

THE REALITIES OF THE SULTAN'S POWER

Nevertheless, there is a great deal about the hierarchical ambitions and surface accomplishments of the Ottoman sultans that suggests a more explicit and institutionally distinct role for appeal than we actually encounter. For in practice it is probable that the decisions of local *kadi*s were very rarely reversed. In order to understand why the empire did not evolve such a role, we must look more carefully at the Ottoman constitution.

The Ottoman sultans claimed absolute political authority and built a system of government to wield that authority. At the capital, the sultans built a large, functionally specialized, hierarchical bureaucracy that culminated in the *divan* of the sultan, an almost daily meeting of the highest officers of the realm. The *divan* was dominated either by the sultan or his grand vizier, the highest political officer of the realm. For our purposes here we need not trace the historically shifting power relations that sometimes made the sultan and sometimes the grand vizier the actual head of state. As we have already noted, the *divan* not only acted to coordinate, announce, and enforce the policies of the central government but as a high court both of first instance and appeal. The *kaziasters* sat in the *divan*. With their participation, the *divan* became the highest court of the Sharia.

The hierarchical and centralized administration of the capital was mirrored by a comparable territorial organization. With exceptions resulting from the circumstances of the conquest of certain of its parts, this organization was fairly uniform for so large an empire. The land was divided into basic units called *timars*, each of which was supervised by and supported a *sipahi,* that is, an armed and equipped cavalryman, and his horse. In the sixteenth century there were about thirty thousand of these. The holders of the larger *timars* were also responsible for providing one or more cavalrymen besides themselves. There were intermediate ranks of *subashi* (roughly captain) and *alay bey* (roughly colonel). In wartime men of these ranks served as commanders of small and intermediate size units and in peacetime as territorial police officials. They held even larger *timars* (*zeamets*). The *sipahi*s and their *subashi*s and *alay bey*s were grouped territorially under *sanjac bey*s, each of whom had his seat in a town and governed his district as well as serving as general of the cavalry division composed of his *sipahi*s. Above them were the *beylerbey*s, or *bey*s of *bey*s, who were governors of their provinces and commanders of the major wings of the army under the direct command of the sultan and grand vizier.

So far what we have described is a very neat structure of centralized empire that looks rather like the Chinese empire and might be expected to exhibit comparable judicial structures. Indeed, since there was a *kadi* in nearly every town, a provincial *kadi* of higher rank in each provincial capital and a *kaziasker* to match each of the two most important *beylerbey*s, the judicial corps followed the territorial pattern of the general government and culminated like it in the *divan*. At the height of the sultan's powers in the fifteenth and sixteenth centuries, great emphasis was placed on the *kadi*s as appointees of the sultan administering the sultan's *kanun* rather than as drawing their authority solely and directly from the Sharia.

Below the surface, however, the Ottoman sultans were very far from achieving the centralization of the Chinese emperors. Shaw indeed concludes that "it was only in the nineteenth century, as the result of Western influence, that Ottoman government in fact secured the kind of autocracy and centralized power that Europe traditionally assumed it had."[26] The

Ottoman state labored under so many incapacities and incompletenesses that they must be itemized methodocically.

First of all, in Islam the title sultan means military leader. In the tribal, Turkish traditions of Central Asia out of which the Ottoman sultans came, the *bey,* or military leader was simply that. He led in war. In peace the Turkic tribes had no chiefs. In a very real sense the Ottoman sultans never escaped these traditions. They wielded absolute authority only over the army and even over it only when it was on campaign. This is one of the basic reasons that the sultans undertook a campaign nearly every summer. The vast bulk of the population, the *raia,* was exempt from military service. So long as it paid its taxes, it remained almost totally untouched by the sultan's authority. The neat territorial organization that ran from *timar* holder up to a *beylerbey* actually only operated when the army gathered for its summer campaigns.[27] For the rest of the year each *timar* holder administered his own lands as an almost entirely independent feudal fief. And each *bey* or *subashi* reverted to ruling his own headquarters town as if it were his *timar,* which in many respects it was. Thus much of the neatly hierarchical structure of Ottoman government was in reality a military structure that became quiescent during most of each year.

Second, the Ottoman sultans had come to power as tribal *bey*s who were only first among equals: The other equals were their Turkic lieutenants, who were fellow nomadic horsemen and fellow Muslims. Turkish, Muslim notables continued to be an important independent power in the empire. To counter them the sultans developed what was surely the unique feature of the Ottoman Empire, the slave family of the sultan. From the families of his conquered European Christian subjects, the sultan drafted young boys, who were then rigorously educated in Islam and trained as servants and soldiers of the sultan. Thus, alongside the old Turkish Muslim elite of notables, grew up a professional army and a mandarinate of governing officials. Each was composed of men who were European and Christian in origin and remained throughout their lives the personal slaves of the sultan, to be disposed of in any way he saw fit. These slaves of the sultan were mingled with the old Muslim notables at many points. For instance, many of the *timar* holders and *bey*s were the sultan's slaves, but old Muslim notables held many governorships and their retainers many *timar*s. Among the scribes, or civil servants, of the capital some were old Muslims and some were slaves.

The central political arm of the capital, however, was recruited almost exclusively from the sultan's slaves. It consisted of the palace staff of the sultan, the grand vizier and his immediate staff, and the central professional core of the army, the janissaries. Just as much of what appears to be hierachcical government turns out to be only a hierarchical army, so much of what appears to be absolute government turns out to be only absolute control by the sultan over his slave family. As the sultanate declined, of course, even this absolutism often proved illusory. The grand vizier or the jannisaries often controlled the sultan rather than vice versa. Even leaving this point aside, however, what is often seen as the sultan's or grand vizier's absolute and arbitrary power over subordinates really existed largely within the slave family and those parts of government controlled by this group. For it was totally dependent on the sultan and isolated from the tribal and Muslim roots of Ottoman society. The sultan's authority tended to drop off very sharply as it entered the realms of the old Turks and the old Muslims. It may be an overstatement to depict the Ottoman ruling institution as neatly split into two parts, the formerly Christian slave family of the sultan, living at his pleasure, and the Muslim warriors and learned men living under the Sharia and custom. Nevertheless, much of Ottoman centralization was really only a family affair.

Third, the centralizing and hierarchical tendencies of the empire were tempered by a vague constitutional theory of balance of powers that, for all its vagueness, is actually reflected in middle eastern institutions. The theory holds that a true empire requires contributions by men of the sword and men of the pen who complement and balance one another. Ottoman central government reflected this theory in the structure of central government ministries and the composition of the *divan*. The three highest advisors to the sultan were the grand vizier on military-political matters, the *nicansi* or chief scribe on administrative matters, and the *seyhulislam* and *kaziaskers* on religious matters. The balancing function was most explicit in territorial administration. The *kadis* were responsible for both the Sharia and the *kanun*, or administrative regulations of the sultan. Thus the *beys* could not act in many matters without the legal authorization of the *kadis*, but the *kadi* had no sword to enforce his judgment and relied on the *beys* for such enforcement.[28]

More generally the ruling establishment of the empire did consist of two parts. One was military and political and centered on the formerly Christian slaves of the sultan. The other was civil and religious and centered on the *ulema*, the body of Muslim religious and legal scholars. In theory they both met at the top in the person of the sultan-caliph. The sultanate was, however, essentially a military-political institution, and the *ulema* was seen as a counterbalance to the secular authority of the sultan. The Ottoman sultans really only began to insist on their status as caliph in the waning days of the empire in an attempt to bolster their sliding political authority. It is true that a *seyhulislam* or other *mufti* or *kadi* who refused to give the sultan what he wanted was likely to find his life highly unpleasant or short. It was also true, however, that major political changes were only considered legitimate when accompanied by a *fatwah* from the *ulema* certifying their religious orthodoxy.

Fourth and last, the seemingly absolute power of the sultan was both limited and superficially dramatized by the Ottoman view of personal responsibility. Within the strict boundaries of the role or status that society had prescribed for him, each individual was supposed to be personally autonomous and responsible for his own acts. The kind of supervision that entailed issuing continuous corrections of a subordinate's errors ran counter to this cultrual ideal. Thus Ottoman administrative control was directed largely into personnel measures. A subordinate was to be left alone to do his job. If he failed, he should be dismissed, or executed, and replaced by someone else who should be left alone until he failed. Under a strong sultan it would be said that a hundred heads of those who had failed sometimes arrived for his viewing pleasure on a single day. Thus the Ottoman government was characterized by dramatic hiring and firing policies but little detailed control over day-to-day administration.[29]

In summary then the sultan's authority was greatest over military matters and over his own slave family and diminished more and more as we move to civil and particularly religious affairs and as we move from formerly Christian European slaves to old Muslim, middle eastern notables.

THE SULTAN AND THE KADIS

The *kadi*s were concerned primarily with civil and religious affairs and were drawn from and deeply embedded in the culture of the old Muslim middle eastern notables. They stayed home when the army went to war. And they were at home in the bosom of Islam, when the government was run by the children of foreign Christians. It is surely no coincidence that when the sultan first searches for an instrument to wield his central authority over the *kadi*s, he chooses the *kaziasker*s—that is, the *kadi*s of the army. Nor that later he chooses the *seyhulislam,* the mufti of his capital city, a city dominated by his slave family. These instruments, however, did not really succeed. The *ulema* maintained its separate authority. At times of crisis a sultan or grand vizier might overwhelm it by sheer force or threat of force. On a day-to-day basis, however, it maintained its independent tradition of learning and law. It provided the *mufti*s and *kadi*s who followed that tradition as a special reserve of authority against whatever pretentions to absolute authority the sultan might have.

Given the Ottoman penchant for supervising administration by hiring and firing rather than direct day-to-day control, the appointment process for *kadi*s was crucial. Here we find that the early and strong Ottoman sultans did seek to centralize the appointing power. In Islam the holder of political power had traditionally had the right to appoint the *kadi*s. As we have already noted the Ottoman sultans established a carefully graded, hierarchical personnel system for *kadis* in which higher *kadis* appointed and dismissed lower ones and the highest *kadis*, the *kaziaskers*, and later the *seyhulislam*, appointed and dismissed the principal territorial *kadis*. The sultan himself appointed and dismissed the highest *kadis* and the *seyhulislam* and so in theory controlled the whole corps. As in other aspects of Ottoman administration, it was this personnel management form of hierarchical control rather than detailed day-to-day supervision and correction of errors that was emphasized. A fully developed appeals system is of course just such a detailed day-to-day supervision and correction of errors. In familiar Western terms, the Ottoman political regime preferred to control its judicial product by reducing the independence of its judiciary rather than instituting a thoroughgoing system of appeal. The trial judge was held in check not by the fear of reversal on appeal but by the fear of loss of his job or even his head.

Ultimately, however, the personnel tactic of the sultan failed, and failed precisely because the *kadis* were necessarily embedded in a traditional Muslim community that was at the periphery of his authority. The sultan was not in a position to challenge the proposition that the *kadis* must be men learned in the wisdom of traditional Islam. As a result the *ulema* continued to dominate the education and the appointment of the *kadis*. The sultan might in some sense ultimately appoint, but he must appoint from among those whom the *ulema* had proposed on the basis of their demonstrated allegiance, not to the sultan, but to the Islamic religious community.

In short, while the *kadis* played an extremely important role in the Ottoman constitution, they were far removed from the central channels of the sultan's authority, namely, the army and the slave family.[30] They were deeply embedded in that portion of Ottoman society most insulated from the sultan's absolutist pretensions, namely, the traditional Islamic community of notables and learned men. The sultans did, nonetheless, seek to impose their control over the *kadis* by both a hierarchical personnel system and an appeals system culminating in the person of the sultan. Both of these devices seem to have been relatively ineffective, however, precisely because they operated at the farthest and weakest reaches of the sultan's power.

In summary, then, in spite of the absence of appeal from the central Islamic juristic tradition which the Ottomans absorbed, there was an appellate process in the empire, closely associated with the institutions through which the sultan sought to centralize political authority. While this appellate process is somewhat obscured by the use of trial de novo on appeal and the intermingling of litigation and complaint jurisdiction, the fact remains that whenever Islamic law and hierarchical government intersect in a relatively stable and long-term way, we do encounter appeal in the Muslim world.

The appeals process is attenuated and obscured, however, precisely because it operated in the sphere in which the government's claims to hierarchical authority were weakest.

## Conclusion

Legal rules and the urge to do justice according to those rules are not absent from the Islamic legal tradition. Quite the opposite. There are rules aplenty, a strong desire that they be applied uniformly, and a strong antipathy to arbitrary judgment. If there is little appeal, it is not because no one cared whether the trial courts did justice under law. The simplest explanation of the absence of appeal in Islamic law is that the Sharia and the courts of the *kadi*s are essentially religious, and that Islam as a religion was not organized hierarchically. Without hierarchical organization much of both the opportunity and incentive for appeal is absent. And most of the pressure for appeal as a lawmaking device was absent because adjustments in law to meet new circumstances could be accomplished by the secular wing of Muslim legal institutions. More generally the Muslim world experienced great difficulty in establishing or maintaining any kind of unity or hierarchy over its vast domains. Where, as for instance in the efforts of the Abbasid caliphs and the early Ottoman emperors, we do encounter attempts at centralization of authority, we do encounter appeal.

In the final analysis the *kadi*s escaped appeals supervision for the same reasons they escaped all hierarchical supervision. Their special identification with the Sharia and their physical and social attachment to the mosque itself, that is, to the very center of the local community of believers, insulated them from the central political authorities. Thus their religious dimension shielded them from the hierarchical authority that normally would have been exerted over them as local legal officials of a central regime. That religious dimension did not in turn lead to their subordination to a central religious hierarchy because there was no such hierarchy. Indeed, in the recurrent collapse of central authority in the Islamic world, the local mosque and its *kadi* became the only constant and ever present receptacle of the religious and political authority of the faith. More often than not the local *kadi*s pulled all sorts of political, economic, religious, and administrative authority away from the central regime. Quite apart from their judicial functions, they seemed to be the only officials with sufficient stability to wield that authority successfully. When local authorities thrive on the confusion of central regimes, and the local authorities happen to be judges, it could hardly be expected that institutions of appeal would flourish.

At the most universal level of historical analysis some observers might wish to attribute the absence of effective hierarchical control in Islam to cultural factors embedded in Islamic thought and the Arab milieu out of which it sprang. Cultural factors would certainly seem to offer the best explanation of the antipathy to lawmaking in the Sharia system. At a more mundane and immediate level, however, it is sufficient to say that in Islam we encounter a peculiar institutional combination of dual legal systems and absence of hierarchy. This peculiar combination accounts for the absence of the institution of appeal that is to be found in almost all other legal system. The Islamic experience suggests again, therefore, that it is not concern for justice under law but concern for political control that is the basic motive force of appellate institutions.

# NOTES

## Chapter 1

1. M. Shapiro, *Law and Politics in the Supreme Court* (New York: Free Press, 1964); W. Murphy and J. Tanenhaus, *The Study of Public Law* (New York: Random House, 1972).

2. T. Becker, *Comparative Judicial Politics* (Chicago: Rand McNally, 1970).

3. G. Aubert, "Competition and Dissensus: Two Types of Conflict Resolution," *Journal of Conflict Resolution*, 7 (1963): 26; R. Abel, "A Comparative Theory of Dispute Institutions in Society," *Law and Society Review*, 8 (1973): 217.

4. Thus courts may be seen as a special case of the dyadic-triadic relationships of Simmel (G. Simmel, *The Sociology of Georg Simmel* [New York: Free Press, 1950]).

5. H. Wolff, *Roman Law: An Historical Introduction* (Norman: University of Oklahoma Press, 1951).

6. C. K. Allen, *Law in the Making* (London: Oxford University Press, 1958).

7. L. Pospisil, *Kapaku Papuans and Their Law*, Yale University Publications in Anthropology, no. 54 (New Haven: Yale University Department of Anthropology, 1958).

8. E. Hoebel, *The Law of Primitive Man* (Cambridge, Mass.: Harvard University Press, 1954).

9. J. Cohen, "Chinese Mediation on the Eve of Modernization," *California Law Review*, 54 (1966): 1201; D. Henderson, *Conciliation and Japanese Law* (Seattle: University of Washington Press, 1965).

10. L. Fuller, "Collective Bargaining and the Arbitrator," *Wisconsin Law Review*, 1963, p. 3.

11. J. Getman, "Labor Arbitration and Dispute Resolution," *Yale Law Journal*, 88 (1979): 916.

12. See F. Sander and F. Snyder, *Alternative Methods of Dispute Settlement* (Washington, D.C.: American Bar Association, 1979); M. Cappelleti, ed., *Access to Justice*, vols. 1 and 2 (Milan: Dott. A. Guiffre Editore, 1978).

13. J. Merryman, *The Civil Law Tradition* (Stanford, Calif.: Stanford University Press, 1969).

14. L. Fallers, *Law without Precedent* (Chicago: Universtiy of Chicago Press, 1969).

15. P. Bohannan, *Justice and Judgment among the Tiv* (London: Oxford University Press, 1957).

16. Pospisil, *Kapaku Papuans and Their Law*.

17. H. Wechsler, *Principles, Politics and Fundamental Law* Cambridge, Mass.: Harvard University Press, 1961); R. Dworkin, *Taking Rights Seriously* (London: Duckworth, 1977).

18. J. Dawson, *The Oracles of the Law* (Ann Arbor: University of Michigan Law School, 1968).

19. Allen, *Law in the Making*.

20. R. Mnookin and L. Kornhauser, "Bargaining in the Shadow of the Law: The Case of Divorce," *Yale Law Journal*, 88 (1979): 950.

21. M. Eisenberg, "Private Ordering through Negotiation: Dispute Settlement and Rulemaking," *Harvard Law Review*, 89 (1976): 637.

22. Ibid.; J. Coons, "Approaches to Court Imposed Compromise—The Uses of Doubt and Reason," *Northwestern University Law Review*, 58 (1964) 750; J. Coons, "Compromise as Precise Justice," in J. Pennock and J. Chapman, eds., *Compromise in Ethics, Law, and Politics* (New York: New York University Press, 1979), p. 191. Compare M. Shapiro, "Compromise and Litigation," in Pennock and Chapman, *Compromise in Ethics, Law, and Politics*.

23. On the problem of certainty and probability in English Law see B. Shapiro, "Law and Science in Seventeenth-Century England," *Stanford Law Review*, 21 (1969): 727.

24. Coons also proposes fifty-fifty splits in cases in which two important public policies are relevant, one favoring one of the parties and the other the other party.

25. M. Gluckman, *Custom and Conflict in Africa* (New York: Free Press, 1959); Hoebel, *The Law of Primitive Man;* H. Jacob, *Urban Justice* (Englewood Cliffs, N.J.: Prentice-Hall, 1973).

26. H. Berman, *Jusitice in the U.S.S.R.* (Cambridge, Mass.: Harvard University Press, 1963).

27. R. Barton, *The Kalingas: Their Institutions and Customary Law* (Chicago: University of Chicago Press, 1949).

28. M. Shapiro, "Toward a Theory of Stare Decisis," *Journal of Legal Studies*, 1 (1972): 125.

29. Cohen, in *California Law Review*, 54: 1201.

30. Allen, *Law in the Making*.

31. G. Haskins, *Law and Authority in Early Massachusetts* (Cambridge, Mass.: Harvard University Press, 1960).

32. A. von Mehren, ed., *Law in Japan* (Cambridge, Mass.: Harvard University Press, 1963); Hideo Tanaka, ed., *The Japanese Legal System* (Tokyo: University of Tokyo Press, 1976).

33. Jacob, *Urban Justice*.

34. J. Casper, *American Criminal Justice: The Defendant's Perspective* (Englewood Cliffs, N.J.: Prentice-Hall, 1972).

35. C. Wanner, "Public Ordering of Private Relations: Winning Civil Court Cases," *Law and Society Review*, 9 (1975): 293.

36. Henry Abraham, *The Judicial Process*, 3d ed. (London: Oxford University Press, 1975); Becker, *Comparative Judicial Politics;* T. Eckhoff, "Impartiality, Separation of Powers, and Judicial Independence," *Scandinavian Studies in Law*, 9 (1965): 9.

37. J. Gibbs, "The Kpelle Moot: a Therapeutic Model for the Informal Settlement of Disputes," *Africa*, 33 (1963): 1.

38. M. Gluckman, *Politics, Law and Ritual in Tribal Society* (Chicago: Aldine, 1965).

39. L. Pospisil, *Anthropology of Law* (New York: Harper & Row, 1971).

40. J. Wigmore, ed., *Law and Justice in Tokugawa Japan* (Tokyo; University of Tokyo Press, 1970).

41. J. Dawson, *History of Lay Judges* (Cambridge, Mass.: Harvard University Press, 1960).

42. Haskins, *Law and Authority*.

43. S. Burman and B. Harrell-Bond, eds., *The Imposition of Law* (New York: Academic Press, 1979).

44. L. Rudolph and S. Rudolph. *The Modernity of Tradition: Political Development in India* (Chicago: University of Chicago Press, 1967).

45. T. Hutchison, ed., *Africa and Law: Developing Legal Systems in African Commonwealth Nations* (Madison: University of Wisconsin Press, 1968); H. Kuper and L. Kuper, eds., *African Law: Adaptation and Development* (Berkeley: University of California Press, 1965).

46. M. Gluckman, "Civil War and Theories of Power in Barotseland: African and Medieval Analogies," *Yale Law Journal,* 72 (1963): 1515.

47. S. Popkin, *The Rational Peasant* (Berkeley: University of California Press, 1979).

48. E. Currie, "Crimes without Criminals: Witchcraft and Its Control in Renaissance Europe," *Law and Society Review,* 37 (1968): 7.; E. Evans-Pritchard, *Witchcraft, Oracles and Magic among the Azande* (Oxford: Clarendon Press, 1937).

49. K. Llewellyn and E. Hoebel, *The Cheyenne Way* (Norman: University of Oklahoma Press, 1961).

50. R. David and J. Brierly, *Major Legal Systems in the World Today* (London: Stevens & Sons, 1968).

51. E. Gruen, *Roman Politics and the Criminal Courts, 149–78 B.C.* (Cambridge, Mass." Harvard University Press, 1968).

52. M. Cappelletti, J. Merryman, and J. Perillo, *The Italian Legal System* (Stanford, Cal.: Stanford University Press, 1967).

53. Casper, *American Criminal Justice.*

54. B. Schwartz, *French Administrative Law and the Common Law World* (New York: New York University Press, 1954), M. Letourneur, J. Bauchet, and J. Meric, *Le Conseil d'etat et les Tribunaux administratifs* (Paris: Armanel Colin, 1970).

55. W. Elliott, *The Rise of Guardian Democracy: The Supreme Court's Role in Voting Rights Disputes, 1845–1969* (Cambridge, Mass.: Harvard University Press, 1974).

56. M. Shapiro, *Supreme Court and Administrative Agencies* (New York: Free Press, 1968).

57. M. Chigier, "The Rabbinical Courts in the State of Israel," *Israel Law Review,* 2 (1967): 147: D. Lev, *Islamic Courts in Indonesia* (Berkeley: University of California Press, 1972).

58. Wigmore, *Law and Justice.*

59. W. Friedmann, *Legal Theory,* 5th ed. (New York: Columbia University Press, 1967; A. von Mehren and J. Gordley, *The Civil Law System* (Boston: Little Brown, 1978).

60. See G. Schubert, *The Judicial Mind* (Evanston, Ill.: Northwestern Universtiy Press, 1965)

61. Abraham, *Judicial Process;* Rene David, *French Law* (Baton Rouge: University of Louisiana Press, 1972.

62. Llewellyn and Hoebel, *Cheyenne Way.*

63. Even Professor Dworkin indicates that courts announce new rules although he would argue they deduce them from legal principles which they discover by methods I do not understand. R. Dworkin, *Taking Rights Seriously*

64. D. Horowitz, *Courts and Social Policy* (Washington, D.C.: Brookings Institution, 1977).

65. M. Landau, "Redundancy, Rationality, and the Problem of Duplication and

Overlap," *Public Administration Review,* 29 (1969): 346.

66. Shapiro, *Law and Politics.*

67. H. Ehrmann, *Comparative Legal Cultures* (Englewood Cliffs, N.J.: Prentice-Hall, 1976).

68. S. Munzer, "Retroactive Law," *Journal of Legal Studies,* 6 (1977): 373.

69. The distinction between appeal by trial de novo and appeal on a record summarizes a broad spectrum of variations. See M. Shapiro, "Appeals," *Law and Society Review,* 14 (1980): 201.

70. Dawson, *Oracles.*

71. J. Frank, *Courts on Trial* (Princeton, N.J. : Princeton University Press, 1949).

72. B. Shapiro, in *Stanford Law Review,* 21:727.

73. Becker, *Comparative Judicial Politics.*

74. M. Horwitz, *Transformation of American Law, 1780–1860* (Cambridge, Mass.: Harvard University Press, 1977).

75. Dawson, *History of Lay Judges.* In some countries there are also officials who fall somewhere between professional judges and lay judges, such as the U.S. commissioners and the German *Rechtspfleger.* See R. Bender and H. Eckert, "The Rechtspfleger in the Federal Republic of Germany," in Cappelletti, *Access to Justice,* vol. 1.

76. J. Hazard, *Communists and Their Law* (Chicago: University of Chicago Press, 1969).

77. See the national reports on China, Hungary, Poland and the Soviet Union in Cappelletti, *Access to Justice,* vol. 1, and K. Kurczewski and K. Frieske, "The Social Conciliatory Commissions in Poland," in Cappelletti, *Access to Justice,* vol. 2.

### Chapter 2

1. On the difficulty of defining the concept see T. Becker, *Comparative Judicial Politics* (Chicago: Rand McNally, 1970), pp. 141–45.

2. See L. Amery, *Thoughts on the Constitution,* 2d ed. (London: Oxford University Press, 1953); W. Jennings, *The British Constitution,* 3d ed. (Cambridge: Cambridge University Press, 1950); cf. L. Scarman, *English Law: The New Dimension* (London: Stevens, 1974).

3. The classic exposition of the English concept of the rule of law is to be found in A. Dicey, *Introduction to the Study of the Law on the Constitution,* 10th ed. (London: Macmillan, 1959). Rule of law notions, of course, cover much broader ground than nonintervention by the political regime in the day-to-day workings of the courts.

4. See note 57 below.

5. Compare, for instance, D. Kennedy, "Form and Substance in Private Law Adjudication," *Harvard Law Review,* 89 (1976): 1685, with A. Chayes, "The Role of the Judge in Public Law Litigation," *Harvard Law Review,* 89 (1976): 1281.

6. The account of English legal history that follows makes no claim of presenting original data. It is drawn from the standard sources, most prominently: F. Pollock and F. Maitland, *History of English Law,* 2d ed. (Cambridge: Cambridge University Press, 1898); W. Stubbs, *Select Charters of English Constitutional History,* 9th ed. (Oxford: Clarendon Press, 1913); T. Plucknett, *Concise History of the Common Law,* 5th ed. (Boston: Little, Brown, 1956); W. Holdsworth, *History of English Law,* vol. 1, 7th ed. (Boston: Little, Brown, 1956); A. Kiralfy, *Potter's Historical Introduction to English Law,* 4th ed. (London: Sweet & Maxwell, 1958); G. Radcliffe and G. Cross, *The English Legal System,* 4th ed. (London: Butterworths,

1964); D. Stenton, *English Justice between the Norman Conquest and the Great Charter* (Philadelphia: American Philosophical Society, 1964); A. Simpson, *An Introduction to the History of the Land Law* (London: Oxford University Press, 1963); S. Milsom, *Historical Foundations of the Common Law* (London: Butterworths, 1969); R. van Caenegem, *The Birth of English Common Law* (Cambridge: Cambridge University Press, 1973). The interpretation placed on these data is, of course, entirely my responsibility and not that of these noted historians. In the notes that follow these sources will be cited by author's name only.

7. See H. Yntema, "Lex Murdrorum," *Harvard Law Review*, 36 (1922): 146.

8. See W. Morris, *The Medieval English Sheriff* (New York: Barnes & Noble, 1968).

9. See W. Morris, *The Early English County Court* (Berkeley: University of California Press, 1926).

10. Holdsworth, 1:66–67.

11. Cf. R. van Caenegem, *Royal Writs in England from the Conquest to Glanville* (London: B. Quaritch, 1959) with Stenton, p. 80.

12. See Holdsworth, 1:17–32.

13. See Plucknett, pp. 144–46; Holdsworth, 1:264–85.

14. On the personal justice of King John, see Stenton, pp. 88–114.

15. See Stenton, pp. 54–88.

16. Holdsworth, 1:51–53, 56.

17. See J. Baldwin, *The King's Council in England during the Middle Ages* (Oxford: Clarendon Press, 1913). In general on the constitutional evolution of the council see G. Adams, *Constitutional History of England* (New York: Holt, 1934); *Council and Courts in Anglo-Norman England* (New York: Russell & Russell, 1965).

18. The early history of the Chancery remains a subject of histotical debate. See W. Jones, Introductions *The Elizabethan Court of Chancery*, (Oxford: Clarendon Press, 1967); B. Wilkinson, *Chancery under Edward III* (Manchester: Manchester University Press, 1929); T. Tout, *Place of the Reign of Edward II in English History* (Manchester: Manchester University Press, 1914), p. 58.

19. See R. Poole, *The Exchequer in the Twelfth Century* (Oxford: Clarendon Press, 1955); Plucknet, p. 155; Holdsworth, 1:231–42.

20. Holdsworth, 1:407, 412–13.

21. Plucknett, pp. 147–51, 155; G. Sayles, *Select Cases in King's Bench*, Selden Society, vols. 55, 57, 58, 74, 76, 82 (London: B. Quaritch, 1936–65); N. Nelson, "Court of Common Pleas," *English Government at Work*, 3 (London: Stevens, 1950): 1327–36; F. Hastings, *Court of Common Pleas in Fifteenth Century England* (Cambridge: Cambridge University Press, 1947).

22. Holdsworth, 1:196.

23. Plucknett, pp. 149–50.

24. See C. Johnson, "The Exchequer Chamber under Edward II," *English Historical Review*, 21 (1906): 726; M. Hemmant, Introduction, *Select Cases in Exchequer Chamber* (London: B. Quaritch, 1933).

25. Alan Harding, *The Law Courts of Medieval England* (London: Allen & Unwin, 1973), p. 60.

26. See J. Cockburn, *A History of the English Assizes, 1558–1714* (Cambridge: Cambridge University Press, 1972), particularly pp. 15–23 on the medieval origins, and T. Barnes, Introduction, *Somerset Assize Orders, 1629–1640* (London: B. Quaritch, 1959); Barnes emphasizes the mixed administrative and judicial functions

of the assizes and thus their continuity with the eyre even as late as the seventeenth century.

27. Holdsworth, 1:274–85; Plucknett, pp. 165–67.

28. Professor Milsom entitles his sketch of the development of English courts "The Centralization of Justice" (Milsom, pp. 1–25).

29. J. de Montmorency, "Danish Influence on English Law and Character," *Law Quarterly Review*, 40 (1924): 324; F. Stenton, *Anglo-Saxon England* 2d ed. (Oxford: Clarendon Press, 1947); M. Bateson, *Borough Customs*, 2 vols. (London: B. Quaritch, 1904–06); Plucknett, pp. 304–14; F. Attenborough, *Laws of the Earliest English Kings* (Cambridge: Cambridge University Press, 1922).

30. On the development of the writs see Plucknett, pp. 353–78; F. Maitland, *Equity and Forms of Action* (Cambridge: Cambridge University Press, 1909); Pollock and Maitland, vol. 2; van Caenegem, *Royal Writs;* G. Turner and T. Plucknett, *Brevis Placitata* (London: B Quaritch, 1951); H. Richardson and G. Sayles, *Select Cases of Procedures without Writ* (London: B. Quaritch, 1941).

31. Milsom, pp. 26–27.

32. Cf. A. Kiralfy, *Action on the Case* (London: Sweet & Maxwell 1951) with Milsom, pp. 256–70.

33. See F. Maitland, *Constitutional History* (Cambridge: Cambridge University Press, 1908), pp. 111–14.

34. Novel disseizin is the most important of the real actions, which include the writs of right and writs of entry discussed in this section. On the real actions and their relation to one another see Simpson, pp. 24–43; Maitland, *Equity and Forms of Action.*

35. On tenures see Simpson, pp. 1–23; Milsom, pp. 88–102.

36. On the nature of seisin see the sources cited in Milsom, p. 386, note to page 103.

37. On the older modes of trial see Holdsworth, 1:299–312.

38. Milsom, p. 120.

39. The development of the jury is summarized in Plucknett, pp. 106–38; Holdsworth, 1:297–356. See also J. Thayer, *A Preliminary Treatise on Evidence* (Boston: Little, Brown, 1898); J. Stephen, *A History of the Criminal Law in England,* 3 vols. (London: Macmillan, 1883).

40. On the growth of the chanellor's jurisdiction see B. Wilkinson, *Studies in the Constitutional History of the Thirteenth and Fourteenth Centuries,* 2d ed. (Manchester: Manchester University Press, 1952), p. 196, and works cited there; Adams, *Constitutional History of England,* pp. 95 ff. Holdsworth's account is often questioned in points of detail and particularly on the issue of the origin of equitable doctrines, but it is surely correct in institutional outline; Holdsworth, 1:396–477. See Jones, *The Elizabethan Court of Chancery.*

41. A contract under seal is one which has been signed and to which the seal of the signor has been affixed as well as certain other formalities undertaken. Common law could enforce such formal contracts, but had a great deal of difficulty with written contracts that had not been formally sealed and with oral and other informal contracts.

42. Harding, *Law Courts.*

43. On the general evolution of the council see note 17 above.

44. On the general history of Star Chamber see G. Elton, *The Tudor Constitution* (Cambridge: Cambridge University Press, 1960); *Star Chamber Stories* (London: Methuen, 1958); C. Scofield, *A Study of the Court of Star Chamber* (Chicago:

University of Chicago Press, 1960); Holdsworth, 1:477–516; W. Jones, *Politics and the Bench: The Judges and the Origins of the English Civil War* (New York: Barnes & Noble, 1971), pp. 103–8; T. Barnes, "Star Chamber Mythology," *American Journal of Legal History,* 5 (1961): 1; "Due Process and Slow Process in the Late Elizabethan–Early Stuart Star Chamber," *American Journal of Legal History,* 6 (1963): 221, 315.

45. Harding, *Law Courts.*

46. See F. Brooks, *The Council of the North* (Oxford: Oxford University Press, 1963).

47. Plucknett, p. 158, is particularly interesting on fourteenth-century developments.

48. Stenton, pp. 7–8, traces the Anglo-Saxon origin of this preference for agreed solutions.

49. This highly complex set of developments is traced by Milsom, pp. 140–211, and Simpson, pp. 44–224.

50. Kiralfy, pp. 117–20.

51. Holdsworth, 1:408–12; Jones *The Elizabethan Court of Chancery.*

52. S. Milsom, "Law and Fact in Legal Development," *University of Toronto Law Journal,* 17 (1967):1.

53. Simpson is liberally sprinkled with confessions that for various land rules either no reasonable explanation is possible, or the origin of the rule is unknown, or the rationale behind the rule is in dispute or the true meaning of the rule was not realized at some time in the past or is unknown at present.

54. Milsom, pp. 140–69.

55. Radcliffe and Cross, pp. 382–83.

56. 14 Edward III, St. 1 c. 16 (1340).

57. On the early history of the legal profession see H. Cohen, *History of the English Bar* (London: Sweet & Maxwell, 1929); Plucknett, pp. 215–30.

58. On English legal education see P. Lucas, "Blackstone and the Reform of the Legal Profession," *English History Review,* 77 (1962): 456; H. Hanbury, *The Vinerian Chair and Legal Education* (Oxford: Blackwell, 1958).

59. Holdsworth, 1:197.

60. See G. Elton, *Tudor Revolution in Government* (Cambridge: Cambridge University Press, 1953).

61. Parliamentary supply usually consisted of a fixed sum of money granted to the king, often for a specific purpose such as fighting a war. To raise the money Parliament would enact a temporary tax, which usually would expire after a fixed number of years or after it had yielded the necessary amount.

62. See H. Bell, *The Court of Wards and Liveries* (Cambridge: Cambridge Universities Press, 1953).

63. The developments of this period are summarized in W. Jones, *Politics and the Bench.* See also A. Havighurst, "The Judiciary and Politics in the Reign of Charles II," *Law Quarterly Review,* 66 (1950): 62, 229; "James II and the Twelve Men in Scarlet," *Law Quarterly Review,* 69 (1955): 522.

64. Jones, *Politics and the Bench,* pp. 45–48.

65. On the relation of the radical law reform movement of the revolutionary period to the longer term, moderate reform movement, see B. Shapiro, "Codification in Seventeenth Century England," *Wisconsin Law Review,* 1974, p. 428; "Law Reform in Seventeenth Century England," *American Journal of Legal History,* 19 (1975): 280

66. Plucknett, p. 248.

67. See E. Barker, *Social Contract* (London: Oxford University Press, 1946), pp. xxvii–xxviii.

68. On Bonham's case see J. W. Gough, *Fundamental Law in English Constitutional History* (Oxford: Clarendon Press, 1955). Cf. R. Mackay, "Parliamentary Sovereignty or the Supremacy of the Law," *Michigan Law Review*, 44 (1923): 215 with S. Thorne, "Dr. Bonham's Case," *Law Quarterly Review*, 54 (1938): 543.

69. Kiralfy, p. 178.

70. See D. Boorstin, *The Mysterious Science of the Law* (Cambridge: Harvard University Press, 1941); M. Shapiro, "Blackstone," *International Encyclopedia of the Social Sciences*, 2 (New York: Free Press, 1968): 81.

71. Milsom, pp. 86–87; Radcliffe and Cross, pp. 127–55.

72. See F. Maitland, "The Law of Real Property," *Collected Legal Papers*, 1 (Cambridge: Cambridge University Press, 1911): 162; Simpson, pp. 163–225; Milsom, pp. 140–210, 391; see also J. Ames, "The Origin of Uses and Trusts," in *Select Essays in Anglo-American Legal History*, 2 (Boston: Little Brown, 1908): 737; K. Digby, *An Introduction to the History of the Law of Real Property*, 5th ed. (Oxford: Clarendon Press, 1897). References to the impact of these complex developments on modern real property law are scattered through R. Megarry and H. Wade, *The Law of Real Property*, 4th ed. (London: Stevens & Sons, 1975).

73. Plucknett, pp. 637–70; C. Fifoot, *Lord Mansfield* (Oxford: Clarendon Press, 1936); Holdsworth, 1:568–73.

74. See, e.g., the last sentence of Milsom's chapter on contracts: "If so, then consideration is a coherent theory of contract mutilated by its passage through tort" (Milsom, p. 315).

75. See references at note 58 above.

76. Plucknett, p. 248.

77. Holdsworth, 1:333–37, 341; Plucknett, p. 138.

78. See B. Shapiro, in *Wisconsin Law Review*, 1974, p. 428.

79. See C. Allen, *Law in the Making*, 7th ed. (Oxford: Clarendon Press, 1964), pp. 441–42; W. Friedmann, *Legal Theory*, 5th ed. (New York: Columbia University Press, 1967), pp. 312–20

80. See W. Jennings, *Parliament*, 2d ed. (Cambridge: Cambridge University Press, 1957).

81. Simpson, pp. 252–61.

82. Holdsworth, 1:633–50, provides a detailed account of the reforms.

83. Holdsworth, 1:377, 644.

84. See J. Gray, *The Nature and Sources of the Law* (New York: Columbia University Press, 1909). Note the interesting comment in Kiralfy's edition of Potter, long a standard work: "It was perhaps typical of Professor Potter's approach that there was...no reference to statutes as a source of law..." (Kiralfy, p. vii).

85. The current organization of the English courts may be found in R. Jackson, *The Machinery of Justice in England*, 7th ed. (Cambridge: Cambridge University Press, 1978). See also R. Stevens, *Law and Politics: The House of Lords as a Judicial Body, 1800–1976* (Chapel Hill: University of North Carolina Press, 1978).

86. See J. P. Dawson, *A History of Lay Judges* (Cambridge: Harvard University Press, 1960), pp. 136–45.

87. Radcliffe and Cross, pp. 277–86.

88. H. Abraham, *The Judicial Process*, 3d ed. (New York: Oxford University

Press, 1975), p. 246.

89. Ibid., pp. 46–47.

90. The classic authority is W. Jennings, *Cabinet Government* (Cambridge: Cambridge University Press, 1936). For an incisive but sympathetic contemporary commentary see S. Beer, *British Politics in a Collectivist Age* (New York: Knopf, 1965).

91. For the growth of administrative tribunals see *Report of the Committee of Administrative Tribunals and Enquiries* (Franks Committee, 1957, Comnd. 218).

92. On remedies in general see H. Wade, *Administrative Law*, 2d ed. (Oxford: Clarendon Press, 1967), pp. 96–152; S. De Smith *Judicial Review of Administrative Action*, 1st ed. (London: Stevens, 1959), pp. 253–458 (hereafter cited as Wade and De Smith). See also W. Robson, *Justice and Administrative Law*, 3d ed. (London: Stevens, 1951); J. Griffith and H. Street, *Principles of Administrative Law*, 5th ed. (London: Pitman, 1973); J. Garner, *Administrative Law*, 3d ed. (London: Butterworths, 1970).

93. See J. Alder, "Time Limit Clauses and Judicial Review—*Smith* v. *East Elloe* Revisted," *Modern Law Review*, 38 (1975): 274.

94. Wade, pp. 76–83; De Smith, pp. 83–91.

95. See Wade, pp. 64, 84–85; De Smith, pp. 248–49.

96. By injunction or declaratory order it may preclude some specific course of action. Wade, p. 47.

97. On natural justice see Wade, pp. 153–98; De Smith, pp. 101–65.

98. Cf. *Franklin* v. *Minister of Town and Country Planning* [1948] A.C. 87 with *Ridge* v. *Baldwin* [1964] A.C. 40.

99. Tribunals and Inquiries Act 1958.

100. Cf. S. Seepersad, "Fairness and Audi Alteram Partem," *Public Law*, 1975, p. 242 with E. Sykes and R. Tracey, "Natural Justice and the Atkin Formula," *Melbourne University Law Review*, 10 (1976): 564.

101. On *ultra vires* generally see Wade, pp. 45–95; De Smith, pp. 55–100.

102. Wade, pp. 219–21, 227–29.

103. Wade, pp. 71–74; De Smith, pp. 190–203.

104. E.g., *White and Collins* v. *Minister of Health* [1939] 2 K.B. 838. See P. Robertshaw, "Unreasonableness and Judicial Control of Administrative Discretion: The Geology of the Chertsey Caravans Case," *Public Law*, 1975, p. 113.

105. Wade, pp. 7–48, 67–71; De Smith, pp. 24–25, 189–221.

106. Wade p. 192; De Smith, pp. 17–19, 41–45, 116–18, 128–30, 28486.

107. Wade, pp. 89–90; De Smith, pp. 83–87.

108. *Associated Provincial Picture House Ltd.* v. *Wednesbury Corp.* [1948] 1 K.B. 357. See A. Wharam, "Judicial Control of Delegated Legislation: The Test of Reasonableness," *Modern Law Review*, 36 (1973): 611.

109. Wade, pp. 89–91.

110. See, e.g., *Taylor* v. *Munrow* [1960] 1 W.L.R. 151; *Smith* v. *East Elloe Rural District Council* [1956] A.C. 736; *Hall & Co. Ltd.* v. *Shoreham-by-Sea U.D.C.* [1964] 1 W.L.R. 151; *Mixnam's Properties Ltd.* v. *Chertsey U.D.C.* [1965] A.C. 735; *Prescott* v. *Birmingham Corp.* [1955] Ch. 210.

111. The first edition of De Smith (1959) expresses profound pessimism about the fate of judicial control of administration. Later editions exhibited some guarded optimism that the retreat had ended. Wade's second edition (1967) chides the courts for their errors of the 1950s and expresses great hopes that they will return to the true path—which for Wade is a relatively active judicial review within the orthodox limits of parliamentary sovereignty. Wade's third and fourth editions (1971, 1977)

profess to see those hopes fulfilled, although on his own showing the cases are very mixed. See M. Shapiro, "Judicial Independence: The English Experience," *North Carolina Law Review*, 55 (1977): 576, 647–48. Other commentators characterizing the recent period as one of activism are R. McInnes, "Jurisdictional Review after Anisminic," *Victoria University of Wellington Law Review*, 9 (1977): 37, and A. G. Kessing, "Administrative Law—Another Retreat," *New Zealand Law Journal*, 1976, p. 467; but both in fact deal principally with English cases that run against their characterization. Two recent articles in the *Economist* (31 July 1976, p. 9; 7 August 1976, p. 10) employ such tags as "new sprouting of administrative law" and "rebirth" while managing to suggest at the same time that little has actually been done and that what little has been is startling given the overall record. Wade's optimism is seconded in D. Yardley, "Abuse of Powers and Its Control in English Administrative Law," *American Journal of Comparative Law*, 18 (1970): 565.

112. [1964] A.C. 40.

113. See Robertshaw, in *Public Law*; 1975.

114. Wade, p. 208.

115. [1968] A.C. 997.

116. [1969] 2 W.L.R. 163.

117. See McInnes, in *Victoria University of Wellington Law Review*, 9:37.

118. *R. v. Secretary of State for the Environment ex parte Ostler* [1977] 1 Q.B. 122.

119. [1976] 3 W.L.R. 641, H.L.

120. See the *Economist*, 31 July and 7 August 1976.

121. See C. Guest, "The Executive and the Judiciary," *Juridical Review*, 36 (1973): 113. Note particularly D. Clark, "Natural Justice: Substance and Shadow," *Public Law*, 1975, p. 27, who concludes "while natural justice casts a lengthening shadow, the shade serves only to conceal the decline in its substances."

122. Wade, pp. 85–89. The *Anisminic* case, while proclaiming the opposite, seems to apply the doctrine even to decisions which enjoy the protection of a statutory clause barring judicial review.

123. See J. Corry, "The Prospect for the Rule of Law," in W. Stankiewicz, ed., *Crisis in British Government* (London: Macmillan, 1967).

124. It is probable that the law lords were seeking the same result by judicial action in *Anisminic* by suggesting that any error of law might be considered an error in the assertion of jurisdiction and thus *ultra vires*.

### Chapter 3

1. For a general introduction to the modern civil law system see J. H. Merryman, *The Civil Law Tradition* (Stanford: Stanford University Press, 1969). See also A. Yiannopoulos, ed., *Civil Law in the Modern World* (Baton Rouge: Louisiana State University Press, 1965).

2. See, e.g., W. Friedmann, *Legal Theory*, 3d ed. (London: Stevens, 1953), pp. 370–79; R. David, Preface to English Edition, *French Law* (Baton Rouge: Louisiana State University Press, 1972); A. T. Von Mehren, *The Civil Law System* (Boston: Little, Brown, 1957), pp. 821–54. J. P. Dawson, *Oracles of the Law* (Ann Arbor: University of Michigan Law School, 1968), pp. 432–502.

3. The history of Roman law is outlined in Hans J. Wolf, *Roman Law: An Historical Introduction* (Norman: University of Oklahoma Press, 1951). A more complete treatment is to be found in H. F. Jolowicz and B. Nicholas, *Historical Introduction to the Study of Roman Law*, 3d ed. (Cambridge: Cambridge University

Press, 1972); their footnotes and bibliography provide an introduction to the vast literature on this subject.

4. Dawson, *Oracles of the Law*, pp. 148–262, provides an incisive account of the reception.

5. On the origins and nature of the Code Napoléon, see David, *French Law*, pp. 1–16; Von Mehren, *The Civil Law System*, pp. 13–22.

6. See Von Mehren, *The Civil Law System*, pp. 22–30, 63–69; *Manual of German Law* (London: Foreign Office, 1950).

7. On the style of European opinions, see J. L. Goutal, "Characteristics of Judicial Style in France, Britain and the U.S.A.," *American Journal of Comparative Law*, 24 (1975): 43; F. H. Lawson, "Comparative Judicial Style," *American Journal of Comparative Law*, 25 (1977): 364; J. Wetter, *Styles of Appellate Judicial Opinions* (Leyden: Sythoff, 1960); L. Prott, "A Change of Style in French Appellate Judgments," in C. Perelman, ed., *Etudes de logique juridique*, (Brussels: Bruylant, 1978), p. 7.

8. Some of the case law argument of French administrative law is reproduced in English in Von Mehren, *Civil Law System* pp. 250–338.

9. The sketch presented in the next few pages can be followed in much greater detail in English in A. T. Von Mehren and J. R. Gordley, *The Civil Law System*, 2d ed. (Boston: Little, Brown, 1977), pp. 590–702; and in French in F. H. Lawson, *Negligence in the Civil Law* (London: Oxford University Press, 1950), pp. 231–82.

10. Cf. e.g., H., L., and J. Mazeaud, *Leçons de droit civil* (Paris: Editions Montchrestien, 1973) with H. and L. Mazeaud, *Traité théoretique et pratique de la responsabilité civile, délictuelle et contractuelle*, 6th ed. (Paris: Editions Montchrestien, 1965).

11. See J. H. Langbein, *Prosecuting Crime in the Renaissance: England, Germany, France* (Cambridge: Harvard University Press, 1974).

12. *Taupin c. Arrachepied*, J.C.P. II. 360.

13. The presumption of responsibility can only be overcome by a showing by the defendant that his thing under guard was in no way a cause of the injury which was in fact entirely caused by someone or something else or that the accident was entirely unforeseeable and unavoidable.

14. *Harty c. Ville de Chalôns-sur-Marne*, S. 1878.II. 48.

15. *Jand'heur c. Les Galeries belfortaises*, D.P. 1930.I. 57).

16. Von Mehren and Gordley, *The Civil Law System*, pp. 102–7.

17. See P. Mimin, *Le Style des jugements*, 4th ed. (Paris: Librairies Techniques, 1970).

18. This description of the Italian experience is drawn from M. Cappelletti, J. H. Merryman, and J. M. Perillo, *The Italian Legal System* (Stanford: Stanford University Press, 1967), which probably somewhat overemphasizes the role of academic doctrine and underemphasizes the role of precedent in the contemporary Italian style.

19. The debate is briefly sketched for English-speaking readers from the French and German sources in Von Mehren, *The Civil Law System*, pp. 57–70.

20. This movement is sketched for English-speaking readers in Friedmann, *Legal Theory*, pp. 227–46. The seminal works are F. Geny, *Science et technique en droit privé positif*, 4 vols. (Paris: L. Tenin, 1914–24), and E. Ehrlich, *Soziologie und Jurisprudenz* (Aalen: Scienta Verlag, 1973; first published 1906). See also M. M. Schoch, ed., *Jurisprudence of Interests: Selected Writings* (Cambridge: Harvard University Press, 1948); F. Geny, *Method of Interpretation and Sources in Positive Private Law* (St. Paul: West Publishing, 1963); E. Ehrlich, *Fundamental Principles of*

*the Sociology of Law* (Cambridge: Harvard University Press, 1936).

21. Cappelletti, Merryman, and Perillo, *The Italian Legal System,* pp. 191–97.

22. The details of the organization, staffing, and jurisdiction of French civil courts is to be found in H. Solus and R. Perrot, *Droit judiciare privé,* vol. 1 (Paris: Sirey; 1961). The detailed organization and jurisdiciton of German courts is set out in the "Law Regulating the Organization and Structure of the Courts" [Gerichtverfassungsgesetz].

23. On the enormous significance of the early creation of judicial bureaucracies on the Continent, see J. P. Dawson, *A History of Lay Judges* (Cambridge: Harvard University Press, 1960).

24. See generally H. W. Ehrmann, *Comparative Legal Cultures* (Englewood Cliffs, N.J.: Prentice-Hall, 1976), pp. 54–79.

25. Cappelletti, Merryman, Perillo, *The Italian Legal System,* pp. 102–9.

26. Ehrmann, *Comparative Legal Cultures,* p. 78.

27. On Continental administrative courts, see H. Abraham, *The Judicial Process,* 3d ed. (New York: Oxford University Press, 1975), pp. 261–69; B. Schwartz, *French Administrative Law and the Common-Law World* (New York: New York University Press, 1954); S. Galeotti, *The Judicial Control of Public Authorities in England and in Italy* (London: Stevens, 1954); H. Lanfer, *Verfassungsgerichtsbarkeit und politischer Progress* (Bonn: Mohr, 1968); L. Neville Brown and J. F. Garner, *French Administrative Law* (London: Butterworths, 1967).

28. See M. C. Kessler, *Le Conseil d'etat* (Paris: Colin, 1968); C. E. Freedeman, *The Conseil d'Etat in Modern France* (New York: Columbia University Press, 1961).

29. Most complaints are heard initially by the Tribunaux administratifs, which are liberally distributed throughout France. About 20 percent of their decisions are appealed. See M. Letourneur, J. Bauchet, and J. Meric, *Le Conseil d'etat et les tribunaux administratifs* (Paris: Colin, 1970).

30. See L. Neville Brown, "De Gaulle's Republic and the Rule of Law: Judicial Review and the Counseil d'Etat," *Boston University Law Review* 46 (1966): 462.

31. Donald Kommers, *Judicial Politics in West Germany: A Study of the Federal Constitutional Court* (Beverly Hills, Calif.: Sage Publications, 1976).

32. Mauro Cappelletti *Judicial Review in the Contemporary World* (New York: Bobbs-Merrill, 1971). For a less sanguine view than Cappelletti's of the Italian Constitutional Court, see Ehrmann, *Comparative Legal Cultures,* p. 144. In general see Walter Murphy and Joseph Tanenhaus, *Comparative Constitutional Law* (New York: St. Martin's Press, 1977).

### Chapter 4

1. J. Excarra, *Le Droit chinois* (Peking: Henri Vetch, 1936), p. 17.

2. See T. Metzger, *Escape from Predicament* (New York: Columbia University Press, 1977).

3. J. Needham, *Science and Civilization in China,* 1 (London: Cambridge University Press, 1956): 518–83.

4. See T. Metzeger, *The Internal Organization of the Ch'ing Bureaucracy* (Cambridge: Harvard University Press, 1973), p. 282.

5. J. Cohen, "Chinese Mediation on the Eve of Modernization," *California Law Review,* 54 (1966): 1201.

6. A. Smith, *Village Life in China* (New York: F. H. Revell, 1899), pp. 280–84.

7. D. Bodde and C. Morris, *Law in Imperial China* (Cambridge: Harvard University Press, 1967), chap. 2 (hereafter cited as Bodde and Morris).

8. Metzger, *Internal Organization,* pp. 167–72.

9. Bodde and Morris, pp. 76–104.

10. The most complete translation of the code into a Western language is G. Boulais, *Manual du code chinois,* 2 vols. (Shanghai, 1923–24). The examples that follow are taken from the translation by Bodde and Morris. See also P. Ch'en, *Chinese Legal Tradition under the Mongols: The Code of 1291 as Reconstructed* (Princeton, N.J.: Princeton University Press, 1979); W. Johnson, *The Tang Code,* vol. 1, *General Principles* (Princeton, N.J.: Princeton University Press, 1979).

11. Bodde and Morris, pp. 517–32.

12. This criminal-civil division at the level of the boards in the capital was paralleled by a similar division in the responsibilities of the local magistrates' secretaries, with the legal secretary handling litigation bound for the Board of Punishments and the taxation secretary those cases destined for the Board of Revenue.

13. Penal provisions of the statues dealing with civil disputes were finally removed in the 1908 revision of the code.

14. No attempt is made here to compare the criminal side of Chinese homicide with the criminal law of the West. The subject is very complex because the Chinese are less likely to admit a defense of self-defense or create categories of excusable or justifiable homicide but are likely to consider a far wider range of mitigating factors in the reduction of sentences than are usually considered in the West. Moreover, it is not clear that death resulting from family discipline by a parent over his or her children is homicide at all except in a few special instances.

15. Perhaps the death penalty for homicide in the West also arises out of an attempt to regularize and provide official terminations for the blood feud, but if so, that conflict resolution rationale has long since been overwhelmed by the deterrent one while in Chinese law the notion of *ti ming* continued to be consciously articulated. See Bodde and Morris, p. 35.

16. Appeal was not required in civil cases though it was in serious criminal cases. Civil appeals were heard by the financial commissioner at the provincial level and rarely were sent on to the capital. Bodde and Morris, p. 119; David Buxbaum, "Some Aspects of Civil Procedure and Practice at the Trial Level in Tanshui and Hsinchu from 1789 to 1895," *Journal of Asian Studies,* 30 (1971): 262–63.

17. R. H. Van Gulik, tr., *T'ang-Yin-Pi-Shih, Parallel Cases from under the Pear Tree; a Thirteenth Century Manual of Jurisprudence and Detection* (Leiden: E. J. Brill, 1956), pp. 170, 176.

18. Buxbaum, in *Journal of Asian Studies,* 30:266 ff.

19. Hsiao Kung-chuan, *Rural China: Imperial Control in the Nineteenth Century* (Seattle: University of Washington Press, 1960), p. 215.

20. This parable is reported as a "curious piece of advice" in a reprinting of what is apparently an early twentieth-century report in H. S. Bhatra and Tan Chung, *Legal and Political System in China* (New Delhi: Deep & Deep, 1974). They attribute the report to one Byron Brenan C.M.G. but give no indication of when or where it first appeared.

21. If this all seems a quaint Orientalism, it is strikingly similar to the technique of the motorcyle cop who flags down a speeder and then tells him that although he was going 50 in a 25 mile an hour zone, the ticket will show a speed of only 35 so that the fine will not be so large. The motorist is then left feeling grateful for the benevolence of the policeman and conscious that a compromise has been reached rather than feeling an absolute loser before an implacable preexisting speed rule.

22. Hsiao, *Rural China,* indicates about one district magistrate to 250,000 people.

See also T'ung-Tsu Ch'U, *Local Government in China under the Ch'ing* (Cambridge: Harvard University Press, 1962), pp. 4–7.

23. J. R. Watt, *The District Magistrate in Late Imperial China* (New York: Columbia University Press, 1972), pp. 143–44, 171–72.

24. See Ch'U, *Local Government,* chap. 4.

25. Ibid., p. 128.

26. Ibid., p. 94.

27. See Metzger, *The Internal Organization,* pp. 347 ff.

28. Bhatra and Chung, *Legal and Political System in China,* p. 47

29. Watt, *The District Magistrate,* pp. 143–44.

30. Bodde and Morris, pp. 113–43.

31. Bodde and Morris, pp. 254, 367, 445.

32. This discussion is drawn largely from Ch'U, *Local Government* and Watt, *The District Magistrate.*

33. In theory education was open to all and entry into the service democratic. In practice the long periods of preparation, the repeated taking of exams often at a distance from home, the long wait for appointment, and the prevalence of appointment by purchase meant that most civil servants were drawn from the ranks of the gentry, that is, those families with substantial economic resources and some educational attainment. However, most authorities agree that there was little stable aristocracy in China, most families holding on to favored economic, social, educational status for only three or four generations.

34. Ch'U, *Local Government,* pp. 122–24.

35. Ibid., pp. 117–18; Bodde and Morris, p. 119.

36. Van Gulik, *T'ang-Yin-Pi-Shig,* pp. 49–54, 60–61; Buxbaum, in *Journal of Asian Studies,* 30:263 ff.

37. Ch'U, *Local Government,* p. 125.

38. Buxbaum, in *Journal of Asian Studies,* 30:263 ff.

39. Ibid., p. 264; Ch'U, *Local Government,* p. 174.

40. Ch'U, *Local Government,* pp. 31, 47–50, 65–66, 68–70, 79–81, 87, 89.

41. Some indication of the difficulty of litigation for villagers is indicated by the fact that in the nineteenth century in one district studied about 60 percent of urban plaintiffs saw their cases to final disposition as compared with 20 percent of rural plaintiffs. Buxbaum in *Journal of Asian Studies,* 30:265.

42. Van Gulik, *T'ang-Yin-Pi-Shih,* pp. 102, 112.

43. Van Gulik reports such a case (ibid., p. 120).

44. Imperial policies toward the imposition of various systems of collective responsibility on the villages and supervision by representatives chosen from among the villagers themselves were complex and shifting. For the details see Hsiao, *Rural China.*) B. McKnight, *Villages and Bureaucracy in Southern Sung China* (Chicago: University of Chicago Press, 1971). On this and related topics see F. Wakeman and C. Grant, eds., *Conflict and Control in Late Imperial China* (Berkeley, Calif.: University of California Press, 1975).

45. Van Gulik, *T'ang-Yin-Pi-Shih,* p. 58; Hsiao, *Rural China,* pp. 290–94.

46. Martin C. Yang, *A Chinese Village* (New York: Columbia University Press, 1945), pp. 179–80.

47. Hsiao, *Rural China,* p. 268; Yang, *A Chinese Village,* p. 185.

48. Ch'U, *Local Government,* p. 175.

49. For instance Hsiao notes that when a dispute arose between residents of two villages, the elders of both might gather jointly to mediate it but if they failed, the

dispute would probably end up in the magistrate's court (*Rural China*, pp. 309–10.)

50. Making a false claim is itself an offense under the code.

51. That the villagers recognized that their customary law jurisdiction was somehow at odds with imperial jurisdiction is indicated by the fact that they compelled the defendant's mother to sign a paper consenting to the sentence (Hsiao, *Rural China*, p. 288).

52. Hsiao, *Rural China*, pp. 293–94, 342–43.

53. Yang, *A Chinese Village*, pp. 165–66.

54. Cohen, in *California Law Review*, 54:1221–22.

55. Sybille van der Sprenkel, *Legal Institutions in Manchu China* (London: Athlone Press, 1962) takes the view that mediation was the dominant mode of dispute settlement (p. 78–79) but then quite revealingly says that private dispute settlement ranged from completely private mediation at one end of the scale to public adjudication at the other (p. 117).

56. Ch'U, *Local Government*, p. 182.

57. Hsiao, *Rural China*, p. 65.

58. Van Gulik (*T'ang-Yin-Pi-Shih*, pp. 178–80) reports a case in which a mortgage holder refused to return a title deed when offered final payment and the owner litigated to recover the deed. See also S. Shiga, "Family Property and the Law of Inheritance in Traditional China," in D. Buxbaum, ed., *Chinese Family Law and Social Change* (Seattle: University of Washington Press, 1978).

59. Van Gulik, p. 176. *T'ang-Yin-Pi-Shih*, p. 176.

60. Ch'U, basing himself on the treatise of Wang Yu-huai, indicates that land cases were settled by consulting the title deed (*Local Government*, p. 98).

61. Buxbaum, in *Journal of Asian Studies*, 30:263 ff.

62. Buxbaum, in *Journal of Asian Studies*, 30:267, reports a case in which a magistrate cancelled a case following the receipt of an official complaint because successful mediation had occurred after the complaint had been filed. However, apparently because the complaint had been filed, the private mediators required the parties to sign a bond to abide by the mediation which they used to support their request to the magistrate that the litigation be quashed.

Chapter 5

1. See M. Rheinstein, ed., *Max Weber on Law in Economy and Society* (Cambridge: Harvard University Press, 1954).

2. The survey of the Islamic legal system that follows is drawn largely from J. Schacht, *Introduction to Islamic Law* (Oxford: Clarendon Press, 1964); N. J. Coulson, *History of Islamic Law* (Edinburgh, Edinburgh, University Press, 1964); E. Tyan, *Histoire de l'organisation judiciaire en pays d'Islam*, 2 vols. (Paris: Sirey, 1938–43); D. B. MacDonald, *Moslem Theology, Jurisprudence, and Constitutional Theory* (New York: Macmillan, 1913). See also M. Khadduri and H. J. Liebsney, *Law in the Middle East* (Washington, D.C.: Middle East Institute, 1955); N. J. Coulson, *Conflict and Tensions in Islamic Jurisprudence* (Chicago: University of Chicago Press, 1969); G. E. Van Grunebaum, *Theology and Law in Islam* (Wiesbaden: Harrassowitz, 1971); J. Schacht, *The Origins of Muhammedan Jurispurdence*, (Oxford: Clarendon Press, 1950); Daniel Lev, *Islamic Courts in Indonesia* (Berkeley: University of California Press, 1972); Ahmad Bin Mohamed Ibrahim, *Sources and Development of Moslem Law* (Singapore: Malayan Law Journal, 1965).

The English spelling of Arabic and Turkish words is a problem for experts. I have employed common English spellings in the singular and added "s" for plurals.

3. The well-known "codification" efforts of such Ottoman sultans were basically collections of their *kanun*s, that is, the administrative regulations that they issued. In all but name many of these were laws, but they were denied the official status of law and so did not enter the *Sharia*. While they were administered by a partnership of *kadi* and military official, they were actually a part of the secular legal system described later in this chapter. Stanford Shaw, *History of the Ottoman Empire and Modern Turkey*, 1 *(Cambridge: Cambridge University Press, 1976): 62, 83, 88, 100–103, 139*

4. MacDonald, *Moslem Theology*, p. 110.

5. Shafi'i's great work, the *Risala*, is translated into English with an instructive introduction by M. Khadduri, *Islamic Jurispurdence* (Baltimore: Johns Hopkins Press, 1961).

6. See Ahmad ibn 'Abd al-Hallim, *Ibn Taimiyah on Public and Private Law In Islam, or Public Policy in Islamic Jurisprudence*, tr. O. A. Farrukh (Beirut: Khayats, 1968).

7. Coulson, *History of Islamic Law*, pp. 139–40.

8. The Ottoman Empire was officially Hanifa and its law was defined by *The Pearls* and *The Confluence of the Seas*, works produced in the fifteenth and sixteenth centuries, respectively. H. A. R. Gibb and H. Bowen, *Islamic Society and the West* (London: Oxford University Press, 1957), vol. 1, part 1, p. 23. An Indian collection of *fatwa*s produced in the seventeenth century was later widely used in the Ottoman Empire. Gibb and Bowen, *Islamic Society*, vol. 1, part 2, p. 117.

9. Coulson, *History of Islamic Law* pp. 145–47.

10. Schacht, *Introduction to Islamic Law* pp. 24–27.

11. Coulson, *History of Islamic Law* p. 131.

12. Tyan *(Histoire de l'organisation)* presents the most complete account of the non-Sharia courts available in a Western language. A second edition of his work was published in one volume in Leiden by E. J. Brill in 1960.

13. Schacht, *Introduction to Islamic Law* pp. 53–54. *Siyasa* is the Arbic term. The Ottoman sultans exercised their *siyasa* authority by issuing *kanun*s. See note 3 above.

14. Coulson, *History of Islamic Law* pp. 132–33.

15. Gibb and Bowen, *Islamic Society*, vol. 1, part 2, pp. 79, 115. The Ottoman sultans officially proclaim this distinction by codifying a body of *kanun* (sea note 3 above) separate from the Sharia. While for reasons that will be explained alter, the *kadi* enforced both the Sharia and *kanun*, a clear distinction was maintained between the two, and by the eighteenth century the *kadi*s had entirely lost their secular "law and order" jurisdiction to the police authorities (Gibb and Bowen, *Islamic Society*, vol. 1, part 2, p. 87.

16. The Ottoman sultans, who were the successors to the authority of the Abbasid caliphs, are treated later in this chapter.

17. Gibb and Bowen, *Islamic Society*, vol. 1, part 2, pp. 74, 117.

18. MacDonald, *Moslem Theology*, pp. 153–58.

19. Coulson, *History of Islamic Law*, pp. 120–24.

20. Tyan, *Histoire de l'organisation*, 2:141–281.

21. The discussion of the Ottoman Empire that follows is drawn largely from Halil Inalcik, *The Ottoman Empire* (New York: Praeger, 1973); Shaw, *History of the Ottoman Empire and Modern Turkey*, vol. 1; Gibb and Bowen, *Islamic Society*, vol. 1, part 1; A. H. Lybyer, *The Government of the Ottoman Empire* (New York: Russell & Russell, 1966; 1st ed. 1913). Of these Lybyer probably somewhat over-

emphasizes the slave family and thus the absolutism of the sultan, with Shaw providing a useful correctiver in his emphasis on the continuing political power of the Turkish notables. Inalcik, a Turk writing to place the empire in the best possible light for Western readers, probably overemphasizes constitutional theories of checks and balances.

22. The caliphate is a complex and often uncertain concept and institution, particularly after the early period when the Abbasid caliphs held both political and religious authority. See T. W. Arnold, *The Caliphate* (Oxford: Oxford University Press, 1924). The capacity of the caliph to proclaim authoritative religious doctrine was usually referred to yet another title or office, that of *imam*. Secular Muslim rulers often assumed the title caliph as an honorific, usually on the event of some great military victory, but subsequently they might or might not actually claim religious authority as *imam*. The sultans proclaimed themselves to be caliphs but rarely sought to exercise the dominant religious doctrinal role implied by the title *imam*. See Gibb and Bowen, *Islamic Society*, vol. 1, part 1, pp. 26–38.

23. See Uriel Heyd, *Studies in Old Ottoman Criminal Law* (Oxford: Oxford University Press, 1973).

24. Shaw, *History of the Ottoman Empire*, 1:26, 136, 139; Inalcik, *The Ottoman Empire*, pp. 74–75, 89 ff.; Lybyer, *The Government of the Ottoman Empire*, pp. 41–42, 219–21 (citing sixteenth-century Western sources); A. Heidborn, *Manuel de droit public et administratif de l'empire Ottoman* (Vienna: Hartung, 1909) p. 389.

25. As personal representatives of the sultan, provincial governors heard and decided cases. The local *kadi*s and other religious men were encouraged to memorialize the *divan* concerning the misconduct of such officials, including their judicial misconduct. Here again little distinction was made between the appeal of a case and the hearing of a complaint against an administrative official. See Gibb and Bowen, *Islamic Society*, Vol. 1, part 1, p. 201.

26. Shaw, *History of the Ottoman Empire*, p. 165.

27. Both weather and the availability of food limited most campaigns to the summer months. The soldiers returned home between campaigns.

28. The basic governmental, territoral unit below the *sanjac* was the *kada*, or judicial district, presided over by a *kadi*. Each *kada* had a *subashi*, whose dual role as military and police official has been explained earlier. The *kadi* depended on the *subashi* for enforcement of his judgments. In theory the *subashi* could not punish without authorization from the *kadi*. In practice he often did.

29. It is noteworthy that, in spite of elaborate financial and accounting staffs and procedures, the Ottomans had no overall budget and exercised almost no supervision over the spending of individual government officials (Shaw, *History of the Ottoman Empire*, p. 264).

30. The essentially religious character of the *kadi*s of the Ottoman Empire is somewhat obscured by the strategies of the early sultans. Essentially that strategy was to recognize and reinforce the fundamental split between government and religion and set the two to balance one another under his own ultimate authority. In the provinces the *kadi* was given authoirty over both the Sharia and the *kunan* and officers of the civil-military government were forbidden to punish without his approval. The *kadi*s were also encouraged to report the misconduct of government officials to the capital. Thus the *kadi* was to serve as a check on the sultan's government. In the capital no grand vizier could hope to survive without the cooperation of the *seyhulislam* and *fatwas* from the *ulema* legitimating his policies. At the same time the *kadi*s were set to watch the civil governors, as holders of government offices, they

were used as intermediaries between the sultan's government and the *ulema*. Indeed among the more orthodox the office of *kadi* was disesteemed because it involved compromise with the civil authorities. This policy of exploiting the dual nature of the *kadi* as religious man and government official to increase the sultan's control over both the civil and religious establishment was more or less successful at various times, but it was neither intended to nor did it in practice result in, the conversion of an essentially religious judge into a secular administrator. See Gibb and Bowen, *Islamic Society,* vol. 1, part 1, pp. 149, 153–55, 201; part 2, pp. 79–80, 86–87, 115, 117, 119–21.

# INDEX

Abbasid caliphate, 195, 206, 221
Abu Hanifa (Hanifite school) 197–99
"Abuse of discretion," 154
Act of Settlement (1702), 99, 102
Administrative law and courts, 27, 29,
  33, 87–89, 111–25, 153–55, 166
Administrative Procedures Act (U.S.)
  117
Administrators as judges, 20–24, 28,
  30, 33, 37, 49–50, 53, 55, 60, 63,
  72–73, 87–90, 171–72, 205–6
Admiralty courts, 97, 102, 105, 108
Adversary proceedings, 1, 12–15, 17,
  27, 33
*Amal*, 204
American law and courts. *See* United
  States, law and courts of
Analogy, 164–65, 199, 202–3
Anglo-Saxons, 70, 78, 79
*Anisminic* v. *Foreign Compensation
  Commission*, 119, 121
Appeal and appellate courts, 7, 37–64,
  77, 90, 101, 103–10, 114, 142,
  148–49, 168, 174–75, 180, 194–222
Appeal by trial de novo, 37–49, 174,
  211, 214, 220
Arbitration and arbitrators, 3–5, 7, 9,
  15, 62, 193
Assize of Clarendon (1166), 77, 83
Assize judges, 77–78, 90–91, 94–95,
  106
Avoidance of litigation, 18, 182–83,
  190–91

Belgium, law and courts of, 134, 143
Bentham, Jeremy, 104–5, 107, 111
Beys, 213, 216–18
Bills, 88–89
Blackstone, W., 101
Board of Punishments, 163, 166–67,
  174, 178, 190
Bodde, D., 162, 164–67

Bologna, University of, 130

Caliphate, 195–222 passim
Cao Dia, 24
Centralization: of law, 78–80; political,
  65, 70–80, 132; of trial courts, 66,
  72–82, 105–6, 108–11, 124, 214–15
Chancellor and Chancery, 21, 74–76,
  85–95, 98, 101, 103, 105–10
Cheyenne, 30
China, imperial, law and courts of, 9,
  14, 20, 22, 24, 52, 57–58, 63–64, 67,
  157–93, 203–4, 216
China, Peoples Republic, law and
  courts of, 9, 63
Church law and courts, 23, 130, 139,
  166, 205–22
Civil law system, 10, 27–29, 33, 35,
  37–41, 44, 55, 58–59, 61, 63–64, 94,
  106, 126–56, 161, 164, 203
Civil war, English, 96, 98–100
Closing of the gate of *ijtihad*, 200, 203
Code: civil, 148; commercial, 133;
  criminal, 148; French civil, 133,
  137–42; general, 126, 128, 131,
  133–35, 163; German civil, 14,
  134–35, 147; Justinian, 5, 128–34;
  Napoleon, 133, 138; Swiss civil,
  145–46
Codex, 128–29
Coke, Sir Edward, 100
Common law and courts, 9–10, 12, 14,
  21, 23–25, 28–29, 35–39, 55, 65–
  125, 131, 135, 141, 164, 167, 203
Common lawyers, 93–96, 102, 105,
  107–8, 124
Common Pleas, Court of, 76–77, 83,
  88, 90–91, 93, 95, 105–6
Communist legal systems, 9
Comradely courts, 9, 62
Conciliar courts, 87–89
Conflict resolution, 1–18, 24–26,